Praise for *The Way of the Bootstrapper*

"Floyd Flake has proven that we can achieve our dreams, regardless of socio-economic background. This inspirational book tells how he did it—through hard work, discipline, and taking responsibility for his life—and challenges the reader to look within and follow his example."

—Walter V. Shipley, chairman, The Chase Manhattan Corporation

"It's hard to pull yourself up by your bootstraps if you don't have boots. From the floor of the House and the pulpit of Allen A.M.E., Reverend Flake has labored on behalf of the least among us. Floyd Flake is a rare commodity: convicted, committed, and compelling."

—Tavis Smiley, author and host of *BET Tonight*

"*The Way of the Bootstrapper* is the story of one man's journey to help the powerless. More than the story of one man's courage, hard work, and strong heart, it is the story of millions of others hoping to make that same journey."

—Ted Forstmann, senior partner, Forstmann Little & Co.

"Reverend Flake sets a powerful example for overcoming obstacles by inner strength, community guidance, and sheer will power. This book charts a course for fulfilling our potential, and every one of us stands to gain from it."

—Leland C. Brendsel, chairman and CEO, Freddie Mac

"*The Way of the Bootstrapper* is an inspiring road map to finding and living our purpose. Reverend Flake offers us the encouragement we all need to develop our individual potential for the greater good."

—Susan L. Taylor, editor-in-chief, *Essence* magazine

"Floyd Flake doesn't just talk the talk, he walks the walk. More than anyone else today he has brought together the disparate worlds of politics, religion, and business. He is the consummate bootstrapper and his successes speak for themselves. *The Way of the Bootstrapper* is a practical mandate for fixing what's wrong with ourselves and our society."

—Bob Johnson, founder and president of Black Entertainment Television

"As a legislator and pastor, and now as an author, Floyd Flake has distinguished himself as one of today's most independent, indispensable, and above all, successful African American leaders. A man of powerful words and equally eloquent actions, he is that rarity—a practical visionary."

— George F. Will, nationally syndicated columnist

"One cannot help but come away from this enlightening and spiritual experience committed to shedding the bad habits of failure and better embracing the habits, traits, and actions of the bootstrapper."

— Congresswoman Maxine Waters, from the foreword

THE WAY OF THE BOOTSTRAPPER

THE WAY OF THE BOOTSTRAPPER

Nine Action Steps for Achieving Your Dreams

FLOYD FLAKE

AND DONNA MARIE WILLIAMS

HarperSanFrancisco
A Division of HarperCollinsPublishers

HarperCollins books may be purchased for educational, business, or sales promotional use. For information please write: Special Markets Department, HarperCollins Publishers Inc., 10 East 53rd Street, New York, NY 10022.

HarperCollins Web site: http://www.harpercollins.com

HarperCollins®, ♣®, and HarperSanFrancisco™ are trademarks of HarperCollins Publishers Inc.

FIRST HARPERCOLLINS PAPERBACK EDITION PUBLISHED IN 2000

Designed by Joseph Rutt

Library of Congress Cataloging-in-Publication Data
Flake, Floyd H.
The way of the bootstrapper / by Floyd H. Flake and Donna Marie Williams.
p.   cm.
ISBN 0–06–251595–0 (cloth)
ISBN 0–06–251596–9 (pbk.)
1. Success.   2. Flake, Floyd H.   I. Williams, Donna Marie.   II. Title.
BJ1611.F53   1999
158—dc21   98–54995
00 01 02 03 04 ❖ RRD 10 9 8 7 6 5 4 3 2 1

This book is dedicated to

My late father and mother, Robert B. and Rosie Lee Flake
My wife, Margarett Elaine McCollins Flake
My children and grandchild, Aliya Mariama, Nailah Lorice,
Robert Rasheed, Harold Hasan, and Nia Renee
My in-laws, Leroy and Lorene McCollins
My living brothers and sisters, Robert, Dorothy, Faye, Linda,
Donald, Ralph, and Sandra

CONTENTS

ACKNOWLEDGMENTS

I thank my wonderful wife Elaine, and my four beautiful children, Aliya, Nailah, Rasheed, and Hasan for being loving, understanding, and supportive during the many nights that I sat up writing this book and for being by my side through all the ups and downs of life.

For many years I thought about writing a book, but I thought I would never have the time until the Rev. Dr. Myles Munroe of the Bahamas Faith Ministries prophesied two years ago that I would write a book before the turn of the century.

I owe a debt of gratitude to Marshall Mitchell for guiding me to his former classmate and childhood friend, Imar Hutchins, who became my literary agent and negotiated a good contract for me with Harper Collins. I thank his partner in Simply Said Literary Agency, Dawn Marie Daniels, for her priceless editorial direction toward making this dream a reality. Many thanks are also due to my co-author, Donna Marie Williams, whose tireless work provided the foundation on which this manuscript was built.

I am grateful to the staff at Harper San Francisco for their generous support in making this project possible. First and foremost to Diane Gedymin, publishing director, for her strong commitment to me and this book. A special debt is owed to Mark Chimsky, executive editor, and his assistant, Eric Hunt, who ushered me through the editorial process of writing my first book. Thanks also to my wonderful marketing and publicity team of Meg Lenihan, Mark Tauber, and Karen Bouris. Also thanks to Laura Beers, art director, for the design of the cover and Terri Leonard, managing editor, for handling the final editorial phases of the project.

This book could not have come to fruition without the tireless work of Christina London, who had to decipher my terrible scribbling and stay focused during my many long hours of dictation. Thank you for giving up Saturdays, evenings, and early mornings of sleep to help me meet the timetable for the project. Also thanks to Gill Photographers for the cover photograph and for all their assistance to my church over the years.

It was a blessing to have Maxine Waters, a good friend, say yes when I asked if she would write the foreword. I am thankful that Bill Bennett, in spite of his busy schedule, consented to write the introduction.

Many special thanks to the members, staff, and leadership of the Allen A.M.E. Cathedral for your patience, inspiration, and encouragement and for letting me serve as your pastor for the past twenty-two years. Without your participation in this great ministry, there would have been much less to write about.

Thanks to the constituents of the Sixth Congressional District for electing me for six terms to serve as your congressman.

I thank God for granting me favor, grace, love, and mercy that I might live long enough to be able to produce this book.

FOREWORD

I served with the Reverend Floyd Flake in the United States Congress. I have come to know him as a warm, positive, and generous man who is highly respectful of others. He always approached each day with a smile, high energy, and hard work. He is an independent thinker with big dreams and high aspirations. His accomplishments both in the political arena and as an educator, community developer, and spiritual leader speak for themselves. He is a doer—he's a bootstrapper. In this book, Pastor Flake generously shares his knowledge and spirit for all who are desirous of knowing "how to," "when to," and "who dares to."

Floyd and I differ on some issues, but I have always felt a kinship with him. We both come from large families—there were thirteen children in each of our families. We both held jobs at a very early age. Our parents were southern and under-educated but strong survivors. Reverend Flake is a proud man. His dress is impeccable. He is perfectly groomed, slim, and in good health. He embodies all of the qualities of a good leader. He does not simply talk the talk—he, indeed, *walks the walk!* I have visited his church, Allen A.M.E. Cathedral, and his community. Having read this book, I now understand better his spiritual roots. He was destined to become a minister.

Upon reading this book, I discovered a refreshing, straightforward discussion and formula that could have easily been entitled, *Life's Lessons* or *The Formula for Managing Life.* Reverend Flake gives real meaning to the phrase, "pulling yourself up by the bootstraps." Pastor Flake shares with the reader his life from early childhood to the present. We learn the value of his family, friends, and mentors in his development. His spiritual richness has given him the vision and power to accomplish and achieve great successes for his congregation and his community. Pastor Flake further details the accomplishments of men and women he considers great bootstrappers. A combination of his own experiences and the role models he weaves throughout this book will serve as a guide to help others become bootstrappers. Pastor Flake's sincere respect and love for every human being and his strong belief that we can all realize our full potential if we but employ our God-given talent is extremely uplifting and inspiring. The importance of family, education, hard work, and determination is beautifully and realistically portrayed by Pastor Flake, the husband, father, minister, educator, former-elected official, and leader.

We often hear generalities from accomplished leaders about what people should do, but seldom do we get detailed instruction and advice. On pages 66–67 of this book, there are twenty-one questions to help one make an assessment of one's life. He further discusses values and characteristics we are generally familiar with such as patience and faith but he also introduces new and powerful ideas such as "claiming what's yours." I loved the definitions of the "claiming prayer" as opposed to the "begging prayer." He restates the words and teachings of our elders, and we are reminded of their wisdom. We also realize how much further we would be in our own development if we had listened to this wisdom. The responsibility theme resonates throughout this book as Pastor Flake generously shares both the high and low points in his life. One cannot help but come away from this enlightening and spiritual experience committed to shedding the bad habits of failure and better embracing the habits, traits, and actions of the bootstrapper.

The Oprah Winfrey profile and her climb up the ladder of success—her discipline in taking control of her body and her weight—the discussions of Vesta Williams, Flo Jo, and others, puts a real face on the description of the bootstrapper. The well-defined characteristics of high-visibility personalities who overcame adversity and pushed beyond the artificial limits magnifies the way of the bootstrapper. It becomes so clear you will find yourself nodding your head in agreement and speaking aloud, "Ah-hah! Yes, that's the way of the bootstrapper."

Congresswoman Maxine Waters

INTRODUCTION

You can know a lot about America by studying its language. In fact, we can learn much about ourselves from the words, phrases, and slogans we see and hear every day. At the end of the twentieth century, what are some of our slogans? One of the watchwords of our time is "whatever." "Break all the rules" is another popular cliché. In fact, quite a few of America's largest and most respected corporations promote similar ideas. Neiman Marcus warns us that there are "No rules here," while Woolite tells us that "All the rules have changed." These phrases, small as they may be, suggest that we are a people opposed to rules and guidelines. Many people have expressed concern about the lowering of standards, but now we are faced with campaigns urging their destruction. This is not a good thing.

Thankfully, there are people out there who want to change this. Reverend Floyd Flake is one of them. He urges us to get rid of these new slogans. But he is not seeking to replace them with new-and-improved ones. On the contrary: he wants us to return to the best ideas from the past. He echoes the lessons most parents and grandparents lived by. They are commonplace lessons that have made America the greatest country in the history of the world. That is what makes this book so refreshing. *The Way of the Bootstrapper: Nine Action Steps for Achieving Your Dreams* is full of timely and timeless adages that bear repetition and adherence:

- Work together
- Seize opportunities
- Take the lead
- Respect your elders
- Know yourself
- Love your country
- Pull yourself up by your own bootstraps

Granted, many Americans will not want to hear what the reverend has to say. These ideas may sound out-of-date to us. Many would call them quaint. They are certainly not easy to live by. But, according to Floyd Flake, they can improve your life. And he is right. He is a living testament to that. From humble beginnings in Houston, Texas, Floyd Flake put himself through college and the seminary. He then became pastor of one of the most popular churches in New York City and a member of the United States House of Representatives. Floyd Flake is a man who walks it like he talks it.

Reverend Flake and I have often discussed education, and, in many ways, that is the subject of *The Way of the Bootstrapper.* Not education in the academic sense—reading, writing and arithmetic—but moral education, what Thomas Jefferson called "the improvement of one's morals and faculties." Too often we focus on the education of the head. We must be equally concerned with the education of the heart. The lessons in this book are aimed at the heart. But simply reading the lessons will not make you a better person; you must make the effort to apply what this book teaches. That requires work. Real, hard, time-consuming work.

"The beauty of bootstrapping," Flake writes, "is that you don't need much." All you need is a belief—a state of mind—that is determined to take responsibility for your words and deeds. You may not start from the best of circumstances, but it is a distinctly human ability to overcome challenges and obstacles in our path, to go beyond others' expectations. Bootstrapping encourages you to do just that: to reject the idea that because you are poor, you cannot get good grades, or that, because your parents neglected you, you can't have a healthy relationship with others. God gave man the gift of free will. And while concrete material circumstances may affect our options, each of us always remains free to choose whether to act responsibly and morally.

Inculcating personal responsibility is perhaps the most important part of growing up American. For we are a self-governing nation. That means more than just having a limited government; it means that we are a nation of men and women who are capable of ruling ourselves. Too often, we whine and blame others for what goes wrong. We find fault with much in our society but are unwilling to take the time to become involved with solving problems. We complain that our children are not learning enough in school but refuse to check their homework. We worry about teenage pregnancy but do not speak out against it. We elect, and then reelect, leaders for whom we profess mistrust. But in a democracy, the electorate is as important—and as responsible—as the elected. Our leadership matters, and it matters a great deal whom we elect, not only in terms of the agenda he sets but in terms of the example he sets as well.

We often hear people accepting credit. Paradoxically, few people are so willing to accept responsibility when something goes wrong—"It's not my fault!" But problems, we all truly know, often are our fault. As Aristotle teaches in the *Nicomachean Ethics,* we determine the type of person we become by our actions. If we choose to act cowardly, we become cowardly. If we choose to speak truthfully, we become truthful. If we choose to act responsibly, we become responsible. And in the process we become a better, fuller, happier human being.

Reverend Flake and I do not agree on everything. In fact, we disagree on some things he says in this book. But we share a belief in the fundamental importance of human life and personal responsibility. Listen to what Reverend Flake has to say. Read his words and lessons. Study them carefully. But also take the next step by incorporating them into your everyday life. Make yourself a better person. Murmur not at the ways of providence. Pull yourself up by your bootstraps.

January 15, 1999
William J. Bennett

PART 1

✴

THE BOOTSTRAPPER'S WAY

WHO IS THE BOOTSTRAPPER?
A PROFILE

What is bootstrapping? It is the *process* of achieving success by making it, against the odds, through self-directed action. It is a *mind-set* that allows you to rise over and above the ordinary and become an extraordinary person by taking responsibility for your own thoughts, feelings, words, actions, and life circumstances. It is a *value system* that directs your relationship with yourself, your neighbors, and the environment. A bootstrapper functions like a soldier in boot camp, who through basic training is always preparing and getting ready to take on any situation that represents a potential challenge in the pursuit of his or her goals. A bootstrapper takes the heat, humiliation, suffering, and pain of the moment in preparation for the joy, peace, and happiness of the future.

Bootstrapping is a way of taking responsibility for and building your own life while bringing reality to your dreams. You can be kept down only if you don't see those metaphorical boots that offer you a way out of your current predicament. Bootstrappers do not see themselves as victims but have confidence in their ability to rise beyond the limited expectations that others may have imposed on them. They develop inner strength from their experiences and sufferings, which allows them to persevere even in the face of challenging odds.

I would like to share with you a bit of the story of my life, to give you an example of how bootstrappers learn from and use their experiences.

My first memory of my early childhood in Houston, Texas, is from about the age of three. I remember hearing singing and praying coming from our living room. The melodious sounds of "Jesus Build a Fence All Around Me" and "Oh, How I Love Jesus" were coming from a "prayer band" that visited our home weekly to conduct worship services when my mother was unable to attend church. She could not attend on a regular basis because the first six children in our family (of which I am the third) were born within seven and a half years. The impression that the prayer band made on my life was not limited to a mere introduction to religious teaching or training but also played an integral role in my ultimate call to the ministry. I reenacted their prayers and songs and mimicked their preaching starting at this early age.

I am now fifty-four years old, but I still remember a very painful experience I had at the age of four. This experience taught me a valuable lesson about discipline, respect, and love. Our house sat on brick blocks, which meant that there was at least one foot of crawl space beneath it. We had explicit instructions never to play under the house. However, my inquisitive nature made me venture into this forbidden territory. I heard my mother calling me but did not respond, knowing that I had broken a rule. Thinking that she had gone into the house, I eventually crawled out, only to see her waiting, strap in hand. I dashed into the house, with her in pursuit, and accidentally fell on a space heater, which burned my arm. Within seconds, my mother's temperament changed as she lifted me up and rushed me next door to Uncle Robert, who drove us to the doctor. In an instant, she had changed from disciplinarian to concerned mother showing love and compassion for her ailing child. I still have an eight-inch scar on my arm, which is a constant reminder of the requirement that is placed upon us to respect persons who are in authority, expect retribution when we have acted incorrectly, and know that we are loved even as we endure discipline. Any successful bootstrapper should allow these three principles to be a part of his or her arsenal for dealing with life.

The atmosphere in the community where I grew up was one of respect. We called all of the adults in the community by titles and first names. My immediate neighbors were Mrs. Dorothy and Mr. Van (Williams), Mrs. Ruby and Mr. Goree (Turner), Mrs. Ossie Lee and Mr. Frank (Hardeman), and Mrs. Doris and Mr. Buster (Kendall). You dared not call them by their first name without prefacing it with a title. The level of respect was such that neighbors had the right to discipline you for misdeeds, although in most instances, they reported you to your parents, who disciplined you accordingly. We could not deny their charges because they were adults, and calling an adult a liar was a sign of disrespect. The slogan that has become popularized today, "It takes a village to raise a child," was more than rhetoric; it was a reality of our everyday life. I acquired many of the values I still have today because I lived in an environment where community support structures and systems were in place. The operative construct was that of an extended family where everyone participated in helping to raise one another's children.

At the age of five, I was admitted to the George Washington Carver Elementary School. I thought it unusual that Daddy had taken a day off to accompany Mother and me to school, but I learned later in life that they had gone to plead with Mrs. Reed, the principal, to let me enter in September, although my sixth birthday would not come until January. I remember Mrs. Reed having me say my ABC's and count to twenty. I suppose that was her way of testing to see if I was ready for school, since I had not attended kindergarten. Fortunately, since Mother was a housewife, she had time to teach us the basic rudiments of education. She was living proof that even when parents have a limited education, their desire for the success of their children is no less than that of other parents.

On the second day of school, I had to ride the bus and failed to accurately calculate the time of the bus ride. I had an accident running from the bus to the outdoor toilet in the corner of our backyard. I expected to be severely disciplined for having messed up my clothes, but instead, my mother merely made me pump water from the well and heat it so I could bathe in our aluminum washtub. Not only did we not have running water, but having moved from Third Ward (which was in the city) to Acres Homes (which was in the country), we now had a wood stove in the living room and kerosene space heaters in the bedrooms. We used to huddle around the stove until bedtime, and then, dressed in flannel pajamas, sleep under two or three quilts that Mother had made from rags.

Often, when we did something wrong, Mother would send us to get "switches" (twigs from our willow tree), which she would then use to discipline us. This process represented both a psychological and a physical whipping. There was no "sparing the rod and spoiling the child" in our home. The worse psychological whipping was when we did something bad enough to be told, "Wait until your daddy gets home." My parents were not abusive, but if the magnitude of our actions suggested a need for stern discipline, then there was no way of getting out of a whipping plus losing certain privileges, like attending a party. My last whipping came at the age of thirteen after a neighbor reported that my friends and I had put sugar in his gas tank. Since Daddy was not home at bedtime, I thought that I had gotten away with something, but at 5:30 the next morning I had a rude awakening. It was not often that Daddy had to be the disciplinarian. We hated his whippings because he would start with a long lecture about how much he loved us and how whipping us hurt him more than it would hurt us—something I did not understand until my wife, Elaine, and I had our own children. Since Daddy was a mechanic, he knew how much time and money it would cost for him to repair the neighbor's car. So, when he took me into the bathroom, I knew this would be a long lecture and a serious whipping. He was obviously very effective, since it was the last whipping that I ever received. I stopped hanging with my friends. Instead, I managed to keep busy with various jobs, including busing tables at a restaurant, doing a paper route, mowing lawns, picking cotton, and helping Daddy clean office buildings. Little did I know that these early experiences were laying the foundation for molding me into a bona fide bootstrapper.

When I was growing up, we had a different mind-set and outlook on life from that of many people today. There were very few neighbors on my block who had telephones, and those who did had party lines (shared by a number of homes). The Williamses, our next-door neighbors, had a black-and-white television, and once a week we were permitted to go over and watch it with their kids.

My father could afford to buy only used cars, which he did not allow any of the children to drive. His thinking was that the car was necessary for him to move between his jobs, and therefore he could not afford for us to put any entertainment miles on it. Our lives were not managed by technology nor consumed by sitcoms and video games. Most of our time was spent trying to survive. All of the children in the family started working at a very young age, beginning with tasks at home. For the most part, at home there was no distinction between what were traditional boy or girl jobs. We were all taught to cook, wash, iron, and sew. My success strategy and bootstrapper spirit were born out of this environment. We were developing as bootstrappers without even knowing it. Eventually the strategies developed in our youth served as the foundation for the emergence of a mind-set, work ethic, and attitude that contributed enormously to my future success and that of most members of my family. Although Mother and Daddy have been interred, their bootstrapper mentality and spirit still serve as guideposts in my life. Given my humble beginnings, there are many people who are amazed by the successes that I have had in my life. They do not fully comprehend or understand the spirit of a bootstrapper. Inner strength, determination, motivation, personal responsibility, and the will to succeed are powerful forces that are operative in the life of a bootstrapper.

Since I was raised in the deep, segregated south, one of thirteen children, eight of whom lived together in a tiny two-bedroom house, it might seem impossible for me to have risen above what many would call a disadvantaged background. This is even more amazing when my parents' education is factored in; they did not get beyond the fifth and sixth grades. They were not allowed to attend school from the early spring until after the cotton harvesting season in the late fall. But they were determined that our lives would be better than theirs had been, given the opportunities that were available to us, which they never had.

Although I was bused past segregated white schools, it was my good fortune to encounter four excellent teachers in a four-room, wood-framed school out in the country. They challenged me to expunge words like *can't*, *inferior*, and *second-class* from my vocabulary. They taught me to ignore the fact that my books had been used for a number of years by white students who had passed them on without a space left to write my name, were missing some pages, or were so filthy that it was almost impossible to read them. The teachers instilled within us the idea that the content of the books was more relevant than their condition.

I shall never forget Mrs. Livingston, Mrs. Grice, Mrs. Dawson, or Mrs. Valentine. Without them setting high standards, challenging me to meet their high expectations, demanding moral fortitude, and placing a high premium on excellence, I am certain that my successes would have been limited. I can recall the sacrifice that Mrs. Grice made when I was in the fourth grade and could not attend school for a year because of a disease called eczema. Her home was seventy miles from the school in one direction, and mine fourteen miles away in another direction. Yet, because of her commitment, she brought homework to me each Friday before driving to her home. I had no computers or new books, I wore secondhand clothes, and I ate plenty of meatless meals, but none of these things could deter me from the pursuit of excellence and my goal of being the first in my family to graduate from college.

Leaving Houston to attend Wilberforce University in Ohio represented a major transition in my life. Because I did not have the benefit of a full financial aid package or parents who could assist financially in my pursuit of a college degree, there was no doubt in my mind that my desire to get a college education would require working my way through school. I am grateful to God and my parents for the bootstrapper spirit and mentality that was instilled within me. Because of it, I was resourceful enough to get a job in the school cafeteria on my very first day at the campus. At five o'clock each morning I faithfully made my way to the cafeteria to assist the cooks in preparation for breakfast. Because of my work ethic and my need to make as much money as possible at ninety cents an hour, on most days I returned to serve on the lunch line, and I even worked the dinner shift when possible. Eventually I assumed the additional responsibility of cleaning the cafeteria at night. Study time was very limited, but I was still determined to be the first in my family to receive a college degree. That burning desire kept me going, even though I often fell asleep on my books. The first year was rough, with what had become a full-time, labor-intensive job; the change from a mild climate to snow and cold weather, plus being far from home, wreaked havoc on my health. I ended the first year with a 2.1 GPA, which was disappointing.

After my first year, I returned home for the summer with no expectation of ever going back to Wilberforce. My brother-in-law found me a summer job at Alright Parking, which paid 1.75 dollars per hour. That, combined with what I earned at a part-time job waiting tables, where I made good tips, seemed to be good money. I was ready to forget about my dream of being the first in the family to graduate from college. But there is a saying that church people often quote: "God moves in mysterious ways." A series of mysterious events started to happen. One day while I was parking a vehicle, the brakes did not hold and I wound up crashing through the front of a shoe store across the street. Several weeks later, a prostitute accosted me at a bus stop, and when I refused to go with her, reached into my pocket and took my money. I started getting the feeling that God was trying to tell me something, but I was adamant that a return to Wilberforce was totally out of the question. However, the mysteries continued.

The two events that really changed my whole outlook on life occurred during that summer. One of my friends, with whom I waited tables, got fired because he refused to dance with the daughter of the owner of the restaurant. When he refused, she informed her father that this "nigger" had flirted with her. The truth did not matter, since such behavior was not tolerated in Texas at that time.

The second event occurred shortly thereafter. A woman approached me in the parking lot during the lunchtime rush hour, stating that she had parked earlier and been short-changed. According to company policy, all reimbursements were to be made by mail after the evening checkout if we found that we had excess monies at the end of the day. Rather than accepting my explanation, the woman called a policeman from the street. He immediately suggested that she have me arrested. I, along with two other attendants, tried to tell him the company's policy, but he refused to listen. He insisted that the woman have me arrested, even against her protests. But he proceeded to completely demonize me, calling me "nigger" and "boy," and before long the officer had convinced the woman that I should be arrested. As we rode to the police station, he talked at me and continued to call me names. When he realized that I was a college student, things did not get any better—as a matter of fact, they got worse, and he began calling me a "smart-ass nigger." I had never had an experience like this before, and I honestly thought that he might kill me before we got to the station house. Fortunately, when we arrived at the station, a company lawyer appeared within moments after I had been fingerprinted and placed in a cell. I was scared to death, but as I examined this little cubicle with a metal bed and a toilet with no private enclosure, all I could think about was getting out and going back to Wilberforce. Several hours later, I was back on the job, believing that God had fixed it so that I would realize that my future was dependent upon getting a good education.

Although I had not saved enough funds to reenter school when September came, nothing could keep me from taking that long Greyhound bus ride back to Ohio. I moved onto the campus and took a full-time job in the cafeteria. For the next five years, first enrolled as an undergraduate student and then for two years as a seminary graduate student, it was my good fortune to hold various cafeteria jobs, wait tables at parties for the president and deans, and wait tables at the Biltmore Hotel in Dayton, Ohio.

In the third year after my return to school, my mother's non-gender-specific treatment of jobs paid off. A French professor, Mrs. Marie Ware, suffered a heart attack and needed someone to be a live-in housekeeper. This gave me an opportunity to live rent-free for two years. Things were still difficult because of my mammoth workload, but every time I thought about quitting, I would remember the searing words of that police officer and would dig a little deeper to find the strength to go on. I decided that I would never let myself be defined or limited by the ignorance and prejudices of other people. As a bootstrapper, that experience made me work that much harder and feel more determined to do everything in my power to make it against the odds and achieve my dreams.

Bootstrapping was the strategy our forefathers and foremothers used to raise families, work the soil, start new businesses, run the government, and care for those less fortunate. They motivated and energized themselves and others with the phrase "pull yourselves up by your bootstraps." They knew that no matter how much or how little they had, it was enough, when combined with their faith and hard work, to create their own realities. They believed that God had given them everything they needed, individually and collectively, to survive. Bootstrapping defined their work ethic, their success strategies, and their philosophy of life.

What a difference a few decades make! Today, when you tell people that they should pull themselves up by their bootstraps, they will accuse you of blaming the victim. They argue that sociological imperatives mitigate against the possibility for success, especially for those who live in inner cities. This attitude has contributed to a condition of malaise that has caused people to believe that the government and others are responsible for taking care of them. They do not get excited about the prospect of assuming the responsibility for their own destiny. They feel overwhelmed by the magnitude of problems, challenges, and tasks that they must face and manage in order to succeed.

The beauty of bootstrapping is that you don't need much. You don't need to win the lottery, or receive an inheritance or help from rich relatives to turn your dreams into reality. Bootstrapping is a spiritual journey rooted in faith, guided by the divine, and moved by the spirit that is within. No matter what your circumstances or where you stand on the socioeconomic ladder of life, you already have everything you need to become a bootstrapper. So, what are you waiting for?

You also don't need fancy electronic gadgets to be a bootstrapper. We are living in technology's dream when it should be the other way around. We think that we can impose order upon the universe with certain results and without consequences, but God created the universe to create a higher order within us. We think that we can fix our lives by simply chanting a positive affirmation or taking a fantasy cruise, when the reality is that sometimes it takes years of hard work to achieve a goal, overcome past mistakes, or handle the unfavorable cards that life seems to have dealt us.

Don't get me wrong—I enjoy modern conveniences: a car with so many power instruments that half of them go unused, a refrigerator that has precluded the necessity of circling the block looking for the iceman, and telephones: cellular handphones, car phones, and digital phones with call waiting and voice messaging, which enable me to communicate with people all over the world whenever I choose. Without the assistance of technology, it probably would take longer for even the most avid bootstrapper to succeed. But, because bootstrappers are driven and motivated, they succeed with or without these aids. Personally, I have not allowed gadgets to determine my outlook on life. Bootstrappers are not slaves to gadgets. As a matter of fact, I wrote this book just as I did my doctoral dissertation, in longhand, because I am not yet computer literate.

While some people feel they need gadgets in order to succeed, others turn to modern self-help success strategies. These are the product of our illusions and childlike desire to have total control over our lives. Our so-called backward, primitive, uneducated, slow ancestors knew how to work hard and control the things they could while letting go of the things they couldn't. It seems that in many ways they had much more wisdom than today's generation.

The Superior Success Strategy

A strategy is simply a plan that is designed to achieve a goal. It is the way to get from one stage in life to another. Each time you take a step, you should already have started planning the next one. Soon you will reach a comfort level where there is consistent movement as you act upon your ideas. This allows you to propel yourself from one strata of success to another. You must watch out for the booby traps, because they can slow you down, but don't let them stop you. If your job is unfulfilling, your strategy might be to go back to school. If you have been in the company a long time, you might consider creating you own job by starting your own business using the same skills and abilities that you have previously made available to enhance the success of others. Successful bootstrappers are most effective when they refuse to be boxed in. If you feel that you are in a box, use the time wisely to develop a success strategy that helps you to get out and move on toward your future. The bootstrapping program described in this book is a superior success strategy for many reasons:

- Bootstrapping helps you to realize that you probably have all you need to get started: a sound mind, a vivid imagination, and big dreams. You need not be rich or even well connected. Just make a commitment to yourself to use all the power within to maximize your potential. Let me show you how to use what you have to get what you need and want in life.

- Bootstrapping helps you to assume personal responsibility for your own life, by taking control of your thoughts, emotions, words, actions, and life circumstances. The assumption of personal responsibility will provide you with the necessary power to accomplish your life goals.

- Bootstrapping will help you to get out of the box that is smothering your ambitions, darkening your pathway, and prohibiting your growth. Bootstrapping is not "owned" by any political ideology, religion, age group, gender, or race. Its strategies can be used by anyone at any time and in any place. Bootstrapping has been used by immigrants, the physically challenged, the racially disadvantaged, victims of the gender caste system, welfare recipients, homeless people, and just plain ordinary people with great ideas, a will to work, and an attitude of believing in success. It has been used to build wealth, start companies, teach children, develop communities, feed the homeless, and more. If you have the tenacity of Bill Gates, the dedication of Mother Teresa, the imagination of Maya Angelou, or the fearlessness of Dr. Martin Luther King, Jr.,—or any number of other positive attributes either singly or en masse—then you already have the essential tools for a solid foundation from which to launch a successful future.

- Bootstrapping is adaptable to a changing world and our ever-changing life circumstances. No matter where you are in the process of achievement, bootstrapping allows you to constantly fine-tune and redefine your goals as you become more in tune with your life purpose and respond to challenges and obstacles along the way.

- Bootstrapping demands of us a high moral standard as we pursue our dreams. There is nothing wrong with competition, but when it lacks a moral foundation, it can be destructive. Bootstrapping challenges us to have the courage of our convictions, to make the right decisions and do the right things, even if it means that we sometimes stand alone.

- Bootstrapping shows us how to develop relationships that help others grow and achieve.

- Bootstrapping challenges us to conduct our activities not merely for ourselves but also for the benefit of others and future generations. Ours is the richest and most powerful country in the world, and there are plenty of opportunities and resources for us all.

The Way of the Bootstrapper will show you how to develop patience, which is a vital necessity, since everything will not happen instantaneously. There will be times when you must just slow down, take your time, and wait. I know your life is fast paced, but you owe it to yourself to set time aside to examine strategies that have helped to create many astounding success stories. There is no need to reinvent the wheel. I am living testimony to the bootstrapping strategies described in this book, which have been proven time and again in my life—and without a doubt, they can work for you as well!

By historical, sociological definition I should not have attended college, let alone graduated. It would have been impossible to imagine that I would build a career that included being sales representative for the Reynolds Tobacco Company and marketing representative with the Xerox Corporation, as well as holding dean positions at both Lincoln University in Pennsylvania and Boston University. I am still flabbergasted at the fact that I was a member of Congress, sat on the House Banking and Finance Committee, and left Congress on my own terms. Even with my vivid imagination, there was no reason for me to believe that I would be able to lead a congregation in growing from a membership of fourteen hundred to one of over eleven thousand. Although I had a vision for community ministry and economic development, when offered the opportunity to pastor in Queens, New York, my mind could not conceive what God would and has wrought through the Allen ministry. After developing more than fifty million dollars in construction projects including housing, stores, a school, and a cathedral, I am still working on new projects to build. With a workforce of over eight hundred, the Allen A.M.E. Church, the cathedral, and its subsidiary corporations represent a paradigm for community and economic development that is being copied by churches all over America. Yet, the bootstrapper in me is yearning to do even more.

Several years ago, when I went back to seminary to earn a doctor of ministry degree, my children wanted to know why. They felt that being a U.S. congressman and pastoring a large and prestigious church were sufficient and that there was nothing to be gained by getting another degree. I told them that I was doing it not as much for me as for them and others who consider me a role model. It was imperative in order for them to understand that education is a lifelong process. Furthermore, my pursuit of the doctor of ministry degree encouraged and inspired my wife, Elaine, who also enrolled and received her doctorate a year later. Bootstrappers are not satisfied when they believe that there are other things yet to be done, other fields to be conquered and new dreams to be realized.

You might think that mine is the quintessential rags-to-riches story. You know the story: the Horatio Alger type hero single-handedly overcomes all forms of adversity to rise to the top. We love this idea of the self-made man. In fact, these stories have drawn and continue to draw people to America. Haitians and Cubans who risk their lives on the wretched seas do so because of the promise that America offers. Russian Jews and Europeans fleeing from political oppression come believing that America is still the land of opportunity. Latinos come to these shores from Puerto Rico and Mexico in hope of a better life. Africans and Caribbeans come believing that American democracy offers them a way out of poverty and political oppression. They all believe in the promise and possibility of being able to succeed on their own merit. Sadly, some are disappointed, but others grab hold of the bootstrapper spirit and make it in spite of the odds against them.

We enjoy reading about a person's solitary stride into success. One individual against the world. One person overcoming obstacles. One person going the extra mile. A leader of people and a follower of none. No job is too menial, because our hero knows that it's but a stepping-stone to achieving his or her goal. This person has all of the potential to become a bootstrapper. With little else but the clothes on their back and the boots on their feet, they pull themselves up by their metaphorical bootstraps and out of the squalor and negativity of childhood experiences and beat the odds. We love the story because it gives us hope.

The characters and settings may change, but the theme remains the same. The story of the self-made individual gives us hope because it helps us to believe the same could happen to us. It is the story that organizes all of our social activities and ethical mores, and it builds our faith. We love our self-made individuals. We are seduced by the charm of their public successes. But there's one problem with this story:

There's no such thing as a self-made person.

I don't care if you're talking about J. Paul Getty, Thomas Edison, Harriet Tubman, Bill Gates, Booker T. Washington, or Floyd Flake—the self-made individual is a fantasy, a myth, a caricature we have made up to justify our actions, direct our activities, and feel good about ourselves.

I could say that I built a four-million-dollar school, a twelve-million-dollar senior citizen housing complex, and a twenty-three-million-dollar cathedral in Queens by myself, but I didn't. The faithfully tithing members of Allen A.M.E. Church caught hold of my dreams and provided the spiritual support and financial leverage needed to make it happen. I was not solely responsible for helping 162 people become homeowners. The city and state governments, The New York City Partnership, Benjamin Developers, Bluestone Builders, Raleigh W. Hall, Harry Simmons Architects, a dedicated staff, and countless others helped to make it happen. The Allen Church and Allen Neighborhood Preservation and Development Corporation worked in synergy with me and others to bring these dreams to reality. My strong political and business relationships, even before my election, provided invaluable support in helping to make things happen. But no way can I take full credit, because I could not do it alone.

One of the most important elements in my life as a bootstrapper has been the love and support of a wife and four children. They have created a peaceful home atmosphere where thinking, dreaming, and working can take place. My wife, Elaine, is my best friend and critic. Because she is much more detail-oriented than I am, her analysis is always helpful. She has been my partner in marriage and ministry in helping to build a successful family and church. She understands my bootstrapper mind and ways and periodically registers concern about my hectic schedule. Yet, she continues to encourage me, supports the majority of my decisions, and has found ways to periodically slow me down by placing vacations and dates on my itinerary as a means of making certain that I have opportunities to relax.

A good friend of mine, the Rev. Cecilia Williams Bryant, once stated that I function in such a hectic manner because I am afraid of reliving the poverty experiences of my youth. I tend to think that there is some truth in the statement. So here I am, the quintessential bootstrapping workaholic, running from an impoverished past, up the ladder of success. Each week I write two sermons and preach them at two of the three Sunday services that I attend. My responsibilities include overseeing the church and its projects, corporations, and employees. In addition, I travel frequently throughout the world to speak before other churches, business groups, schools, and community organizations. It gives me great joy and a sense of pride to know that I have overcome many odds to attain a reasonable portion of success. However, I realize that without faith in God, some great mentors, a supportive church and community, and a loving family, none of these things could have been done.

Yes, it's true, we alone are responsible for our own lives, but in everyone's rags-to-riches story is the mentor, the coach, the loving parent, the great teacher who *helped us help ourselves by challenging us to be more than we thought we could be or more than we were*. These supporting characters opened doors, shoved us, shook us, pulled us, gave us critiques or helping hands, and said the right words at exactly the right moment. In my life, for example, in addition to my mother, father, grandparents, and teachers, there were some other central characters who represent positive role models by virtue of the examples they set for me. They helped to develop my bootstrapper mind-set.

The Rev. O. L. Dawson is the pastor who began giving me leadership roles in the church when I was ten and accepted me into the ministry at the age of fifteen. He stands very tall as someone who helped me to shape my understanding of religion, faith, moral values, and responsibilities as guiding principles in my life. I spent Sundays traveling with him to the various places where he preached. Then I would go home and conduct my own special worship services during the week. My sisters, dressed up in some of mother's old clothes and high-heeled shoes, served as my choir and congregation. I would kill rodents and bury them, having made a cross from popsicle sticks to serve as grave markers. Never in the history of humankind have rodents had such a great send-off as they received from the eulogies I prepared and preached.

Mrs. Jewel Houston, who taught history at my high school, helped me to develop a real interest in the value of education. She was the mother of three children and treated me as if I were her fourth child. As the book steward of the school, with the responsibility for distributing books to the various classes, she gave me a volunteer job in the bookstore. For one period each day I either worked or studied under her direct supervision. On Saturdays and many evenings after school, I traveled with her around Texas to youth meetings. It was Mrs. Houston who, when I was fourteen, sent me on my first trip out of the state, to Kittrell, North Carolina, to attend a youth conference.

One of my role models was the Rev. John Hurst Adams, who was president of Paul Quinn College in Waco, Texas. He was in his twenties at the time, and I found it unbelievable that someone at that age could be so intelligent and powerful. At Kittrell College, I met the Rev. Philip R. Cousin, who was also in his twenties and president of that college. I realized then that I wanted to be a preacher and college president when I grew up. Both now serve as bishops in the A.M.E. Church.

A stalwart in my life was the Rev. W. D. Williams, who, having heard me preach at a youth service for the Wesley Chapel A.M.E. Church, where he was pastor, decided to take me to his alma mater, Wilberforce University, and enroll me in school. My mother never understood why it was necessary to go all the way to Ohio to get an education, but I realized that if I stayed home, in a house full of kids, I would not be in a great atmosphere for studying. Furthermore, most of my friends who stayed home and went to the local colleges dropped out without graduating. Without the Rev. Williams's insistence, I probably would never have left Houston, and only God knows what would have happened in my life.

At Wilberforce University, I had the opportunity to meet the Rev. Ulysses A. Hughey, who pastored St. John A.M.E. Church in Xenia,

Ohio. This was a critical time in my life, because I was struggling with whether to continue in my pursuit of ministry. The Reverend Hughey spent a great deal of time on campus interacting with the students at the student union. He had heard me preach, but he had heard from some of my friends that I was neglecting the ministry and not attending church on a regular basis. When he confronted me I informed him that it was impossible for me to attend church because of my early Sunday work schedule in the cafeteria. That did not matter to him. He told me emphatically that he was assigning me to be his youth minister at fifteen dollars per week, and he expected me to be in church each Sunday. I served in that capacity for four and a half years in the two churches that he pastored during that period. Since he was a former college and seminary professor, he was quick to critique my sermons, many times before allowing me to leave the pulpit. This proved to be an invaluable asset to my ministry. He did more for my ministry than anyone I have ever met, because his criticism forced me to work harder and to always be prepared. Furthermore, he helped me to develop a greater sense of responsibility and commitment to the ministry.

I quit seminary after two years to get married for the first time. Most people thought that we were too young and financially unstable for marriage. Yet, like many young couples, we took the approach that love conquers all. We soon faced the reality of how difficult marriage is when people are struggling financially. I worked, attended school several nights a week, pastored on weekends, and sold various products in whatever free time I had. I went door-to-door selling pots and pans, vacuum cleaners, and stereos. My wife also worked full time, attended school, and accompanied me on my pastoral duties.

The church that we initially pastored was one hundred miles from Dayton, in Kenton, Ohio. We would leave early on Sunday mornings and return late at night. Ultimately, I received the appointment to Lebanon, Ohio, which was thirty-five miles from Dayton. The trip was shorter, but outside of regular weekly visits with my wife's wonderful parents, who treated me like a son, we had very little social life. A year after our marriage, I accepted the job as dean at Lincoln University, in part because it included tuition credit for my wife and we felt that a change of scenery would be good for us. However, it wasn't long before my work schedule at the university extended into the evenings, and in addition, I began pastoring the Second Presbyterian Church of West Chester, Pennsylvania. Moving my wife away from her family to an isolated campus in the country proved to be disastrous. The marriage did not survive.

Somehow, by the grace of God, I managed to keep mind, soul, and spirit together. It was hard to get a good night's sleep, so I would work from morning until late evening, when exhaustion would overtake me. I met interesting young ladies who gave tremendous emotional support, but I found it difficult to establish meaningful relationships. I had built an impenetrable shield in the hope of never being hurt again. At the time I did not think of marriage as being an option in the foreseeable future. Obviously, had I kept that attitude, I would have missed the blessing of the wonderful experience that my second marriage has afforded me over the past twenty-three years. Bootstrappers are just like everybody else. They suffer the same types of hurts, pain, frustration, and guilt that others experience. Bootstrappers are not exempt from questioning or passing judgment on themselves. But they stop short of allowing these things to keep them mired in a state of depression or hopelessness. They have no time for pity parties or feeling sorry for themselves. For them every experience, good or bad, represents another rung in their ladder to success.

Moving to Boston represented more than a career change for me. The change of scenery was a necessary part of my therapy in moving beyond the divorce. There I met the Rev. (now Bishop) John R. Bryant, whose support, encouragement, and model of worship opened my eyes to new ways of defining the ministry. St. Paul A.M.E. Church in Cambridge, where he served as pastor, was alive with a vitality, vibrance, and community outreach that involved many of the students who gathered there from the surrounding colleges and universities. The power and spiritual dynamism of that ministry prepared me for the eventual call that came from Bishop Richard Allen Hildebrand, who asked me to come to New York and pastor Allen A.M.E. Church. Having received a recommendation from Bishop Vinton R. Anderson, he entrusted me with the leadership of the Allen A.M.E. congregation, whose pastor, the

Rev. Donald G. Ming, had been elected to the office of bishop. It was unusual for a thirty-one-year-old pastor to be assigned to such an esteemed church.

I met Elaine at John and Cecelia's home. She was a member of the choir at St. Paul A.M.E. Church and assisted Cecelia with their son, Jamal. Our relationship was platonic for the two years in which she became my best friend. My impenetrable shield was shattered, and in August 1975, I shared my feelings with her. On December 28th of that year, we were married in Memphis, Tennessee, at her home church, St. Jude Baptist.

When we moved to New York in August 1976, Elaine was expecting our first child, who was born in November, but she fully supported the relocation because she felt that I would be happiest when I was a full-time minister of the gospel. In essence, she realized that the bootstrapper spirit within me had surfaced by virtue of the excitement that I was expressing for this new challenge. My adrenaline was flowing, my pulse was racing at an accelerated pace; I was in bootstrapper heaven facing the new possibilities inherent in the Allen pastorate. Even with my exuberance, experience had taught me not to neglect my marriage. So, Elaine became a partner early on in the ministry. We worked together on many of the proposals that were funded and served as the foundation for the current Allen ministry. With her educational background, she formulated the plans for the founding of Allen Christian School, where she has been the educational director since its beginning in 1982.

Even bootstrappers need some help along the way. We are not isolated beings freely floating through space and time. We are all interdependent and interrelated. As we receive help, we are obligated to give help to others. Without this reciprocity, we may achieve a goal or two, but we cannot find fulfillment or lasting happiness; there can be no social cohesiveness, no sense of civilization or connection.

No one goes it alone. Remember when you were lent a few dollars just when you needed it? Or maybe a trusted friend helped you to figure out a problem. Maybe someone said a kind word or uplifted your spirit with an unexpected gesture. Where would Bill Gates be if IBM hadn't agreed to let him make the operating system for that first fledgling PC?

There would be no Microsoft, Windows 98, or any of the other spectacular technology that has derived from his creativity. Where would John H. Johnson be without that five-hundred-dollar loan from his mother? *Ebony* magazine would be just another faded dream. Where would John D. Rockefeller have gotten if he hadn't finally convinced a Cleveland commodities businessman to give him a job as a bookkeeper so that he could learn the business?

Even the government has been a partner in providing assistance to many Americans who have found success. Ross Perot, in spite of his haranguing about the size and power of government, received his start through government support. The difference between a bootstrapper and others is that they may receive government help, but they refuse to become totally dependent on it. A bootstrapper views government assistance as a leveraging tool that moves whatever he wishes to accomplish from a means to an end. Many of the railroads that were built in the 1800s would not have been built without government help. Human effort and vision, plus free land and subsidies, made cross-country transportation possible and helped people to help themselves. The Allen A.M.E. Community Development programs accept government assistance through housing subsidies and contracts for various services, but it doesn't end there. It leverages its own church resources from tithes and offerings to create public-private partnerships. Successful bootstrappers know how to leverage government resources for the good of people and communities by building coalitions for success.

The West was settled not by self-made, gun-toting outlaws, as the movies would have us believe, but instead by courageous men and women of all races who received a lot of help from the government to help themselves. The same thing can be said of farmers. Men and women applied their skill and effort to plant seeds, till the soil, and harvest the crops, but without land grants and subsidies from the government, many farmers may never have gotten started. They received help so they could make life better for themselves and others. Some of the greatest examples of government-supported programs are the development of the military-industrial complex and the Chrysler bailout. Bootstrappers are not reticent to help taxpayers get the full benefit of their dollars reinvested back into their communities for the delivery of goods, services, and jobs. Bootstrappers take what they receive and apply their toil, sweat, tears, intellect, energy, gifts, and talents to make what they already have even greater.

Are You a Bootstrapper?

There are two types of people in the world: people who *do* and people who *won't*. The people who *do* usually become the movers and shakers of society. They are the ones who make things happen. They are the producers, builders, and providers who make a difference in the lives of people. They devote every fiber of their being to making dreams come true—theirs and others. People who *do* don't have time for gossiping, watching television, or attending nonessential meetings. They don't moan, groan, or complain about the hand life has dealt them. They are action-oriented people, always moving, planning, and implementing. They may slow down for the bumps in the road, but before long, they are back to full speed. They may take detours when necessary, but they quickly find their way back to the road that leads them to their destiny. When they face difficulties, they simply take a deep breath, roll up their sleeves, and work their way through them. People who *do* come from every race and every religious and socioeconomic background. You can recognize them by the look of determination on their faces and the purposeful stride in their steps. They seem to always be going somewhere.

People who *do* wield a powerful magnetism. This magnetism has nothing to do with whether they are nice or mean but everything to do with the laserlike focus they give to any activity. Whether they are liked or disliked is irrelevant. Some people who *do* are hard to live and work with, yet they have a knack for attracting to their lives the people and circumstances that will ensure their own success and the success of others. They often are talked about, both negatively and positively, yet they are admired because they know how to get things done and make others feel good about the things they do.

People who *do* are charisma personified. They may be envied, but no one can deny that they have that special something. Their charisma is the direct result of their action-oriented personality and is manifested in leadership skills that attract and inspire people to high levels of enthusiasm and support for those things that have meaning and purpose. People around them work harder just to keep pace. People who *do* are like the rising sun that lights up the room and brings in the day. They are continually moving, with energy to burn. They can't sit still or relax; their mind is always busy thinking about the next task, the next project, or the next program. They fidget, they pace, and they generally get by on little sleep. Even when they are asleep, they are restless and uneasy because they are convinced that they really don't have time to sleep when there is so much to do, so much to think about. Before they've finished one project, they've already started on the next, stirred by a desire to move hastily toward fulfilling their driving ambitions.

Now I said that there are two types of people in the world. The second type are the people who *won't*. Not people who *don't* or people who *can't*, but people who *won't*. People who have the skills, talent, education, vision, and know-how to achieve their dreams but just refuse to get up and get busy. These are the people who *won't*. In my line of work, I get more calls from people who *won't* than from people who *do*. People who *won't* are those who expect you to do their work for them. They are more often than not trying to get something for nothing. They procrastinate and create alibis and excuses about why they are not performing. Their greatest nightmare is to be compared to a doer, whose every effort seems to be measured by some level of success.

People who *do* are bootstrappers. They say it takes all kinds to make the world go 'round. Maybe so, but I've learned that the people who *won't* get in the way of people who *do*—at least, they try to. My faith dictates that I love everybody, and I make every effort to do so. But at this stage of my life, I am able to choose whom I work with. People who *do* cannot work with people who *won't*, because those people keep them from getting their work done. People who *won't* increase the workload of people who *do*. It is too time-consuming dealing with people who merely want to talk about what doers are doing or attack what they have done. A bootstrapper is too busy growing and pursuing new goals to worry about people who *won't*.

My greatest joy comes from doing things that lend themselves to bringing fulfillment to myself and others. As a bootstrapper I consider myself a doer, not a talker. Therefore, my work speaks more loudly for me and about me than I could ever speak for myself. Bootstrappers can articulate with great substance and eloquence of speech, but if given the choice, they would prefer to "walk the walk" rather than merely "talk the talk." A bootstrapper is more interested in creating a sustainable product than self-promotion.

Are you a doer? Do you like to take action rather than just sit around and talk? Do you prefer working toward solutions to problems rather than complaining about them? Do you have that burning zeal, desire, and determination to succeed, not only for yourself but also for the betterment of society? Then, congratulations, you are a bootstrapper. Welcome to the club!

THE NINE ACTION STEPS: AN OVERVIEW

When undertaking any new endeavor, it helps to have guidelines to assist you in turning your dreams into reality. By setting goals, developing plans, implementing procedures, and fine-tuning your schedule and activities, you'll provide a solid foundation for your new endeavor. That's the only way to ensure that all your decisions and actions will flow from the same value system. However, you must be careful to maintain some flexibility in case of unanticipated changes. In fact, I encourage you to not overcompartmentalize your life activities. From time to time we've all been guilty of having one set of values for our life at the office and another for personal relationships. This splits our focus and drains our energy. Our lives become less than honest. My strong recommendation is that you use bootstrapping in all areas of your life—personal, family, and professional. That is a sure way of maintaining a consistency and focus that will enable you to stay the course and place you in a position where others see you as a person who is reliable and trustworthy. You will discover that you are going to need this credibility to achieve your goals.

The guidelines presented in this book are organized into three tiers: personal activation, collective execution, and global acceleration. Each tier, or section, contains three action steps. The journey begins inward with self-assessment exercises and "ends" with us maximizing the highest potential in our lives and inspiring others to do the same. In reality, there is no ending, because the way of the bootstrapper is an upward spiral that propels a person to reach the highest heights possible while going through life.

About the Action Steps

When you consider the fact that there are many individuals who are successful today because of their own initiatives and the assumption of personal responsibility, you should realize that you too, can achieve more successes in your life. You need not wait any longer to begin your own bootstrapping process. Now is the time to give up procrastination and begin writing a new chapter in your life. Bootstrapping can help you to bring reality to your dreams and aspirations.

Consider the fact that entire communities have saved themselves from violence, drug infestation, and other problems by using this program, and you'll begin to appreciate the magnitude of the process. Because of its magnitude, I've broken this book down into nine distinct and manageable action steps so that you won't feel overwhelmed. Each step will guide you with exercises and ideas that you can use to change your life. Read each action step thoroughly and complete the exercises. I strongly recommend that you do the steps in order, because they build on one another.

Before you get started, read the following overview of the bootstrapping program. This will give you a good idea of what to expect in the next sections.

Activate!

Before you can sell yourself to the world, you must start within with an introspective search of your soul. Michael Jackson phrased it this way in the title of one of his hit songs: "I am starting with the man in the mirror." You cannot effectively meet your needs or anyone else's if you do not reckon with yourself first. William Shakespeare challenges us with the words "To thine own self be true." Have you ever wondered why the flight attendant mandates you to put on your oxygen mask before trying to help anyone else? This can serve to remind you that you can't help anyone else until you first help yourself. Even though the person in the mirror (that's you) may have shortcomings and failings, you should be challenged to use all the power that is within you to turn those weaknesses into strengths. You should work to know as many truths as possible about yourself; otherwise, what others know about you can ultimately become destructive when used against you. So, get rid of your pretensions and get ready to start on the successful journey toward fulfillment. Putting first things first means starting with your own "self-needs analysis."

The three action steps in this section will activate your thinking and creativity to develop a firm foundation for positive, lasting change. If you are looking to improve your life, you cannot afford to skip these steps.

Action Step 1. Know Yourself

The first step in becoming a bootstrapper is honestly and objectively assessing your strengths and weaknesses. This will help you in discovering your mission in life and achieving the goals that you set for yourself. Each person is put on the earth for a reason, but it is up to each of us to uncover what that reason truly is. You have a purpose in life, but you will never identify it until you truly know yourself. Start acting like a detective, and search every phase of your life until this very moment for the clues to your true identity. Unfortunately, many people never do this, and as a result, they meander through life without tapping into the fullness of their potential.

In order to assess your strengths and weaknesses and to find out what your mission in life truly is, you must look deep within. Face those tough issues about yourself that you have tried to avoid. Most people think they know who they are and what they believe in, but often when they are forced into unanticipated situations, they are astonished at how little they know about themselves. Getting to know yourself also means getting to know what you truly believe, not just what you pay lip service to. Often, the two are in conflict, and that is why your best efforts are undermined. Some of us need to take a reality check so we can make changes in our actions. We must change our habits before we are consumed by our own negative behavior so that we can portray an image that is more representative of who we are.

People often make the mistake of using their roles, titles, positions, or life circumstances to define who they are. I function as a husband, father, minister, politician, columnist, and businessman, but these roles do not define me. People often think that who they are is measured by their roles and titles. I take the position that *what* I am called does not define *who* I am. Who I am is defined by what I do, not the roles I fill. Successful bootstrappers are content to let their work speak for them. In a world and time where change is an inevitable way of life, you must work toward building substantive, sustainable accomplishments if you intend to be more than a mere survivor.

What if you change careers several times, as many do today? How then will you understand your identity? Does your identity shift every time you change jobs or get a new title? If you rise from poverty to wealth, the changing conditions will obviously necessitate functioning at a different level, but even then you should always be cognizant of who you are and not run the risk of losing your values, your integrity, and your identity. Shifting your identity every time your circumstances change is not the most efficient way to live, yet so many have made this very serious mistake.

Before you can achieve your goals or manifest your dreams, you must commit to the process of getting to know yourself. It has been reported that most human beings use only a tiny portion of their brain power. It makes you wonder what happens with the unused portion. Getting to know yourself will help you to solve the mystery of who you are and allow your mind to transcend what you have previously believed to be your limitations. This process not only helps you to pay more attention to your conscious thoughts and perceptions but also helps you to deal with those old subconscious motivations that have been sabotaging your efforts.

Action Step 2. Claim What's Yours

Every individual has needs, wants, and deep soul desires. Yet many never get out of the starting block because they don't know where the finish line is. During the years that I served as a college dean, I saw many students who entered college merely to please their parents but did not have the faintest idea what they wanted to do or be in life. Many of them ultimately dropped out of the institution because they had not been able to clarify their goals. If you have no idea which goals to pursue— and this is common—you probably will never get out of the gate. You may even become victimized by the paralysis of analysis that has broken so many dreams and grounded so many aspirations.

Recognition is the key to unlocking the second action step in the bootstrapping process: you can't claim what is yours until you identify what you are seeking. Next, you must acknowledge the extent to which you are willing to make sacrifices today as a means of ensuring your successes tomorrow. Each of us has been blessed with a spiritual inheritance, and that's our birthright from God. Our spiritual inheritance evolves from the beginning of our lives, when we receive God's spirit, which is the breath of life. That makes us a living soul. It is the one thing that places every person on a plane of equality. It's yours to claim, but you must realize it is there. Even if you cannot see it in substantive form, you must believe that it is yours, pursue it, and work diligently to bring it into reality. You must maintain a moral value system that allows you not only to claim what's yours but also to keep it.

Action Step 3. Plan Your Destiny

Every year I speak to thousands of smart men and women across the country from every racial, ethnic, and economic background, and the story is the same. Though smart in the academic sense, with a strong desire to succeed and brimming with potential, they have not produced the results that they have been longing for. They have looked for help, and even when they have received it, they have not been successful in implementing their plans. Like many of us, they have not come to fully understand who they are.

Opportunities are the raw materials of potential that a bootstrapper has to work with. Potential is the promise that has not yet come into being. It is the possibility that is latent and undeveloped. Without a plan to point you in the right direction, you will never know the fulfillment that you desire. Your promise, potential, and possibility will lie dormant, and because of a lack of cultivation, it will never become actualized. People often skip planning, but no company intent on growth, prosperity, and longevity would ever skip this crucial step. No builder would start construction without it. No nation would dare not plan for the future. We must treat our lives in the same way that companies, builders, and nations do. We must plan our destiny and work the plan to success. Even with the world's concerns about the Y2K problem, people are still planning for the next century.

Many wealthy people became rich because they had a plan. Buildings are constructed from architectural plans, clothes from patterns, and meals from recipes. Since our lives are more important than any of these, it seems that developing a plan should be as natural as drinking water or getting a reasonable amount of sleep. Planning is an important action step because it lays out the blueprint and charts the course for a better life. However, I would caution you, as a builder or developer, to always be mindful that even the best-thought-out plans are subject to change. But a plan is necessary because it helps you to concentrate on your objectives and focus on how you intend to meet your goals.

When I came to Queens, New York, in 1976, to pastor Allen A.M.E. Church, we had about fourteen hundred members. The community surrounding the church was basically middle class, but the scourge of drugs and crime had caused it to be seen as a community in decline. Every newspaper article about the community was slanted to focus on its negatives. It would have been easy to give up on the community and lose hope of its possibility for recovery. But I would not accept the definitions that others gave to the community. Instead, I saw it as a fertile field of opportunity. Many people thought that change would never happen. But today, twenty-two years later, we've built our membership up to more than eleven thousand people, making Allen Church one of the largest churches in the country. The church is also a nationally recognized model of economic self-improvement and self-help. Allen Church was there even as the community was declining. The difference between then and now is that we have become more of a catalyst for change. Other communities can do the same. I have met with countless clergy groups around the country, in seminaries, and here in the church, encouraging them to begin planning for the next millennium by taking responsibility for their communities.

If thousands of immigrants can come here to the "land of opportunity" with dreams, plans, and a determination to succeed and take advantage of the opportunities that these communities offer, then those who are native-born ought to realize that they can do the same thing. With a good plan it is possible not only to rebuild communities but to create sustainable jobs for the good of their residents and make the notion of welfare-to-work a more feasible reality.

Execute!

We tend to forget that the early settlers in America came to flee religious oppression. They were inspired to join together and take their burning desire for religious freedom to a new land. America has always been a place where people were able to combine their individual strengths and personalities in a synergy that benefited them, both individually and collectively. From the pilgrims to the slaves and the modern-day immigrants, one of the great strengths of Americans has been their willingness to work together. Our ancestors succeeded because of a bootstrapping spirit that superseded the limitations of their communities. Even if those communities were called ghettos, they were like paradise compared to where the immigrants came from. These people pooled their time, energy, money, and resources to create a better life for each and every one. Today's immigrants have learned that there is strength in numbers. The models that they build are similar to those of our foreparents, who understood that success is almost impossible for those who function in a vacuum. The African American church in America understands that its survival has been based upon its willingness to work toward the collective inspiration of its people. It has always promulgated a program of bootstrapping and self-help as a paradigm for liberation.

The three action steps in this section emerge from the historical foundation of faith upon which this nation was built and many lives transformed. You say you don't have the time to help, learn from, or work with others? If you intend to develop into a real bootstrapper, you cannot afford not to align with like minds, kindred spirits, and zealous souls who share your vision. The quality of your life depends on it!

Action Step 4. Work Together, Build Together

What is the true spirit of collaboration? Many of our efforts don't even get off the ground because we don't really understand what the process involves. Many a community-wide effort has failed when all the responsibility ended up on the shoulders of one person. The civil rights movement of the sixties has not been able to retain or reclaim its passionate fervor because of the death of one man, Dr. Martin Luther King, Jr. True collaboration is built not on egos, personalities, or emotion but on a shared vision, commitment, and purposeful action.

In this action step, you will learn how to work with others effectively so that your individual and collective efforts can be maximized. You will learn how to choose your friends and colleagues wisely. You need people who can bring skills, influence, commitment, and more to the table. You must be around positive thinkers who can share in a trusting relationship. This may go against the grain for many who are in the habit of letting others choose their friends for them.

Bootstrappers have learned that in order to build successes, emotion must be cultivated with intelligence in order to avoid making the critical mistakes that have led to the destruction of many. Bootstrappers know where they want to go and how they intend to get there. They choose their relationships carefully and generally live, work, and relate with people who are moving in the same direction.

I know a little something about working with others from my eleven years in the U.S. House of Representatives. A major part of the job involves persuading others to share your view and vote your way. I mastered the art of bipartisanship when I realized that political differences should not stand in the way of progress. Many of my successes in Congress came about by virtue of my ability to work with people who did not necessarily share my political ideologies.

In this action step I'll share with you some of my success strategies for team building, effective communication, and negotiation. A good bootstrapper is aware that success means working with others, even when they don't share all of your ideas. It means working outside of the box so that the interests of many are met.

Action Step 5. Seize Opportunities

Bootstrappers are masters at seizing opportunities, and if there is no opportunity, they'll create one. This ability is what separates the people who succeed from the people who stay stuck in dreams, good ideas, procrastination, laziness, and failure. Some of the best minds with the greatest ideas have seen others with lesser talent but tremendous drive and ambition prosper from the same ideas. The difference? The ability to observe and the boldness to take advantage of a chance meeting, a bit of information in a magazine, a new product. When you are focused on your goals and you have a plan to achieve them, you'll suddenly awaken to the field of opportunities that have been surrounding you all along.

Taking advantage of opportunities, or opportunism, has gotten a bad rap. We've all heard stories about barons of industry who compete at cutthroat levels. What we don't hear about are the individuals and companies who succeed quietly and with integrity. Rarely do we hear about the nice guy or gal finishing first, but it can be done. It is being done every day. These bootstrappers take advantage of opportunities, but they do it in a way that hurts no one. This positive opportunism is a win-win situation for everyone. The good news is that you can seize opportunities with integrity; in other words, you don't have to walk over others or stab people in the back as you're climbing the ladder of success.

Opportunities are often hidden in the most unlikely situations. Often, when we experience an uncomfortable event, such as downsizing or illness, we immediately view it as a negative. Bootstrappers who have the knack for recognizing and creating opportunities can turn a negative situation inside out and transform it into something that helps them to succeed.

I submit that you cannot succeed in life without the ability to seize and create opportunities. Maybe an opportunity has presented itself to you and you are unsure what to do about it. If you don't know how to take advantage of opportunities, or if you lack the boldness it takes, never fear. In this action step, we'll be discussing how to seek, identify, and create opportunities. It is my hope that by reading this section, not only will you get some practical suggestions, but your own creativity will be stimulated and you'll be brainstorming and taking action in no time!

Action Step 6. Deal with Crisis

No one enjoys bad times, least of all bootstrappers. We are built for action, so when a setback occurs and we are forced to retreat and reflect on what has happened, this can go against the grain. But into everyone's life a crisis will fall—so get ready. In fact, if you are trying to do something positive with your life, I guarantee that someone or something will try to hinder you. It's the nature of the game, so expect it.

There is no quick way out of a crisis. In fact, some have spent years managing theirs. Some companies run on what's called "crisis management." They never seem to emerge from problems, yet they thrive.

We all know some person whose life is like a great soap opera. It seems as if every day there's a new story to tell, some new sad song to sing. You may not want to live like that, and I surely wouldn't advise it, but the hard fact is that life will sometimes sour on you.

In this section, I'll discuss some of my own setbacks and crises and how I dealt with them, how I used them as a platform to view my life, my goals, and my future. Every successful person I know has had to wade in troubled waters, so if you are in the midst of your own personal trial or tribulation, you are in good company. As you read through the stories in this section, take heart: it doesn't rain forever. Your attitude, whether positive or negative, will make all the difference in the magnitude and duration of the crisis.

Accelerate!

In this section, we're putting our foot on the pedal and accelerating our efforts. Global acceleration takes all the action steps we have learned and puts them in motion on a grand scale. This section contains the last three action steps.

Global acceleration is a rapid movement of our ideas communicated in meteoric time sequences with new and advancing technology. This is when life really gets exciting, because anything can and usually does happen. The action steps in this section use obstacles as springboards, launching us into realms that climax with feelings of excellence, accomplishment, and joy. We come to believe that we can deal with anything that life throws our way. That is what global acceleration is all about—making a way out of no way.

Action Step 7. Take the Lead

If people aren't ridiculing whatever I'm saying or calling it "hopeless," "impossible," or "crazy," then I feel like I'm doing something wrong! Real leaders present ideas and possibilities that have never been tried before. Many times, they find it necessary to force people out of their comfort zones in order to reach the fullness of their potential. I sometimes have to say things that are unpopular to my congregation or lead the church in doing something that we've never done before. That's what it means to be a leader. You'll stand out from the rest because you assume responsibility for initiatives that affect the lives of many people.

Leaders have different styles, but they all must have one thing in common: a passion for change. They have courage; they take risks that lead to extraordinary feats of daring. Some leaders are well known, and some are not—but all assume the responsibility for making dreams happen against the odds. Bootstrappers are leaders! Some are born, and others are made, but all of them stand out because they are not always conformists who "go along to get along." They set the agenda rather than follow it.

In this action step, you will learn how to reach deep within and draw out your natural leadership abilities. Chances are, you've already been assuming leadership on projects at work, or you take the lead at home, at church, or in your community. In this step, you'll learn about the different styles of leadership and how to refine your own abilities.

Action Step 8. Stretch!

There will always be some people who don't want to change. It's easy to just stay put and be comfortable in mediocrity. But it's a real challenge to push yourself to go further. Pushing yourself is exactly what you have to do, and bootstrappers know this. That is why they are aggressive, enterprising, and not given to procrastination. They take the basic approach that yesterday is gone and tomorrow is uncertain. Therefore, today must count for something. You have to realize that the only person you should compete with is yourself. Instead of resting on your laurels, you should always be pushing yourself to achieve new heights and excel beyond the norms that others have established for you.

In this step, we'll take another look at the goals you set for yourself in action step 2. Now is the time to reflect on what you've done and determine what you could have done better. As you work through the program, new dreams will come, and there won't be enough time in the day to get it all done. But you'll find a way.

Action Step 9. Create a Lasting Legacy

When you test your limits like this, you raise the standards for yourself and for generations to follow. In turn, you are challenging others to do their best. Bootstrappers create lasting legacies because their focus is not just on getting through the day or "working for the weekend" but on building for the future. Instead of leaving a mess for future generations to sort through and clean up, you'll want to create blueprints and build paradigms as solid foundations for future success. This is one of the fundamental tenets of bootstrappers: not only do they want to be successful, but they are interested in the success of others. Material success is just one small part of the equation. At the core of the bootstrapper's drive is the desire to create a legacy that will long outlast the physical.

Throughout this book, I will continue to tell you my story, not to boast but to prove to you that it doesn't take as much as you think to achieve big dreams. Everything that you need, God has already placed within you. I had the extra blessings of great parents, a supportive family, and a strong community. You may not come from a family that is similar to mine, but you can still overcome the odds if you acquire a bootstrapper spirit. Many of the blessings that are manifest in my life came through the very same bootstrapping program that I am laying out for you here. It is part of my lasting legacy to pass on the bootstrapping program to anyone who is willing to listen.

Writing this book is another step of the bootstrapper's program for me. It involves launching into a new arena that I have never experienced before. It is a part of my continuing desire to prove that bootstrappers know no boundaries or limitations but are willing to stretch the borders of their minds by seeking and taking on new challenges. This project represents the opening of another door in a career that, by most definitions, has been successful and fulfilling. Now that I have seen this door, the bootstrapper spirit within me demands that I go in, explore, experiment, and work toward becoming a successful author.

Being a bootstrapper means starting to take your dreams out of the clouds and bring them into the reality of your life. It means using what you have got to get what you truly want—not symbolic wants born out of social conditioning, but desires that God has placed deep within your soul.

If all you have is a vision, courage, and the will to succeed, you have the power to make your dreams come true. Stick with me and work the program. The facts of your life may be overwhelming to you right now, but just remember: they are not the whole truth of your life. Your truth includes God's good plan for you and the deepest desires of your soul. Now use your imagination, grab hold of your bootstraps, and pull. It's time to lift yourself up into a new reality where the good life awaits!

PART 2

ACTIVATE!

In the life of any society there are key moments that, for better or worse, create massive change. A critical mass of discontentment is reached, and people are activated to rebel against the status quo. Activation occurs first on the individual, then on a collective, level. Activation is the result of a great motivating emotion of such raw power, such force that you are utterly compelled to action. The emotion is so strong that you feel as if you have no choice but to do something. The time for talk has passed; the time for action is now.

The decision to leave home and go away to college was a difficult one for me. I had to overcome the fear of being in a totally new environment, physically separated from my family. I had to resolve the question of how to pay for my education. I needed to face my concerns about whether I would be able to compete academically. After the Reverend Williams took me to Wilberforce in May, it seemed that September came too quickly. But, even with my uncertainties, at the appropriate time I was on the Greyhound bus, taking that long ride that would change my life.

From all I had heard about life "up north," I expected that I would never again face some of the prejudices that I had dealt with in Houston. It did not take long to realize that this trip would present constant reminders of what I was hoping to leave behind. In Oklahoma, Missouri, and Indiana, I found myself still going in the back rather than the front doors of restaurants, and using toilets and drinking fountains that had the COLORED sign emblazoned on them.

The personal activation of leaving home to go to college provided an opportunity for me to expand the cultural dimensions of my life, to broaden the level of my understanding and widen the horizons of my limited scope. There are some things in life that you don't really know until you take action and move from your places of comfort. Most of the things that you need to succeed in life will not come to you; you must find them, you must go to where they are, you must take action by getting off of your hind parts and making them happen. Otherwise, you may become captive to the nightmares that have replaced your dreams because of your inaction. A bootstrapper must act on his impulses, aspirations, dreams, ideas, and thoughts. Nobody can do as much for you as you can do for yourself. This is your moment, the sixty seconds that can change your life, but you must stop procrastinating and act now.

I am often asked the question, "How are you able to get so many things done?" The simple answer is that between 5:30 A.M. and 11:30 A.M. on most days, I am vigorously engaged in programming a number of functions as effectively as possible. I have learned to use time wisely so that I am not merely going through the motions of life. My orientation is focused on consistently pursuing some goal. My schedule is daunting and challenging, but not overwhelming, because I don't waste time. When I am home writing or preparing sermons, it is not unusual for me to also be preparing dinner. My telephone conversations are specific and short. I am able to watch the morning news while exercising, and my other television viewing is very limited. I am a bootstrapper, so there is no time in my life for sitting and idle talk or gossip. I have a social life, but even that is usually managed and generally scheduled. When a meeting is unproductive, is repetitive, or lacks focus, I find an appropriate time to head for the exit.

I have been blessed with an ability to compartmentalize the important and essential things that need my personal or immediate attention from those that do not. People who work for me actually work with me, in an action-packed, result-oriented process, focused on the attainment of positive results. They learn to walk faster, think more positively, react more quickly, and act freely with confidence. Being active, functioning, moving, and working with vigor, energy, and spirit helps me to stay physically fit, mentally alert, and morally strong. New ideas are constantly springing up in the recesses of my mind, and as they are revealed, I write them down for immediate or future action.

At a meeting of the FannieMae Foundation Board, of which I am a member, we received a report that African American and Latino home-ownership lagged far behind that of Whites. Since home ownership is a key element in building stable families, generating capital, and revitalizing communities, I felt it imperative that I personally get involved in trying to close the gap by helping these groups pursue the "American Dream." So I did a commercial for the foundation. Allen Church, through one of its corporations, has built 160 new homes. My appeal to the Allen congregation is for the members not only to tithe and give offerings of 10 percent to the house of God (the church), but also to give 10 percent to themselves and save money for the down payment on a home. I have challenged them to take action for their future, and many who never thought they could own a home are now proud homeowners or are working toward the fulfillment of that dream.

A year ago, while watching news about the stock market activity for the previous day, I wondered how many members of the congregation invested in stocks and bonds. Raising the question in a Men's Club meeting the following Monday night, I was shocked that out of over one hundred men, only five or six had an investment portfolio beyond insurance or a bank savings account. We took action by starting an investment club that was open to the entire church membership. Three hundred people invested in the club. Now there are twelve investment clubs, focusing on different segments of the market. These are the kinds of phenomenal results we get when we act on our ideas.

Activation can change the way you think, live, and function—so what are you waiting for? There is no reason that you cannot take action on your dreams and desires. Real bootstrappers don't just think about what they would like to do; they take action.

Activation will help you overcome the well-meaning social theories and programs that were designed to help people and institutions recover from economic disaster and injustice and springboard them into self-sufficiency. These programs have backfired into a pervasive, self-destructive mind-set of dependency and blame. This mind-set prevents us from assuming responsibility for our thoughts, words, and deeds. When we abdicate responsibility, we give away our power. And when we give away our power, we become dependent on others for our survival. Activation helps us change the definitions of our reality. In philosophy, I was taught that "the active, creative mind is the source of all reality."

Today, as we stand on the threshold of a bold, new era, once again I feel the swelling of emotion. Bootstrapping through personal activation is making a comeback. There are still so many problems to solve, but we know we are up to the task. There may be great discontentment, but there is also great hope. We are being activated to change not only our life circumstances but our methods. You know that we are on the brink of something great when a military man like General Colin Powell takes the lead on volunteerism, an inspiring move in our capitalistic society. We are now learning to include values, spiritual principles, and morality the way we conduct our businesses, run our government, raise our children, and develop our communities. We are learning that caring for the environment and making money need not be mutually exclusive. We are beginning to understand that helping others to help themselves is an investment in social capital, and when we invest in others, we make our society strong. Most important, we are learning that change must first occur from within before positive, lasting change can be made in our life circumstances. We are being activated to reclaim our bootstrapping heritage.

Enough Is Enough!

In the life of every individual there are also key moments that, for better or worse, create a change in attitudes, beliefs, and life circumstances. It is in these key moments that change is born, takes shape, and produces either misery or joy in our lives. Key life moments are powerful and emotionally intense. They stir our sleeping spirits, energize our bodies, inflame our imaginations, and incite a riot of activity. The good news is that you can create a key life moment right now. You can reclaim your power by activating yourself.

The bad news is, that's not usually how it goes. Life change is often motivated by heartbreak or tragedy. Seldom are we inspired to change when we are happy. Most often we have to be depressed or anxious or bored. We have to be poor or sick or overweight. We have to be brokenhearted or on the receiving end of a physical attack. We have to be in dire straits before we feel that peculiar stirring of our spirits, the inner activation that makes us get up off the couch, forces us to turn off the TV, put away the calorie-filled desserts, cut up the credit card, and make a lasting change.

We claim our power when we get up on our throne of personal responsibility. That means the buck stops with you when it comes to *your* thoughts, *your* feelings, *your* words, *your* deeds, and *your* life circumstances.

If we are going to accept responsibility for our lives, then we've got to stop blaming God, the devil, the government, our parents, our cultural and social background, or our race for our own poor decision making and impoverished life circumstances.

Let your reading of this book be a key moment in your life. Let it activate you to make positive, lasting change. That you are dissatisfied with your life is a good thing. A restless spirit is a blessing. That is God taking you by the shoulders and lovingly yet firmly shaking you and waking you up. God is trying to get your attention because you deserve to live a better life.

Personal Activation Need Not Be "Politically Correct"

There are as many ways to get activated as there are people in the world. Self-help books may suggest ways to get motivated, but true motivation comes from within. In action step 1, you'll be doing some self-assessment exercises to help you discover or be reminded of your true soul desires. Your soul is where you'll find the buried treasure of your own unique passions that will stir you to action. Until then, think about the areas in your life that are poor to mediocre. What would it take to make you take that first step? What mitigating factor would be strong enough to override your fears and inertia?

Take, for example, weight loss. It seems that everyone I know wants to lose weight, and they all have their own reasons. About six years ago I wanted to enhance my health and fitness, so I bought a treadmill and work out on it every day. Even when I don't feel like it, I work out because I want to stay healthy. I've added a Nordic bike, weights, and an abdominal machine. Each morning or evening, whether on the road or at home, I exercise. I have found that when I exercise at 5:30 A.M., I am able to mentally organize my whole day while getting the full benefit of maintaining my health. When my schedule precludes morning exercises, evening exercise helps me to bring the day to a close with a very positive experience that makes it easier to get a good night's rest.

To achieve my health and fitness goal, it was also necessary to change my eating habits—no more quarts of ice cream before going to bed.

Singing star Vesta knew she needed to lose weight but never felt truly activated to do so. Neither her ample size nor the big clothes hanging in her closet motivated her to get her eating under control. It took the loss of a recording contract to wake her up. Although she was beautiful and talented, her obesity was anathema in the image-driven music industry. It took the loss of income to activate her to get her body in shape. She started exercising and eating wisely and eventually lost more than one hundred pounds. Not only does she look and feel good, but the weight loss gave her the confidence she needed to get her career back on track and land a lucrative recording contract.

Now, some might say that Vesta didn't lose weight for the "right" reasons, such as health, but personal activation has nothing to do with political correctness and everything to do with your unique motivating, activating passion. The threat of ill health is enough to keep me working out every day; money did it for Vesta. My co-author wants to look cute. Whatever gets you going is valid. Ultimately, it doesn't matter what other people think. Personal activation is personal; this is all about *you*.

Tragedy As Personal Activation

What happens when your entire life is turned upside down by a totally random, unexpected event? You may not have control over the event, but you can and must control how you respond to it.

One day in 1980, thirteen-year-old Cari Lightner was walking down a city street. That walk would be her last. She was killed by a hit-and-run drunk driver. After police identified the perpetrator, it was discovered that he had four prior drunk driving arrests and two convictions.

The loss of a child is a parent's worst nightmare. Imagine trying to deal with such a senseless death. No one would deny Cari's mother, Candy, her grief. No one would blame her if she had allowed her daughter's death to overwhelm and paralyze her. Cari's death could have been prevented by stronger laws. This enraged Candy Lightner, and her anger activated her to advocate for tougher laws and a tougher judicial response to drunk driving. Then she motivated others who had also lost loved ones to join the movement. Today, Mothers Against Drunk Driving, MADD, has hundreds of chapters and millions of members worldwide. One tragic event activated one mother, and then millions more, to get the laws changed.

Some tragedies we have no control over, but others we do. For years now, doctors have been telling us that smoking is bad for our health and that lung cancer is a preventable disease. Yet thousands continue to die as a direct consequence of smoking. Despite all the research, the nation acts recklessly. If you know you need to lose weight, work out, stop smoking, then why don't you? What's going on? We have the information; we know what to do. The link that connects our knowledge to action is missing. That missing link is a combination of belief and passion. You can have all the information and desire in the world, but if your underlying beliefs are undermining your best efforts, you will not succeed. You cannot work against what you believe. Belief + passion = personal activation.

In this section you will be exploring some of your most sacred beliefs and how they hinder and help you. What you will discover may surprise you. Why wait and let tragedy activate you? Write down the following sentence, post it everywhere, and commit it to memory:

I have the power to activate myself!

That's right! You don't have to wait for cancer, heart disease, or a car wreck to compel you to action. When you decide that you want your life to be different, when you commit, with all your heart and passion, to making a change, then you will make a change! When you get fired up about making change, nothing can stop you. You will be like a force of nature. Recently, hurricane George stormed through the Caribbean and the southern states, leaving death and destruction in its wake. Unfortunately, too often we label passion as negative, like a destructive storm. "Chill out," people say—but I say, get fired up! Passion is positive and activating. Don't wait for tragedy to strike. Take responsibility and activate yourself.

Necessity, the Mother of Personal Activation

Madame C. J. Walker was arguably the most famous African American female millionaire before Oprah Winfrey. The myth is that her discovery of the straightening comb led to her success, but that's not true. She didn't discover the straightening comb, but she did create the first line of hair care products for African American women. What inspired her to take the leap of faith in a racially hostile climate? Madame's hair had begun to fall out, and she was desperately trying to create an ointment that would prevent balding! Thomas Edison, Alexander Graham Bell, Bill Gates, Daniel Hale Williams, Albert Einstein, Marie Curie, and all the great inventors were inspired to devote years of their lives to creating a product or technology because they saw the need for it. Necessity, the mother of invention, is also the mother of personal activation.

At Allen A.M.E. Church, we were driven to take the education of our children into our own hands because their needs were not being met in the public school system. Elaine, as a former public school teacher, felt that we could offer a better equal educational opportunity to every child by building our own school. When I introduced the idea to the congregation, they were excited but assumed that we would look to the government for financial assistance. When I said that we would build the new school from the ground up with our own church resources, some of the enthusiasm waned. This was in 1976, before reports on public school education had revealed the magnitude of the problem. Many of the members did not believe that we could raise the money, or that we'd find enough students to fill our school. Fortunately, there were enough people who believed we could do it. They became activated and led the congregation in raising over 1.9 million dollars. With a 2.1-million-dollar loan from a consortium of African American banks, the school opened in a brand-new building in 1982. Rather than having a shortage of students, for the past seventeen years we have averaged more than one hundred annually on the waiting list. Similarly, Marva Collins founded Chicago's Westside Preparatory School after years of experiencing frustration as a public school teacher. Many of the problems facing education today can be solved if more people will become activated.

One recent phenomenon that has created a great need in our society is corporate downsizing. Our parents taught us that if we went to school and worked long and hard, the company would take care of us in retirement. Corporate downsizing has been a rude awakening. No one's job is secure. When it comes to the bottom line, everyone is dispensable. Millions of workers have been released into the marketplace, and this has created a two-sided coin of crisis and opportunity. Out of necessity, many women and men have been activated to start their own companies. The number of small home-based businesses, the fastest-growing segment of the U.S. economy, is increasing at a rate of more than 10 percent per year. Approximately twelve to fifteen million people are operating their own businesses out of their homes, in part because of corporate downsizing—and that number will surely double, perhaps even triple, in the next century.

Successful home-based entrepreneurs are extraordinary bootstrappers. They combine passion for their work with an ethic of self-sufficiency. They are masters at networking, negotiation, and communication. They have learned how to use their limited resources to maximize their bottom line. The really good ones even give back to their communities. For many, getting laid off was the best thing that ever happened to them. Downsizing activated them to take a risk. If they had remained in a secure job, they might never have felt the push that they needed to start their own company.

Setbacks and Failures:
The Quick Paths to Personal Activation

What we need in this country is a new definition of failure. Instead of viewing failure as a character defect or something to be ashamed of, we should recognize it as a part of the path to success. Failure often provides just the springboard we need to make a dramatic change in our lives. Failure makes us look at how we've been doing things. Failure provides crucial feedback on what we did right and what we could have done better. Failure allows us to learn from our mistakes and apply those hard-earned lessons to future planning.

In 1965, I applied for a promotion at Lincoln University from my position as director of student affairs to an open position as dean of students. The director of admissions also applied for the position and was appointed to it. I felt like a failure. I had worked hard for the university and believed that the position should be mine. When the president spoke with me, he indicated that the only difference between our credentials was my lack of a master's degree. However, he gave me a promotion with greater responsibility, as the associate dean working with the person that he had selected for the job. I learned from the experience and went back to school so that I would never be denied another position because of a lack of academic credentials.

Sometimes, what we see as a failure turns out to be a blessing. That was the case when in 1975 I was offered a pastorate of a church in Norwalk, Connecticut. At the last minute, the bishop informed me that the church preferred having a pastor who was married, and therefore he could not appoint me. Four months later, I got married, and seven months later, I received the appointment to Allen Church. I was disappointed initially about not going to Norwalk, but I rejoiced that another opportunity presented itself after such a short period. This time I was ready, although I did not get married for the purpose of qualifying for a church.

In 1992, while serving in Congress, I failed to win a seat on the powerful House Appropriations Committee. I lost in spite of promises from my colleagues to support me on the basis of my seniority. But, by secret ballot, they chose two members from New York who were my juniors. However, having to remain on the Banking Committee turned out to be great for two reasons: I was able to chair the Subcommittee on Oversight and Investigation during the savings and loan crisis, which was a high profile situation. Also, in 1994 the Democrats lost control of the House, and one of the more junior members lost his position on the Appropriations Committee, a position I would have lost if I had been there in his place.

Nobody wants to fail, but nobody is excluded from failure; therefore, we all need to learn from our failures rather than making the same mistakes over and over again. A bootstrapper does not allow a failure to become a permanent resting place but learns to move on with his life.

Today Chris Rock is famous for his razor-sharp comedy, but before he hit the big time, he was just a moderately funny guy. Nothing special. Discovered by Eddie Murphy, Rock was, in effect, an Eddie Murphy wanna-be. He got bit parts in a couple of movies (*I'm Gonna Git You Sucka* and *Beverly Hills Cop II*); then he got the chance of a lifetime to work as a member of the cast of *Saturday Night Live.* By all accounts, his performance was lackluster. Chris Rock didn't seem to know who he was as a performer. In three years, he left the show to work on *In Living Color,* but by then that show was on the decline. As an entertainer, he was floundering. His timing was off, and he was making bad judgment calls.

Chris Rock's key activating moment came one night during a standup performance in Chicago when his opening act, Martin Lawrence, "annihilated" him. "That was a pivotal moment, because I wasn't really prepared. . . . It just made me realize I had to change my whole game."

And that's what he did. Instead of whining, he went back to learn the basics. For a year, he apprenticed himself on the old chit'lin circuit, in the clubs and dives. Along the way he reclaimed the joy of comedy, and in the process he discovered himself and his own unique style and material. Failure activated Rock to become an excellent comic.

There are times when an F does not mean failure but is a challenge to "look again." When students get that dreaded F on their report cards, instead of just punishing them we should use the opportunity for dialogue to help them understand what went wrong. We need to challenge them while also giving them encouragement so that they are not destroyed by this experience. We should take the same positive approach into the workplace. Oftentimes, when something goes wrong, instead of using the occasion to shore up operations, people ladle out blame in massive doses. There will always be plenty of blame to go around, but who will stand up and say, "Let's use this failure to our advantage and learn more about ourselves"? If you don't allow yourself to get bogged down in self-reproach and self-recriminations, failure can be one of the surest, quickest ways to become personally activated. I stated earlier that my GPA in my first year of college was 2.1, but my first-semester average was even worse—1.9. But I knew that in spite of this I was not a failure, so I just worked harder to prove that I could bring my grades up to a higher level.

Personal Activation for the Greater Good

When the members of a society achieve a critical mass in their level of discontentment, often one leader will rise out of the ranks to voice the concerns of the people. Such leaders are personally activated for the greater good. Cesar Chavez advocated for better working conditions on behalf of migrant farm workers. Susan B. Anthony spoke on behalf of women and their voting rights. Martin Luther King, Jr., led protest marches across the country, demanding an end to racial discrimination and hatred. What inspires these great leaders to risk their own lives? Painful childhood memories, a soul-deep hatred of injustice, and natural leadership abilities. Leaders are bootstrappers, and bootstrappers are often leaders. These people seem to be continuously activated, and they have the ability to motivate and inspire others to action. They are often eloquent and action-oriented. Their personal flaws and sometimes unpopular causes serve as lightning rods for criticisms and attacks, but no one can deny their influence and effectiveness in creating change on a massive scale.

Before you can have an effect on the world around you, something must occur inside you. You must discover what's really important to you. If you've spent your adult life trying to keep up with the Joneses, this section will change your life. You will be asked to go deep within to find your true passions, desires, and beliefs. You'll also need to hold your professed desires up to the light of social conditioning to determine whose desires they really are. Do you really want a million dollars, or do you want financial freedom? Do you really want to get married right now, or do you crave more love in your life? It's important to be clear about what you really want, because that's where your passion and activating power reside.

You can either activate yourself or let life activate you, through its trials and tribulations. Self-knowledge, the subject of the first principle of bootstrapping, will unlock the door to success.

ACTION STEP 1: KNOW YOURSELF

Self-knowledge is the key to the kingdom.

When you don't know yourself, you are subject to lose control of your whole life. Many of the kids who join gangs indicate that they do so because of an ability to identify with those who are part of the group. They find their sense of security, though false, among others who are like them and share their ideas. Unfortunately, they give up their own identities and lose themselves within the group. Therefore, the definition of the gang and its activities automatically becomes the definition of who they are. Sadly, many of them, because of the nature of initiation into the gang and the inability to be a freethinker, never reach the point where they learn who they are. I often speak in penal institutions, and inmates tell me that they are incarcerated because they followed the wrong crowd. This problem is also seen in a number of the young teenagers who have babies. They are victims of low self-esteem and a lack of the knowledge of who they are. They have been convinced that becoming a woman requires them to have a child. Tragically, their identity crisis is passed on from one generation to the next because they are not capable of assuming the responsibility that comes with rearing a child.

I was a virgin until I was twenty-one years old because of my fear of getting someone pregnant. Having witnessed the experiences of others, living in the era of "shotgun" marriages, I knew that all of my dreams would be short-circuited if I did not remain chaste. Naturally, when I talked with my peers I gave them the impression that I was very active sexually. Because I knew who I was and what I expected to achieve in life, I found it easier to lie about what I was not doing than to take unnecessary risks that could have hampered me for the rest of my life.

My life has been characterized by an independent will that has allowed me to take strong positions based on my conscience rather than someone else's determination. In college, I watched as friends of mine started smoking "reefers" in the mid-sixties, believing that it would not cause any long-term damage. I adamantly refused to even try marijuana, in spite of the insistence of some of my friends. Eventually, they accepted the fact that this was something I was not going to do. As I look at many of their lives today and witness where they are, I am convinced that mine was the better choice. Some of them were destroyed by the Vietnam War, others by the drug wars, and still others by the war within themselves. The desire to be like everybody else has cut short the lives of so many of my friends.

As a pastor, I have had to make hard choices about how I want my ministry to be defined. Interestingly, I am sometimes relegated to the status of a pariah because of my refusal to be like the majority. I believe that one's ministry must represent not only the highest moral authority but also a quality that is greater than one finds in any other agencies or structures in society. By knowing myself, I have consistently sought to raise the standards of ministry. Though I am sometimes challenged by some who believe that the call to the ministry is the same as any other, the Lord has given me the strength to stand in the face of challenges because of the knowledge that I have of who I am.

It is this knowledge that allowed me to take positions as a congressman that were sometimes contrary to those espoused by the Democratic Party, of which I have been a lifelong member. There are some issues that I refuse to relegate to mere political correctness. My conscience would not allow me to vote for same-sex marriage, although I have historically been a strong supporter of gay rights, civil rights, and human rights for all people. Yet I believe that the question of same-sex marriage transcends politics. Another issue that presented difficulty for me was partial-birth abortions. I am not a believer in wholesale abortion as a means of birth control, but I support abortion in cases of rape and incest. Partial-birth abortion falls into a different category. As the child of a mother who gave birth to me in her seventh month, I could not conscientiously vote for the right to abort in the seventh month. Because I know myself, there are some things that I will not do if I feel that they compromise my morals and principles, which have gained a measure of respect for me from people of many differing political views and ideologies.

Don't misunderstand me; I am not arrogant or conceited, but I refuse to let other people control my life, lead me astray, or pour cold water on my dreams. Once my high school counselor tried to discourage me from attending college, believing that it was an unrealistic desire since my parents could not afford to send me. She did not understand how badly I wanted a college degree or the sacrifice I was willing to make to get it. Some of the older members of the church even discouraged me by suggesting that as a preacher I did not need to attend college. They said, "Just open your mouth and let the Lord speak for you." They did not understand that I wanted to be more than just a preacher, that I believed that ministry required skills consistent with those of leaders in the corporate and academic world. But I knew myself. When you know yourself, you have the strength to keep from being locked in a box without options. To know yourself is to be free from the possibility of letting ideology, ignorance, fear, or anxiety control your life. You can be the person that God intended you to be, utilizing all of your gifts to fulfill the innate potential and possibility that is within you.

Whoever said that ignorance is bliss never experienced the ecstasy of revelation. So much of our life is spent in confusion that when the light flashes on and we experience our *aha!* moment, we feel activated. When we receive an answer to a question that has bothered us for a long time, we are in awe and we feel grateful. Those moments of revelation are like grace, unbidden and unasked for. Our perception shifts just enough to enable us to see an old situation in a new way. We are excited and empowered. In that moment of clarity, we are changed forever.

If you've ever experienced such a rare moment of insight—and we all have at least once in our lives—chances are you weren't looking for it. Deep down you knew something was amiss, but you didn't have the desire or courage to deal with the void. In this section, we are going to immerse you in a process of self-reflection that will create a mental and spiritual receptivity to self-knowledge. You will experience many *aha!* moments as you explore the most mysterious person in the universe— you. But I warn you, once you begin to glimpse the truth of you—your beliefs, values, passions, strengths, weaknesses, wild dreams, and life purpose—there will be no more excuses. No more ostrich behavior with your head stuck in the sand of apathy and inertia. Along with self-knowledge comes the challenge and the mandate to act on what you know. Imagine sitting on a treasure chest and never opening the lid—and there you are, broke, sick, depressed, and in need. That treasure chest contains every answer and resource you need to achieve your dreams, but you'll never make progress if you don't explore what's inside.

There once was a woman who defined her life as "fair to middling." Fair is lower than middling, and middling is light-years away from excellent, outstanding, and fantastic. Her life was neither good nor bad, just mediocre. Not surprisingly, she was bored with her job, her husband, her kids, and herself. One day, a friend suggested that she go into therapy to deal with some problems in her marriage. She told her friend, "My mind ain't broke, so why fix it? I'm doing *just fine* without some quack rummaging around in my brain." On the fair-to-middling scale, where is "just fine"? Better than fair but lower than middling? What's more, the woman told her friend that she didn't want to know. "Know what?" asked her friend. "All that old, dead, and buried stuff," she said.

What was stopping the woman from embarking on a self-seeking mission? Fear, the great enemy and paralyzer of bootstrapping. In this program, you will be required to look within and then act on what you find—despite your fears.

Be honest with yourself: does that woman remind you of anyone? Now, before you judge her and call her a coward, take a hard look at yourself. When was the last time you had a real heart-to-heart with yourself? When was the last time you looked in the mirror and dealt with the situations and relationships in your life that you've not been happy with for a long time? Like that woman, you've probably been coping, just barely getting along.

Before you can achieve your goals, before you can manifest your dreams, you must commit to the process of getting to know yourself. Do you think you know everything there is to know about you? Well, you don't. You don't know the half of who you are. Most of us don't know ourselves, and we surely don't know all of what we are capable of doing.

The most successful bootstrappers I know humbly admit that they have much to learn about themselves. They have acquired the ability to stay centered and focused on the tasks at hand while growing in wisdom and expanding their knowledge and skills. They are both teachers and students, leaders and followers. These are the true Renaissance women and men. They are constantly surprising themselves as they access spiritual strengths, emotional depths, and intellectual heights that they never knew they had. On the other hand, people who are content with their lives and think that they know all that there is to know about themselves stagnate quickly. They may achieve a goal, but in the long run they risk landing on a plateau and staying stuck there. People who are afraid of looking deep within are fearful of change. Authentic bootstrappers approach life as an adventure; thus, they do not let their fears of the unknown prevent them from striving to reach higher heights.

The journey to self-discovery is a high and noble quest. It is a process that will last a lifetime. Learning about yourself is what makes life so interesting, and if you are truly committed to the process, the new things that you will discover about yourself will amaze and delight you. As you make this exploration, you will build confidence in your ability to manifest your dreams. Believe me when I say that you are a wondrous creation. Your circumstances may be mediocre and your life may be lackluster, but do not believe that these are the real facts of your life. Hold on and never let go of the truth. Remember, the truth will set you free. The truth is the big picture of who you are at your deepest soul level.

To get you started on this remarkable journey, I'm going to take you through two journeys of imagination. Albert Einstein said, "Your imagination is your preview of life's coming attractions"—which means your life is about to get rave reviews! Read, relax, and let go. Let your mind soar. If, as you are reading these words, you hit upon a mental block or some emotional pain, great! Fantastic! The dam is about to burst, and that's just what you want. Let loose all those old grudges, the painful memories, the lack of confidence, the jealousies, hurts, angers, and fears. You've been too uptight for way too long. You've been complacent and unfulfilled, and your habitual thoughts and emotional responses to daily routines, intimate relationships, and personal circumstances have kept you stuck in poverty, lack, and mediocrity—but no more. Get ready to fly!

Imagination Station 1

You are walking along a sandy beach. The day is beautiful, warm, and sunny. Sailboats drift lazily on the water, and the sounds of summer fill you with peace and happiness. Suddenly, you trip over an object that is sticking out of the sand. You stoop and dig it out. It's a container of some kind! Sand and caked mud cover its facade, but as you wipe away the dirt, a lovely pattern emerges. You take a tissue out of your pocket and begin to wipe off the dirt and grime. As you wipe, the world as you know it fades from view, and you are standing alone on the beach.

You wonder, what in the world is going on? In response to your thoughts, a voice, which is within you and all around you, says, "You have three wishes. Or you can pick one special wish. Decide now."

You think you must be dreaming, so you play along. You say, "If I have a choice of three wishes, or one special wish, I choose—"

"Wait!" booms the voice. "Before you choose, I have to tell you what the nature of those wishes is. If you choose the three-wish package, you can ask for any material goods, and your wishes will be granted."

"Wait a minute. Do you mean that if I wish for a car or a house or my bills to be paid—"

"Right, your wishes will be granted." You get excited. This is better than winning the lottery. Still, you give the voice a little respect and let it finish talking. "Or you could choose the one special wish. If you choose this wish, you will be granted the knowledge of your total self—mind, body, soul, spirit."

Which do *you* choose?

Imagination Station 2

Imagine that you're in your bed. Your head rests on down-filled pillows. You're in the deep, deep REM (rapid eye movement) phase of sleep, and your dreams are so real you have no idea that you're dreaming. In fact, as far as you're concerned, this *is* real life. You have no knowledge of what awake people call the "real world." You snore contentedly. All you know is that you're in dreamland, and ignorance is bliss. It's what the Temptations call "Cloud Nine." Everything seems real as long as you're asleep.

Then, suddenly, there's a loud, earth-shaking thunderclap, and you are shocked out of your sleep. You are awake, and your heart is beating like crazy. You can't think. For an instant you can't remember who you are, where you are, why you are, or what you were doing just a second ago. You wipe the sleep out of your eyes, and gradually, the real world comes into focus. You think to yourself, "Not that dream again!"

Another night has gone by, and you've spent it dreaming a dream that you've had maybe a hundred times over the past few years. You're tired of this dream and wish you could stop it from coming back, but you don't know how. You feel powerless. The dream has got a hold on you. You're under its spell.

Each of us has had dreams like this, in which we are running or standing in place, unable to break out of the walls closing in on us. It's like what happens to Phil Connors (Bill Murray) in the movie *Groundhog Day*. Phil is a weatherman who has dreams of doing much more than the weather. Unfortunately, for years, he is stuck with the worst assignment of his life—covering the Groundhog Day Festival in Punxsutawney, Pennsylvania. Miserable, frustrated, and bitter, he behaves like a jerk to everyone. Then one Groundhog Day, February 2, his entire life changes. He gets locked in a time warp, and as a result, he gets stuck on February 2, the worst day of his career. Every day becomes Groundhog Day.

Every day is the same, but Phil discovers that he has the power to make changes, in himself and in events. He goes to the doctor, a psychiatrist. For the first time he talks to his co-workers from the heart. He talks about his fears. But his behavior gets worse before it gets better. He tries various tricks to get to February 3, but he learns that tricks won't change his life. He even tries killing himself, but that does no good. At 6:00 the next morning, February 2 starts all over again.

It's not until Phil does some serious soul-searching and discovers that *he* is the groundhog and that he's been living life in the shadows rather than living life to the fullest that the potential for true change begins to awaken within him. Without this type of intensive soul-searching, life is one long winter. The humble groundhog and his shadow have much to teach us about getting out of our ruts and getting on to the next season of our lives.

Back to Imagination Station 1. Which wish package did you choose? If you were smart, you chose the self-knowledge package, and here's why: If you seek to understand yourself first—what makes you tick, your passions, your strengths and weaknesses, your likes and dislikes, your purpose in life, why you think, speak, feel, and act in your own unique way—then you will finally realize that within you is everything that you need to make the other wishes come true. It's the proverbial "I wish for an infinite number of wishes" choice. It's the wish that gives you the power to have it all.

And until you realize that you can actually change the dream, you'll keep on having it. You'll feel that you need somebody to blame. Who are you going to blame? And what is blaming someone else going to do for you? That's right—it will make you feel powerless. It's a vicious circle.

How do you change the bad dream? How do you get out of your rut? Go within. The kingdom is there. What is a kingdom? It's the house, the castle, the temple inside you. However you view it, your life is your responsibility.

Sometimes our dreams, or our life experiences, recur to teach us lessons. Our childhood experiences condition us to a certain way of perceiving the world and behaving, and throughout our lifetime, if we don't wake up, our old conditioning will create a pattern of undesirable situations. The people and places may change, but the situations will stay basically the same.

For many of us, our waking lives are like recurring dreams. We keep doing the same things over and over. We get results, but not the ones we want. You may be in a rut, or you may be in a state of high drama. Names and faces may change, but the results are always the same.

If you stay on automatic pilot, always doing the same things, you'll keep getting the same results. But if you go within, I guarantee your life will change for the better.

Going Within

Go into your closet, and when you have shut your door, pray.
God, who sees in secret, will reward you openly.
Matthew 6:6 (paraphrased)

To get out of that rut of mediocrity, you must go into your private place—your soul's "closet"—and pray for guidance, healing, and a renewing of your mind.

What is this mysterious closet? What secrets does it hold? Most important, how can going there help us in our quest to become successful bootstrappers?

The newer versions of the Bible tell us to "go into our room" or "go away by ourselves, all alone" and pray, but the old King James version tells us to go into our "closet." All convey the same idea, but for me, the closet holds the deeper mystery, and potentially, the more profound answers to my questions. Your closet is where those old boots have been hidden for so long. But before you find them you'll have to go through all the junk. That old junk symbolizes negative beliefs and attitudes, self-limiting emotions and destructive behaviors. But those durable old boots you had forgotten about represent the foundation on which you will rise to new levels of achievement and success.

Every time I go into my "closet" I gain new understanding about myself and my life. My faith in God and myself strengthens. The peace that you get in your "closet" is beyond understanding. This is the place where you meet yourself and your Maker.

The symbol of the closet is a powerful one, because in it lies the secret to our selves and all that we need to succeed. The problem is that there are all sorts of fascinations and distractions that keep us from going within. The world can be a noisy place, which suits us just fine when we are trying to avoid dealing with ourselves. The world holds us spellbound. We are in a hurry to buy more stuff, watch more TV, and hang out with our friends. How can going to this secret place compete with what we see, hear, touch, taste, and smell? How can it compete with money and cars and gourmet food? Who has time to spend in a closet praying and thinking? But let me tell you, you must make time.

Children love to play in their parents' closet, amid all the old clothes, shoes, hats, and clutter. It's like playing in a cave or under a table or in a box. It's the place you went to when you wanted to hide from the world, to be alone to think your thoughts without anyone bugging you. No one was allowed to go there because it was your secret place.

You need that place today. We all need a place that we can call our own. We all need a place where we can retreat from the world to renew our minds, bodies, and spirits. Whether you go to a physical place, such as a park bench or garden, or you seek an internal state wherever you are, going within lays the foundation for the bootstrapper's journey. Without the knowledge gained from such meditative times, you will end up spinning your wheels. You will go whichever way the wind blows, because you'll have no direction of your own. You will fall for anything, because you have not taken the time to discover what it is that you stand for.

Coy Pugh spent one very long night in his closet. The night lasted about eighteen months, and the closet was a jail cell. After he went through a childhood filled with gang activity, theft, pandering, and drug addiction, the law finally caught up to Coy and forced him to deal with his demons. Not having the benefit of a rehab center, Coy went through withdrawal virtually alone in that closet until his system was clean of drugs. He sweated out all the ugliness and trauma in his life. He prayed for healing and guidance. For some, jail provides an opportunity to further develop their criminal skills. For Coy, jail gave him the opportunity to come face-to-face with himself, and as a result, he experienced a spiritual transformation. Today, he is an entrepreneur, pastor of West Englewood United Methodist Church, and the Illinois state representative of the Tenth District in Chicago. He also works with prison inmates to help them get their lives back on the right road. He is a success by any definition of the word, and he continues to grow. However, none of his achievements would have been possible had he not first gone within. Even people on lockdown must decide whether they will spend their lives locked out or use the time to look within for the strength to rise beyond this experience.

Patti LaBelle is a great example of someone who took to her closet in fear because of a health crisis that plagued her family. Her mother and sister had died of breast cancer, and Patti feared that she would not reach the age of fifty. She thought the condition was hereditary. She revealed in her book, "Don't Block the Blessings," that when her sister passed, she had a choice of either canceling a recording date or going ahead with it. People in the studio waited and wondered whether she would show up. She kept that date, and she has also lived beyond her fiftieth birthday. She exemplifies the strength and courage of a bootstrapper who understands that when we are in our dark closets with our fears we cannot afford to stay there. When we open the door and let the light in, we realize that our closets are merely extensions of our rooms. Therefore, there is no need to fear.

My mother dreamed of the day that she would make the trip to Ohio for my graduation, but she suffered a prolonged illness and passed away several months before my commencement. I took to my closet, grief stricken, and emerged empowered to work much harder so that her dreams would be fulfilled. A few years later, Daddy passed, and when I was elected to Congress, I kept thinking of what joy they must feel. Their deaths inspired me to be as productive as possible during my lifetime, knowing that I have no control over when it will end. All of us are charged with the responsibility of making the most of the time that God has given us. Many people have given up when they had to enter the closet of sorrow, especially if they've lost someone who is as close as a parent. This is a time when you must really know yourself if you intend to keep your life on track.

Sometimes going within requires getting away from the noise and seductions of the world. Getting away takes strength and courage. It may mean not hanging out with your friends at the club for a while. You might have to limit your time on the phone. It may mean turning the television off to read some inspirational literature. It may mean participating in a support group. It may mean just sitting on your bed every night for a few minutes to pray.

Whether you're a beginner or an advanced bootstrapper, going within will happen throughout the course of your journey to success. Don't think that once you've reached the pinnacle, you'll no longer need your closet. That's when you'll really need to systematize your quiet times.

Closet Work

Closets hold both skeletons and treasures, and we must be courageous enough to look at both the good and the bad. Like the Good Book says, we have all fallen short. No one is perfect. There are some past experiences in our closets of which we'd be highly ashamed, if ever they were to see the light of day. But no one is going into your closet but you, so c'mon—open the door and walk right in. Talk to God about your hopes, dreams, memories, and fears.

Select a place or enter a state of mind. Your closet can be an actual physical place, like a closet or a room. Or it can be time you set aside for "going off by yourself." Or simply close your eyes regardless of where you are. Many parents do their closet work in their cars, coming home from or going to work. It's the one place where they can think their thoughts in private without being distracted.

Take the time. Some of us get so caught up in the nine-to-five grind and taking care of our responsibilities at home that we seldom take the time to ponder the big questions: Who am I? What am I doing here at this time, at this place? What am I supposed to be doing with my life anyway? Is this all there is to life?

Invest lots of time in your closet. You may or may not get the answers that you're looking for right away, but trust in the process. Give it time. Sometimes when you're least expecting it, a phrase will pop into your mind that suddenly provides the answer to a problem. Or you'll feel a sudden urge to call someone, and that person will help you find the answer.

So take time out every day for this quiet time, even if you can give it only ten minutes. Be ruthless about it. Do not let anyone or anything intrude upon this private space and this special time. Take the phone off the hook and give the children explicit instructions that for the next few minutes you are not to be disturbed. They will try you. One will do or need something that will require your immediate attention. Another will fall and hurt herself. Your spouse may call and, of course, it will be an emergency. That's why I told you to take the phone off the hook! Being selfish about your time alone may go totally against the grain, but for your sake, you must do it.

Zip the lip. For a while, keep your desires and plans to yourself. Even when you're ready to talk, be careful in choosing whom to confide in. Remember the people who *won't?* They're waiting, even hoping, for you to fail. If you succeed, that makes them look bad. They may even put a smile on their face while they're stabbing you in the back. It's like the O'Jays sing: "They smile in your face—back stabbers."

How many diets have been sabotaged because folks made the mistake of confiding in someone they thought they could trust? The "friend" couldn't stand to see you getting thinner and getting more attention than him, so the next thing you know, he's waving brownies under your nose and offering to treat you to dinner at some greasy fast-food joint. As the old saying goes, "Don't put your business out in the street."

Take stock. Right now, go and look into your real bedroom closet. What's in there? What kind of shape is it in—messy, organized, empty, stuffed? Do you even know what's in your closet? Look at your shoe rack. Some people have numerous pairs of shoes, yet they wear the same ones over and over. Sometimes we are more comfortable in the things that we are familiar with than in taking chances on those things that are available to us but that we rarely use. Some of our lives lack fulfillment, not because we lack the things necessary to fulfill us but because we keep doing the same things the same way. The challenge that a bootstrapper faces is how to explore all of the possibilities.

Now, think about your life. Are you happy or not? Content or not? Fulfilled or not? The following list of questions is meant to stir up your spirit and to trigger thoughts, ideas, dreams, and memories that you may have submerged for a long time. As you're going through the list, be kind to yourself. This exercise is not about beating yourself up but about discovering the things that make you tick and that may be holding you back. Write extensively in your journal or talk into a tape recorder. You can even use your laptop. Meditate on the questions, and let your thoughts flow freely. No one's going to grade you on grammar or judge your thoughts. The only requirement is that you be completely honest with yourself.

1. What are my biggest fears? What are they preventing me from doing?
2. Am I holding a grudge against anyone? Why? How does this make me feel?
3. Am I satisfied with my job? Am I satisfied with the amount of money I'm making?
4. Am I a good parent? How could I be a better one? What are my fears and worries about my children?
5. How am I handling my personal finances? Am I in debt, and if so, why? What am I doing to get out of debt?
6. What is the state of my love life? If I am married, is my marriage a good one? If not, why not? If single, how do I truly feel about not being married? How do I feel about the opposite sex, or people of the same sex?
7. How is my relationship with God? Do I pray and meditate every day? Do I treat others as I would like to be treated?
8. What are my real values? What do I believe in?
9. Have I given of my time, money, energy, or resources to help others?
10. Do I take care of my body like I should? Or am I overweight? Unfit? Malnourished?
11. What are my weaknesses? What are my strengths?
12. What is my purpose in life?
13. What makes me happy?
14. If today were my last day on earth, what would I do?
15. If I discovered that I would live forever in this body, how differently would I live my life?

16. What makes me special?
17. What's the one thing I do better than anyone else? How am I God's gift to humanity?
18. Do my friendships nurture me? Am I a good friend?
19. What am I curious about? What am I interested in?
20. What are the things I don't want anyone to know about me?
21. Do I like myself? Love myself?

Skeletons in the Closet

If you're anything like 99.9 percent of your fellow humans, you found a skeleton or two in your closet. These skeletons give us so much trouble. They shame us. They make us feel guilty. And we fear them—suppose someone else finds out about them? The following is an inventory of the skeletons in your closet. I want you to name them to yourself, to identify each one so you can begin to take action on them.

Secrets. They say that confession is good for the soul, and it's true. Have you been holding on to some information that's been tearing you up inside? Do you have a good friend, a therapist, a minister—someone you can trust? Consider sharing this secret. Dilute its power and its hold over you by talking about it. There's an old saying that goes "You're only as sick as your secrets." Don't hold on to information that's wearing you out. It's not worth it. If the secret is someone else's that you've sworn to keep, go back to that person and tell them of your discomfort. Here's a thought that may help you: your secrets are not sacred. What is the worst thing that would happen if your secret came to the light of day? Would you die? Probably not. You might suffer some embarrassment, but on the other hand, you would be free of the shame, guilt, and fear a negative secret can hold over you.

The companions of secrets are usually lies. Lying taints the spirit. It is an offense against the spirit and against the person being lied to or about. Lying creates even more shame, guilt, and fear—especially fear, because the more you lie, the more you open yourself up to the fear of discovery.

Even worse than the secrets we keep from others are the secrets we keep from ourselves. You might tell yourself lies such as "It doesn't matter" or "I don't care," when you know you're hurting inside. Lying to yourself is not a good coping mechanism. Instead, let yourself feel the pain or sorrow. If you don't deal with it now, it's bound to resurface time and again.

Low standards of behavior. Here's an interesting skeleton that every self-respecting bootstrapper must deal with. An example of a low standard of behavior is coming home from work and sitting in front of the TV all night, eating french fries. Another is doing the bare minimum on the job. Or being irresponsible with personal relationships. Or squandering money. Or consistently ignoring your kids.

Bootstrappers have high standards of behavior, and they are their own toughest critics. Even when they are tired, they continue to perform. In fact, that is when they do their best. You can always do more. You can always do better. There is no excuse for allowing yourself to be mediocre. The good news is, you have the power to change.

Low standards of behavior are closely linked to a problem with values. If you know that this skeleton holds a prominent place in your closet, check your values. What is it that you truly believe in and are not just paying lip service to?

Traumatic childhood experiences. Your secrets are not sacred, nor is your past. Anyone who has gone through the trauma of any kind of abuse—mental, verbal, emotional, physical, or sexual—has been victimized. However, no one has to live life as a victim. The decision must be made to live life victoriously, not merely as a survivor or a victim. Since the choice is up to you, you should make a choice before perception becomes reality.

Shame. Most of us keep secrets because we feel shame about something we said or did. When we feel shame, we are disgusted with ourselves. It's the old feeling of "How could I have done such a thing?" Shame is a powerful emotion and can undermine your best efforts at success. Again, confession is good for the soul. The only way to get over shame is to face it head-on. Talk it out with someone you trust. Make amends if you have to. Most important, forgive yourself.

Bad habits. Smoking, overeating, drinking, gossiping, procrastinating, criticizing, nail biting, laziness, backbiting—most of us have at least one of these bad habits in our closet. But if we are to become successful, we must root them out of our daily lives.

Fear. Fear is the great paralyzer. If we let it, fear will prevent us from taking action. Bootstrappers are known risk takers, but this does not mean they never experience fear. They do. The difference is that they take a deep breath and go on despite their fear.

Procrastination. How long did it take you to pick up this book and start reading? A week or two? There's a chance that you're a procrastinator. Don Marquis said that "procrastination is the art of keeping up with yesterday." I also like the old saying "Don't put off until tomorrow what you can do today." A bootstrapper would say, "Don't put off until tomorrow what you can do right now!" As Nike says, "Just do it!"

Procrastination is the thief of your blessings. Procrastinators never get anything done, and then they have the nerve to complain when some ambitious co-worker, family member, or friend raises the performance curve at work or at home. Again, check your values, and then check your actions. If the two don't match, something's wrong. Don't let this low standard of behavior rob you of your blessings.

Grudges. If you've ever said, "I'll forgive, but I'll never forget," you've held a grudge. Scripture teaches that we're not only to forget about insults, hurts, and slights; we're to never bring them up again. Now, that doesn't mean that you shouldn't learn from your experiences. Please learn from your experiences. But don't use up all of your precious mental and emotional energy being mad at someone for something that he did to you twenty years ago, or even yesterday. Life's too short, and you've got too much to do. Grudges sap you of your vital life energy. Worse, while you're still fuming, the other person has gone on to live his or her life. Whatever happened, forgive the person, and then let it go.

Poverty. Many people are ashamed of their poverty and will go to great lengths to keep it a secret. Great stories have been written about men and women who created new identities to try to hide the fact that they were poor. There is no shame in being poor, only in complaining about it and not doing anything about it.

Addiction. There are as many addictions in the world as there are people. The more popular ones are, of course, drugs, alcohol, overeating, compulsive spending, and sex. Recently, the idea has been promoted that certain addictions may be genetic in origin. That may or may not be so, but I do know this: Just because you may have a genetic predisposition toward a certain behavior doesn't mean you have to engage in it. You still have the power within you to resist temptation.

Hidden Treasure in the Closet

Don't stay stuck on the skeletons in your closet, because there is treasure there, too.

If you're like most people, you have no idea of the treasures that lie hidden in your closet. Finding the skeletons was probably a lot easier, but it is just as important to find the good stuff. It is the treasures that will empower you as you strive to achieve your dreams.

At birth, each of us is given a repertoire of powers that enable us not only to survive but to thrive. Life is not supposed to be drudgery, but that's what it becomes if you're unaware of the hidden treasure in your closet. The following is a list of some of the good stuff. We'll be exploring some of these treasures in more detail in action step 5, but for now, just know that you have within you the following strengths, gifts, and resources. Begin to identify your hidden resources to yourself.

Power. We need power to run our cars, homes, and industries. But we also have at our disposal personal powers that make life a thrill. Physical power keeps us healthy and strong. Mental power enables us to reason, analyze, and learn. Emotional power equals emotional maturity. We can learn how to master those unruly, raw materials called emotions. And spiritual power pulls it all together. Here is where we get our guidance to solve daily problems and our inspiration to keep on keeping on.

Values. Our values, those ideas that we profess to believe in and live by, determine how well we conduct our affairs. Not the values we pay lip service to, but the values we truly believe in. If you say that you love everybody but you gossip about your neighbor, your professed values are not in alignment with your actions. Either your values are not what you think they are or you have not developed the courage or moral fortitude to think, feel, speak, and act out of your values. You cannot achieve lasting success in your life if your values and your actions are in conflict. Your credibility in work and love will suffer if you are conflicted about your values and behavior. Work either to develop a new set of moral, life-enhancing values or to align your actions to the values you already profess.

Answers. Before you get answers, you must ask good questions. Asking good questions opens up your mind in new, ever-expanding directions. Before we learn to trust our inner resources, we tend to seek answers from others. We may or may not get good advice. As you mature as a bootstrapper, you will increasingly come to trust the answers to problems that come from within. Make your own decisions. You are just as capable as anyone else of receiving guidance from God.

Motivation. Just the act of waking up in the morning motivates me to make something good of my day. But for those times when you feel down, remember your victories and remember that "this too shall pass." Remember how it felt to succeed at something. Let those good feelings infuse your spirit. While tapes and speakers can give you a boost every now and then, don't depend on others. Learn to motivate yourself.

Energy. We must eat nutrition-rich foods in order to keep our bodies healthy and energetic. To be an outstanding bootstrapper, you'll need all the energy you can get!

Patience. We want what we want and we want it right now! Spending time in our closet gives us patience. Change does not come right away, even when we achieve clarity by going within our closet.

Wisdom. How well do I use the information and guidance that I receive? That's wisdom. Knowing how to sift through all the many choices in life and make the right decisions—that's wisdom. Wise decisions have as their foundation a strong moral framework out of which we think, speak, feel, and behave.

Talents. Talents are God's gifts to us. Each one of us has a special talent, something we can do that just comes naturally. Your talents are the things you can do effortlessly. Your talents provide the clue to your life purpose.

Skills. Skills take a little more work than talents to develop, but they are no less of a joy. According to sociologist Karen Pittman, a sense of mastery is one of the basic human needs. To become really good at something, we have to practice for many years. That's how we become the best athletes, carpenters, cooks, business entrepreneurs, teachers, or pastors. When we get really good at a task, we feel good about ourselves. Our confidence in our abilities is strengthened, and we are challenged to try to develop new skills.

True desires. Sometimes we cannot distinguish our true desires from those we were conditioned to have by childhood rearing or by society. True desires provide another important clue to our life purpose. True desires contain within them the truth of who we are. This is closet work at its finest. When you are able to distinguish between the desires that form the beauty of your soul and the desires that the media, peers, parents, and others instill in you, you will have taken a giant step forward in your personal development. Even more important, when you understand your soul's true desire, you must begin to leave behind those socially conditioned ones that no longer serve you, satisfy you, or direct you to your life's purpose.

Love. Everyone's got their own ideas about what love is. Here's mine:

> *Love is patient and kind;*
> it is not jealous or conceited or proud;
> love is not ill-mannered or selfish or irritable;
> love does not keep a record of wrongs;
> love is not happy with evil,
> but is happy with the truth.
> Love never gives up; . . .
> Love is eternal.
>
> *1 Corinthians 13:4–8*

Without love, forget it. All your successes, all your achievements will mean nothing. Without love, your spirit will dry up like a prune.

When a child is deprived of the physical hugs and kisses of love, he or she grows up emotionally stunted, or worse, psychopathic. Love is essential to health and overall well-being. Don't get so crazed in the pursuit of riches that you forget what is really important, and that is love.

There's a Groundhog in My Closet!

There's a lot of stuff in your closet! Lots more than you may have realized. Just because we've reached the end of this section, don't think that the process of self-inventory is over. You still don't know all that there is to know about yourself—and isn't that great! No chance of getting bored during this lifetime!

As you discover the good, the bad, and the not-so-good about yourself, let the following attitudes help you in accepting and loving yourself despite all your weaknesses, foolishnesses, and faults. Here's what the groundhog taught Phil. It changed his life and got him to the next day a totally changed and renewed man. It can help you too.

Keep it honest. It's not until we take an honest look at ourselves that we can begin to wake up and change our lives for the better.

Accept and be grateful for life as it is. This is a paradox. Ironically, even though you may be miserable, you've got to learn to accept your life as it is. It's teaching you and making you a better person. It's helping to wake you up. When the storms of life hit, learn to take it all in stride. That's how you can begin to develop a cheerful outlook on life.

What's the difference between the pessimist and the optimist? Pessimists allow the world to throw them for a loop. Optimists, on the other hand, see opportunity in every experience and practice a positive opportunism.

Have fun. Stop taking yourself so seriously. Lighten up. Learn to laugh at yourself.

Take responsibility for your thoughts, words, feelings, and actions. No more "it wasn't my fault," "I couldn't help it," or whatever. No matter what the situation, no matter how bad it gets, remember that you are responsible for your own life.

Learn how to truly love yourself and others. "Love your neighbor as you love yourself." Learn to cultivate a love for yourself and others that is unconditional. Despite your faults, learn to love yourself.

Stay true to this process and you will receive the answers you are looking for. You'll even learn to ask better questions. You may have your doubts, but trust in the process. This is spiritual work. There's a difference between the facts and the truth. The facts may say that there's not enough money in your bank account to buy that building. The truth, the answer you will get while praying in your closet, is that you must work diligently to make it happen. You will be amazed at how God will work on your behalf to make your dreams come true. It doesn't matter if the facts say that there aren't enough good men to go around. The truth is that God has given you the desire for marriage and if you trust in the process, He will give you your heart's desire. You may have to look in some nontraditional places, such as church, rather than in bars or at parties. The facts may say that the field that you're trying to break into is too competitive for someone who has no prior experience, but the truth is that while in your secret place you had a strong feeling that you were meant to call a certain company for a job. If you don't do it, you surely won't get it. But if you follow up on your hunch and prepare yourself with information before going to the company, you may be able to watch the miracle happen! I did that before my job interview with Xerox, by going to the library and learning all that I could about the xerographic process. I got the job by having the answer for every question that the interviewer asked and then turning the interview into a dialogue.

Sometimes the answer we need to move forward is slow in coming, but don't doubt for one moment that it will come. You have no idea what activities you've set in motion by going to your secret place. The hard part is waiting. And then when the answer comes, get ready to get busy!

Pull Yourself Up by Your Bootstraps . . .

The greatest obstacle standing between you and success is the skeletons in your closet. For people who persist in blaming everything and everybody for their misery, this is a difficult reality to face.

Your skeletons can not only prevent you from achieving success but also prevent you from enjoying success when you do achieve it. In this section, you've spent a lot of time reflecting on your past and looking within to discover the strengths and talents with which you have been blessed. Since bootstrapping is an action-oriented success strategy, in the next section, you are going to take action. You are going to clean out the two major skeletons in your soul's closet: *unforgiveness* and *guilt*.

Unforgiveness

Are you harboring any ill feelings against someone who may have hurt you in the past? Have they gone on with their lives while you are still grieving? It is time to let go of the past, and all its hurts and pains. Grudges are unproductive. They are old, dead memories that you choose to carry within your heart. The only power they have is to make you sick and unhappy. Peter asked Jesus, "Lord how often shall my brother sin against me, and I forgive him? Up to seven times?" Jesus said, "Seventy times seven" (Matthew 22:21–22). No matter how bad the hurt, it is your responsibility to forgive, and to keep forgiving.

Easier said than done? Not if you change how you perceive the painful event. Your perception has the power to change a negative into a positive. One way to change your perception is to find the lesson in the situation. Events have a way of teaching us, if we let them. If you can perceive the event as educational rather than damaging to body, mind, or spirit, then you will begin your healing. With healing comes the ability to truly forgive.

You may not feel you are ready to forgive. But even if you are not ready, you must. During your prayer time, be honest with God. Tell God that you do not feel you have the capacity for forgiveness in this particular situation. God knows your heart anyway, but it is important that *you* know how you feel. Practice saying, "I forgive this person." Imagine how you might speak to the offending person if you had truly forgiven them.

Now comes the hard part: call the person up, even if you have not spoken in years, and talk out the problem. Use "I" language when referring to feelings: instead of saying, "You betrayed me," say, "When you spoke against me, I felt betrayed." Most important, say to the person, "I forgive you."

I realize that you will not always be able to talk to the person. I've conducted many funerals in which there were hard feelings between the deceased and the living. The living must find a way to make their peace with the dead, despite the great divide that now separates them. If you are separated by death or circumstance from the offending person, write that person a letter. Explain in detail how you felt when you were hurt, and then in your letter, declare your forgiveness.

I've often heard people say, "I'll forgive, but I'll never forget." Jesus said to forgive seventy times seven. This is a profound forgiveness that never looks back at the hurt. However, do look at the situation enough to learn from it so that you never repeat it. There's an old saying that goes, "A people who do not know their history are destined to repeat it." If you don't want history to repeat itself, let the suffering go, forgive, and then learn from the situation.

Guilt

We have all played the victim as well as the victimizer. I don't know which is more difficult, to forgive or to ask for forgiveness. I do know that it is of utmost importance spiritually and in your quest for success to seek forgiveness from those you have hurt. Guilt can eat away at your soul, and if you allow it to grow, it can make you sick psychologically, spiritually, and physically. Even if the offense was not intentional, it is your responsibility to make things right with the other person. If the person refuses to forgive you and you've truly done all that you can do to make amends, then you can walk away with a clear conscience. But you must make vigorous attempts to make things right.

For your own soul's sake, as well as the other person's, take action to right a wrong today. Call up the person, acknowledge what you did wrong, and then—and this is important—ask the person to forgive you. Tell the person that you are truly sorry for your words or actions and that it will never happen again.

We must all learn from our mistakes. That is what being human is all about. If we do not learn from our mistakes, if we repeat them again and again, we are destined to fail in our pursuit of success. The nation's prisons are filled to capacity with people who are being forced to pay the price for hurting others. Many inmates never get over their resentment for having been caught in the act, and still more are bitter, but there are a few who seek to make the best of the experience by learning from their mistakes and striving to become better people. True repentance has the power to heal and make us better. It clears away the emotional obstacles that are preventing our spiritual growth, achievement of goals, and enjoyment of life.

ACTION STEP 2:
CLAIM WHAT'S YOURS

Claiming what is yours is your declaration of intent to pursue a goal.

When I was a boy my father would pack us kids into his car and take us riding through some of the wealthiest neighborhoods in Houston. The homes were big and beautiful, and the seed of desire was planted deep within me. I knew that one day I'd have to get a big house also. Even though I didn't know about the aggressive method of prayer I call "claiming what is yours" back then, the idea of living in a home like that claimed me. My siblings and I learned from our parents that we could one day have anything we wanted, but we would have to work hard for it. I didn't know how I'd make this dream come true—all I knew was that somehow, some way, at some point in my life, it would happen. I never felt deprived or frustrated because I didn't have a big house or a nice car, because I knew that it was only a matter of time till I'd get those things. When I was older and cutting lawns in some of those affluent neighborhoods, I still knew that my dream of one day owning a similar house would come true.

Interestingly, I never considered this desire for the good life to be in conflict with my religious beliefs. Many people feel that to be a Christian you have to be poor and stern, but for me, ministry, wealth, and joy were never in conflict. I don't believe or preach the "pie in the sky after you die" theology. Heaven is found not merely in the reward of the afterlife but in the heavenly environment that you create in this life. Many of my biblical heroes, like Abraham and Solomon, were wealthy, so I knew I'd be in good company. Fortunately, the strong work ethic, character, and values that my parents bequeathed to me made my quest for the good life a balanced and moral one. For some people, money is everything, but for me, it is the means to an end. For me, the acquisition of money has been nothing more than a way to enjoy the good things in life and to help others.

It never occurred to me that I didn't deserve to have a big house or a successful career. "Low self-esteem" has never been reinstated into my vocabulary since way back when my teachers made me take it out. During my thirty-eight years in ministry, I have come to realize there is a great sense of inertia among people who have low self-esteem and don't believe that they have the power to claim what is rightfully theirs. Claiming what's yours is more than a wish, desire, or expression. It is the willingness to work toward the implementation of your objectives in pursuit of your goals. You cannot allow the struggle for survival to keep you down and out; you must set your sights on the stars. Believe in your heart that you can fly. Believe that the sky is the limit, like an eagle you can soar.

Earlier we talked about people who pray to win the lottery, but there are just as many people who feel that they don't deserve to have any more than they already have. Their only exposure to the good life comes from television, which makes it seem light-years away. They say things like, "I'm satisfied with living at home with my parents, or in my studio apartment," or "As long as I can feed myself and my kids, I'm happy." Don't depend on the lottery—you can use those dollars more wisely by investing them or putting them into your bank account. You may not save a million dollars, but you will be surprised at how much you can accumulate over time. If you smoke or drink, for instance, imagine how much money you would have today if you had saved the cost of the pack of cigarettes you smoke every day, or the alcoholic beverages that you drink regularly. If you spend your money this way, you might as well set your dollar bills on fire or flush them down the toilet.

Who among you hasn't imagined the luxury of flying first class and not having to deal with crowded seats and peanuts? Who hasn't dreamed of owning nice clothes that make you look rich and feel good? Who hasn't longed for the respect that comes from a job well done?

Who hasn't fantasized about calling the boss and telling him what he can do with his job? I think people try to convince themselves that they are content with their lot because they don't feel they deserve more and they're afraid of failing if they try to improve their situation.

Deep down inside you, there is a desire that captivates your attention, and you know it's true. It keeps breaking into your imagination; no matter how hard you try, it just won't leave you alone. You must act on it, because it is determined to stay with you. Maybe you have never talked about it to anyone, but it is there nevertheless. Maybe you are afraid you'll get ridiculed, so you keep it a secret.

Now is the time to honor that desire, because it is trying to lift you out of misery and mediocrity. If you keep ignoring it, you will continue to merely exist as you watch others achieve the same things that you desire. You begin to wonder why you did not act on it when it first came to your mind. Only by giving proper attention to your desires can you begin to identify and claim those things that you want. Your desires are not evil, ridiculous, or impossible to attain. They are your compass, pointing you in an upward direction! Become a bootstrapper—act on your desires and enjoy the fulfillment that is yours.

Desire

At the age of twenty-nine, while still single, I bought my first house. It was not the big one that I had desired from the days of my youth, but it was a start. It was a little two-bedroom Cape model on Cape Cod in Wareham, Massachusetts, on a property that abutted a lake in the back. Some of my friends thought it was a crazy idea to buy a house while I was still single. But it seemed to make sense to me, since I had been investing so much of my money in clothes, cars, and other depreciating assets. I really could not understand how they thought marriage was a prerequisite for home ownership. The point that I am making is to get out of your mind all of those stereotypes that keep you from fulfilling your desires. If you believe that something is yours, go for it and get it. That's the way of a bootstrapper.

Earlier, we looked at several crisis activators that propel people up into the stratosphere of challenge and opportunity. However, not all experiences have to be tragic. Desire is the granddaddy activator of them all.

What is this thing called desire? Desire is not just a hope or a wish. It is not an idle fantasy or a distant dream. Desire is an unfulfilled hunger that has the power to get you up and moving. When you don't feed this hunger, you starve your dreams and aspirations to death. That's just how intense an emotion desire is. In our society, we usually equate such hunger with the need for sex, but this narrow understanding of desire has limited potential to activate us.

Unrealized desire leaves a void in our souls. Nature abhors a vacuum, so what rushes in to fill the void? Compulsion, addictions, mindless activities, boredom, and depression. Many people get addicted to sinful behaviors not because they are inherently evil but because they don't know how to deal with the void in their lives. They are afraid of it, so they do anything they can to escape it. But hear me now: you can't escape the desires that are in your soul. As my grandmother would say, "An idle mind is the devil's workshop."

Unfulfilled desires will become like a call from a distant shore. You hear the sounds, but you can no longer identify what they mean. If you let desire atrophy, it will waste and wither away, just like any muscle in your body would if you did not exercise. If desire is ignored it becomes like a match soaked in water. There is no fire left in it. Ignored desire resists compartmentalization. It infects every area of your life. If you have ignored your heart's desire to start a business and opted for the nine-to-five grind, your choice will probably have a negative effect on your marriage, work ethic, community service, relationships, and everything else. Your entire life can turn gray and boring as you find yourself becoming more insecure, jealous, and envious because others have attained what you still desire. You even run the risk of getting sick, because unrealized desire can lead to depression, which compromises your immune system. The good news is that even if you have run away from your heart's desire but still have periodic reminders of it, it is not too late to explore it to the fullest. Don't be afraid. I'm telling you, God put it in your soul to elevate you to a higher quality of life. Since tomorrow is not promised, you should cease your procrastination and act on your desires today.

There is a good side and a bad side to desire. If unrealized desire is dangerous, desire run amok can be even more so. When we were children, we saw toys, desired them, and threw a temper tantrum if we couldn't get them. Do you remember your mother giving you "that look," as if you had lost your mind, and then either ignoring you or snatching you into a state of reality? Part of growing up and becoming a mature adult involves managing our desires and learning how to harness their power to enhance the quality of our lives. If you don't manage your desires, in the end you will cause pain and suffering to yourself and others. By then, Mother may not be around to give you "that look" which expressed her displeasure and warned you that you had better get your act together.

If you do not control your desires, they will control you. They may even destroy you. Many a fallen leader once truly desired to serve others, but then the desire for power, money, or sex (the big three) took over and hastened the fall from grace. Greed and lust are the shadow sides of desire. That's what the Bible meant by "the love of money is the root of all evil." Money is not evil; it's the blind desire to get it at any cost— without regard for consequences—that's the great sin. If you are not grounded in a strong value system and have no clear understanding of moral principles, desire becomes a one-way street to destruction.

Be honest with yourself and study those skeletons you found in your closet. We all have a few. If you do not work to overcome your weaknesses, then your desires become your greatest downfall.

On the positive side, desire gives us the energy to pursue life, liberty, and happiness. But to take desire for granted is to risk being the fool. You must respect the explosive power of desire. Desire can be an activator that motivates bootstrappers to work overtime to complete a job or stay up late at night as often as is necessary to finish an important project. Bootstrappers learn how to channel their strong desires in a positive way that enables them to pursue their dreams with integrity and drive.

Unraveling Desire

When a bootstrapper sets his or her sights on success, it is desire that imagines the goal and fuels the process of achievement. The bootstrapper knows that her appetite and cravings can be satisfied only by engaging the body, mind, and spirit in a synergy of effort that results in the goal being attained. Recognizing desires, honoring and respecting them, involves going back to our closets and asking ourselves what this passion is really all about. Most people make the big mistake of feeling, then claiming, then acting. There is a big step missing here. Before you can claim what is yours, you must unravel the true meaning of your desire.

It is not enough to have a strong hunger. You must know what will satisfy the hunger. Have you ever eaten something, thinking that it would appease your hunger, only to finish and find yourself still craving something else? If you do this, you'll only feel more frustrated and irritable and probably eat a lot of other things that are not so good for you. Some of us try to satisfy our hunger with what are essentially snacks when we really need a full meal.

Sometimes we might have a strong desire but mistake its meaning. We sometimes mistake jealousy, envy, or competition for desire. Or we think we want a million dollars, when what we really want is to live in a safe neighborhood, take frequent vacations, and have the assurance that we can satisfy our basic needs for love, friendship, shelter, food, and clothing.

There are many desires, but the ones that get the most attention are love, money, and sex. Claiming what's yours without self-knowledge can lead to disaster, so before we start claiming, let's explore how you really feel about these attention-getting desires.

Love

My parents' marriage lasted for thirty-seven years, until death parted them. Now, that's love! I am certain that they had their moments of tension and disagreement, but love kept them together. Their love for each other and for their children, and their mutual respect, kept divorce from becoming an option. We would do well to honor the value of love in our relationships, just as we do so many other things that are inconsequential and unimportant. Love is the foundation for building a lasting relationship. The apostle Paul, in his letter to the Corinthian church, said,

"But now abides faith, hope and love, these three, but the greatest of these is love" (1 Corinthians 13:3). If we substitute into this text the three desires just mentioned, we say, "Now abides love, money, and sex, but the greatest of these is love." With the divorce rate so high today, I feel certain that there are many who have no idea what constitutes love.

The emotions that we call love are infrequently backed by commitment, trust, and fidelity. Love is more than emotion; it is the power that enables us to endure with another through sickness and health, poverty and wealth, thick and thin—whatever conditions arise. In our marriages, we must live the words of Adam to Eve in the Garden of Eden: "This is now bone of my bone and flesh of my flesh" (Genesis 2:23).

The desire to be loved and to love is natural. God put that desire in us, and it is good. Love desires, like any other emotions, can get out of control when they are not grounded in values. It is not enough to attract or be attracted to someone; you must share values and spiritual views. Attraction is primarily a function of the physical: what you see is what you want. It comes and goes. Love comes from and goes to the heart; therefore, it is everlasting.

I can't tell you the number of men and women who talk to me about their longing for companionship or their dissatisfaction with their marriage. The grass always seems greener on the other side; single people want to get in, and married folks want to get out. We must once again reclaim the sanctity and serenity of covenants and vows in both our conjugal and communal relationships. Marriage is wonderful, but you should not feel loveless or unfulfilled because you happen to be single. As best-selling author and lecturer Iyanla Vanzant, the Yoruba priestess, recently stated on the Oprah Winfrey show, being single means you are available and open to opportunities.

Before you make another move, stop and think about your thoughts, feelings, beliefs, and past and current behaviors regarding love. Write your answers to the following questions in your journal.

1. What is your definition of love?
2. What do you feel are your responsibilities in a love relationship? What are your mate's responsibilities toward you?

3. What attitudes, beliefs, and love behaviors did you inherit from your parents? Do they serve you in your love relationship?

4. What are your hopes for the future regarding your love relationship?

5. Are your values and your behaviors in sync in your love relationship?

6. How do you feel about emotional intimacy? Are you comfortable with it or afraid of it?

7. Have you been able to maintain a long-term relationship? Why or why not?

8. Does your desire for a mate come from a soul desire or from social conditioning? How do you know?

9. Is love fair? Does love hurt?

10. What are your overall feelings about people of your sex or the opposite sex?

11. Are you cynical or hopeful about love?

True love is strong enough to carry a couple through any ordeal. That's why it is so important to start acting on our love desires rather than just feeling them. Bootstrappers, whether in a nuptial bond or not, are as aggressive in love as they are in the other pursuits in their lives.

Money

One of the preeminent desires that people have is to make lots of money. For some, "a lot" means enough to live comfortably and pay the bills on time. For others, it means millions of dollars. As we hear about the wealth of Fortune 500 executives, star athletes, and entertainers and models, we fantasize about what we would do if we had their money. We desire millions without asking ourselves why.

Go back to the list of questions that you answered in the last section. If you want a lot of money, ask yourself why. Don't feel threatened by the question. I believe God intends for you to have as much wealth as you can handle. I am asking you to explore this question so that you will not be unhappy when you get what appears to be a "lot" but is in fact a "little" when compared to someone else's fortune. How much is a lot to you? Do you truly think that it will make you happy? Will it solve your problems? Money can mess you up if you acquire it without having the benefit of honest self-reflection. The Beatles were correct when they suggested that there are some things, like love, that money cannot buy. Money is not a substitute for peace of mind.

Go back into your closet and ask yourself the following questions about money. Write the answers in your journal.

1. Are you satisfied with your financial situation? Why, or why not?
2. Are you a good steward of your money? In other words, do you respect your money? Do you manage your money wisely?
3. If you were to hit the jackpot, would you manage your money any differently? Or would it mean more of the same (more debt, more mindless shopping)?
4. Does money frighten or intimidate you? Unravel your fears about money.
5. Are you ashamed of your financial health? Are you able to talk freely and openly about your finances?
6. Do you feel you are worthy of having money?
7. Is your debt high? How do you feel about that?
8. Write down some of the messages you received about money during your childhood. How did your parents manage their money? How did they feel about money? What beliefs and values, negative or positive, did you inherit from them?
9. If you won the lottery, what would you do with the money? Get it out of your system: write it down.
10. Get to the root of your money hunger. What do you truly want that you think money can buy you? Freedom? Safety? A comfortable home? A good car? Nice clothes? Or is it even deeper? Are you seeking respect, prestige, status, even love?

This was not a test. I want you to explore your feelings about money because this is a big issue for everyone. If your pursuit of success is to have half a chance of becoming reality, then you must first understand what's truly driving your behavior. Only then can you begin to intelligently and definitely claim your good. You must be able to maintain a healthy, moral perspective whether you are rich or poor. Being wealthy doesn't mean what it once did for some people. Many are leaving great-paying jobs on Wall Street in search of the fulfillment that has eluded them while they concentrated on building a strong financial foothold. When root passions and consciously stated desires are in conflict, you'll end up spinning your wheels and doing a lot of ineffectual busywork.

Don't claim anything until you're sure it is what you want. In other words, be careful what you ask for, because you very well may get it. Take, for example, a gentleman named Phil, who came into sudden money after a distant relative died and left him one hundred thousand dollars. He was sorry about the relative, but not too sorry, because he had not really known her. Now, Phil was one of those folks who had always prayed to receive "a lot" of money, and suddenly, there it was. Phil said, "I've been poor and now I'm rich, and rich is better!"

As soon as the money was deposited into his bank account, Phil got to spending. Did he pay off his incredibly high debt? Invest the money? Start a retirement fund? Buy property? No! He promised himself that he would pay off his debt, but he wanted to have a little fun first. The spending spree began with him writing a four-thousand-dollar check for a custom-made suit. He bought a high-end car and went on vacations to Europe (first class all the way). At the end of two years, Phil was in even more debt than when he first received the inheritance. In fact, he ended up filing for bankruptcy, and his home went into foreclosure.

What went wrong? Phil got his prayer answered, but he never stopped all his old, irresponsible money habits. Sure he was worthy of the good life, but he didn't take care of business first. Phil was using money to deal with something else, and until he does some serious closet work, he'll never know what that need is.

A year ago, I met with the young adults in the Allen Church and asked what type of seminars and programs they were interested in having us include in the ministry. These bright, talented, young professionals placed at the top of their list a workshop on money management and investment. In a meeting of the Men's Club, the members too felt that this topic needed to be addressed. Out of these discussions evolved the Investment Club, which has now grown to twelve clubs with over three hundred enrollees. We discovered that the majority of the enrollees had traditionally invested in passbook savings accounts, certificates of deposit, and insurance policies. They have now become financial boot-strappers who meet weekly and discuss financial strategies.

Perhaps it's time for you to start looking at ways of becoming a financial bootstrapper. It is the only way to ensure your future financial security and independence. Lay a good, solid foundation of self-knowledge from the beginning so that you can fully enjoy the fruits of your labor when they come—which they will. Get a financial counselor, rid yourself of the burden of debt, join an investment club, and read all the information that you can about ways to maximize your money. Manage your desires by constantly referring back to your system of values. Often, our spending goes out of control because we allow the pursuit and spending of money to override our values.

You might remember that I mentioned tithing in an earlier section. I brought many debts into my marriage to Elaine, but she taught me the value of tithing, which has helped us to be disciplined as we manage our financial goals successfully. All of our resources are packaged together for the good of the family and to the benefit of our church and community. Although we have not yet reached all of our financial goals, we have a strong beginning because we are following our plan. You should develop your financial plans and strategies with the same spirit that you pursue other bootstrapping goals so that when retirement comes and you are living on a fixed income, you will not be worried about what the politicians do with Social Security. Build your own security and let Social Security be your source of extra spending money rather than your primary vehicle for support.

Whatever your desires, use this same method of questioning. The goal is to get a deeper understanding of what drives you, and to strengthen your beliefs and values even as you build your financial security.

Sex

It seems that wherever a group of men are gathered, eventually the discussion finds its way to the topic of sex. We are surrounded by sexual images on television, in movies, and at bookstores. Even the church is not exempted from confronting seemingly taboo subjects. It is no wonder that we have a generation of young people who are consumed by thoughts of sex. No longer do they wait until adulthood, as I did, to experiment with sex. They start at a very early age. This is contributing to a burgeoning population of children raising babies. There are many grandmothers who are paying the price for their children's sexual promiscuity. Having been pressed into service rearing another generation of children, the grandparents provide all of the essential services that should be provided by the parents.

I have seen too many people's lives damaged by ill-advised affairs. The parties who are victims of sexual infidelity and betrayal experience great difficulties in putting marriages and relationships back together. In order to be a successful bootstrapper, we must learn to control our urges and manage our way through the temptations that could ultimately lead to our destruction.

Obstacles to Claiming

By now you may feel clear about what you desire and what you want to claim. Let's make sure that the way is clear so that your prayers are not hindered by your own doubt and indecision. We can do this by looking at some of the obstacles that can block our blessings.

Blaming

I've been ministering to folks since I was a teenager, yet I am still amazed at the lengths to which people will go to excuse their own irresponsibility, immaturity, and poor judgment. Rather than be adult and own up, saying, "I was wrong" or "I messed up" or "I did it," people would rather make excuses for their behavior. People participate in pity parties because they don't want to admit to themselves or others that they messed up.

Shame and blame are kissing cousins. We can't stand the feeling of failure, which makes us feel ashamed; therefore, we seek out scapegoats to assume responsibility for our own frailties and shortcomings. All the major "isms"—racism, sexism, and so on—are blame and shame taken to a collective level. Blaming others enables people to justify their own bad behavior. Instead of saying, "I'm sorry," and then correcting their behavior, they project their own insecurities and sins onto others. Blame and shame on an individual level is bad enough, but scapegoating groups of people using such arbitrary indicators as skin color or gender can cause real damage, from glass ceilings to discrimination to genocide.

Don't get me wrong. Stuff happens. Every once in a while, life throws you a wild card just to see if you are paying attention. When those times come, all you can do is pray this common prayer:

God grant me the serenity to accept the things I cannot change,
the courage to change the things I can,
and the wisdom to know the difference.

But even in the worst circumstances, you have the power to decide how you will react to and perceive an event. If we get nothing else from talk shows, we can learn that the one thing that keeps us stuck in a rut is blaming others for our misfortune. The ones who heal and go on with their lives are the ones who have been able to stop the finger pointing. They went into their closet and did the hard heart work to find out exactly how they contributed to the problem. That is how I was able to get beyond my first marriage. When you're able to come face-to-face with your own weaknesses and misdeeds, you will be well on your way to achieving joy in life.

You are a blamer if you say things like:

Where did the time go?
I've had a run of bad luck.
The sun was in my eyes.
It wasn't my fault!
She/he did it.

We'll blame the sun, the moon, and the stars for our troubles rather than taking responsibility for our own lives.

Many corporations have a culture of blame. Rather than using the inevitable human errors to provide valuable feedback, people in some companies engage in a system of blame, which works to obscure the lessons and hinder learning: Who made the mistake and how can we punish the person? How can we let everyone know that we didn't make the mistake? In the meantime, a golden opportunity to learn has been squelched.

Do you want to be right, or do you want to be happy? Do you want to blame everything and everybody for your misery, or do you want the opportunity to claim your good? Do you want to be right, or do you want to achieve your goals? Do you want to win, or do you want to achieve your goals?

Own up! Don't despair. If you've been a blamer all your life, there's help for you. The first step is to realize that your life is your own. Instead of feeling overwhelmed by the responsibility, you should feel empowered, because now, finally, you can do something about your mess. The power to change your circumstances has been in your hands all along!

The next step is to admit where you went wrong. Think about it: What's the worst thing that could result from such an admission? You might be embarrassed, but you can handle that.

One of the big mistakes people make when they are first cured of blaming others is that they blame themselves for everything that's gone wrong in their life. Assuming responsibility for your life does not mean blaming yourself. Blaming yourself is the same as blaming other people. Getting to the root of your problems is not about blaming, which leads to shame, guilt, and scapegoating. A better approach is to honestly assess your missteps without judgment and with love. When you intelligently analyze where things went wrong, then you can decide how to get back on track.

How to change a blaming personality? Change your perspective. My wife, Elaine, has a powerful perspective on this issue, and if you can wrap your mind and heart around it, your life will change in an instant. She says that "perspective is how we view, understand, or interpret reality." Perspective determines how we feel about ourselves, our loved ones, and our acquaintances. It even determines how we treat others and relate to God.

The power of perception is never more obvious than in a marriage in which one situation is interpreted in two different ways. The husband perceives that the wife is lazy and bossy, but the wife feels overworked, emotionally abandoned, and voiceless. The wife perceives that the husband is harsh, insensitive, and uninvolved, but the husband perceives that he is present, affirming, and a loving family man. Elaine says, "Perspective is reality for us, and reality is often contingent upon our perspective. Your reality can change; your situation can turn if you simply change the way you think."

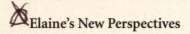 Elaine's New Perspectives

By changing your thinking, you can go from . . .

- Being miserable to being filled with joy.
- Living in fear and dread to having a life full of courage and hope.
- Always seeing the downside to being able to see the bright side.
- Being angry and bitter to being at peace and pleasant with everyone you meet.
- Being selfish and insecure to being giving and self-confident.
- Failure to success.
- Victim to overcomer.
- Negative to positive.
- Outsider to participatant.
- Being irresponsible to being responsible.
- Mediocrity to excellence.
- Procrastination to accomplishment.
- Struggling to thriving.

Some people feel trapped by their environment, while others are motivated to change their environment. Some folks feel overwhelmed by life's problems, but others take everything in their stride. The difference is perspective.

Self-defeating perspectives come from having only a handful of facts about a situation, rather than the truth. Where do you get the truth? By going within. Your perspective can either imprison or liberate you. Your perspective can make you feel either defeated or victorious.

As Elaine says, "With a change of perspective, you may still not have the money you need, but you'll at least know that all your needs are met. Your children may still not be acting right, but you can keep your wits about you. You might have been through terrible relationships in your past, but you don't have to carry that old baggage with you in your future. Your situation may not change right away, but you can still have a smile in your heart. You can begin to look at your problems as opportunities for God to work wonders in your life."

Before you can start claiming, you've got to stop blaming. To stop blaming, simply change your perspective. Here's how you do it:

Identify the source and cause of your shame.
Forgive yourself and others.
Bless the problem, those who may have hurt you, and yourself.
Learn from the lesson that your shame has taught you.
Affirm your worth. You are a good person.
Resist the temptation to blame others for your misfortune.

You have the power to choose. Regardless of what happens in your life, you can choose to experience it in a life-enhancing way. In the last section, you found those old boots in your closet. Now it's time to step up to the plate and put them on, and take responsibility for your life.

Lack of Patience

We live in a society of instant gratification. We don't even have to get out of our cars to get food anymore. All we have to do nowadays is pull up to the window, order, pay, and drive off.

Instant gratification leads to impatience, the great enemy of the bootstrapper. "I've got to get this done, and I've got to get it done now!"

Perfectionism

One thing I've noticed about most bootstrappers is that they like to control every facet of every task. They find it hard to delegate responsibility. It is said that while in office, Jimmy Carter was so involved with the details of management that he even kept tabs on the scheduling of the tennis courts.

My co-author knows an entrepreneur who epitomizes bootstrapping, right down to this problem of having to be right, trying to control every outcome, and driving everyone crazy in the process. He is enjoying moderate success in his chosen field, but he could probably double his profits if only he would let go and let his employees do their job. That way he could be out and about getting more business instead of getting bogged down in minutiae.

Simmering beneath the behaviors of the perfectionist is the emotion of fear—fear of failure and loss of control. If you are stuck on having to be right and in control all the time, you won't be able to claim what is yours even when it's staring you in the face, because you can't see it for all the worrying about the other stuff. Learn to let go.

Lack of Faith

Imagine going on a job interview with the belief that you're not going to get the job. Or trying to buy a house with no faith that you're going to get it. What's the point of claiming what is yours and pursuing your dreams if you don't even believe they're going to happen? But that is what so many of us do. When you let doubt creep in and infect your faith, you lose your power. "Faith is the substance of things hoped for, the evidence of things not seen" (Hebrews 11:1). In other words, our desire is good enough. We can rest assured that our desires will come true.

What a promise, and at the same time, what a test! When everything seems to be going wrong, it is difficult to keep the faith, but you must.

Lack of faith will steal the thunder from your claiming prayer. Your faith gives it the power to manifest.

Claiming Your Good

Now we get to the fun part, and if you've done the hard heart work, this is fun well deserved. This is the part where you get to dream your dreams and to declare them as your own. Claiming is the part where you get to be a co-creator with God. Ultimately, faith in God will make your dreams come true, but that doesn't mean you get to sit on your backside all day and watch soap operas. No, it's time to get busy. Bootstrappers are masters at identifying their desires and claiming their good. They have a goal, and they keep it uppermost in their minds. Their days are organized around the achievement of their goals.

What is claiming? Claiming is an aggressive style of prayer where you acknowledge the result even before you receive it. Different stages of the bootstrapping journey require different forms of prayer. Sometimes you need to be quiet and listen for guidance. But at other times you must become a prayer warrior and claim your good.

The Bible says that "the Kingdom of heaven has suffered violent attacks, and violent men try to seize it" (Matthew 11:12). Many people are put off by bootstrappers because they appear so driven, and they are. Even their prayers are fierce, because their desire is so strong.

Claiming is a powerful style of prayer. Claiming your good is your declaration of intent to pursue a goal. Claiming acknowledges God as the ultimate resource and yourself as God's channel for good and righteous action. Claiming is an affirmation that you can say at any time of the day or night. Contrary to the begging prayer, in which you're constantly bugging God for something that you want, or the meditative prayer, in which you're listening for an answer, the claiming prayer declares before God, the angels, and the universe that you are expecting miracles, opportunities, and help along the way. The claiming prayer positions you in a constant state of reception. You are willing to take responsibility for your life and work hard to achieve your goals. Once you've claimed a thing, you can't go back to doubting that your dreams will ever materialize.

On the other hand, the thing you've claimed may have to move over for something better, so you need to be on the alert and stay flexible. Just because you claimed a thing doesn't mean you can't change your mind. Seldom are we given the complete picture of our life's journey. We have to be like detectives, searching for clues along the way. Most important, we have to have faith in the process. There will be setbacks, course changes, and forks in the road along the way. That's natural and normal, so expect it. What claiming doesn't allow for is merely sitting down and crying when things don't go your way. Blaming others for obstacles that have been set in your path is against the bootstrapper's code of ethics. Mature bootstrappers learn to view the obstacles as opportunities and springboards to success.

Suppose your passion is to teach children. Even though your computer job is paying you a good wage, you decide to take a risk and claim a teaching job because that's what you've always wanted to do. You know exactly what you need to do: enroll in a four-year university, register with the education department, get money for tuition, books, and other expenses, allot a certain amount of time to take classes. However, halfway through the second or third term, you realize that you don't want to teach after all. You love education, and you want to help children, but you don't want to be in the classroom. You want to go into administration or educational research, or you want to figure out a way to use your background in computers to teach kids. Now, are you going to let the fact that you claimed a teaching job make you go stubbornly along your way and get that teaching certificate, or are you going to step back, reflect, pray, and change your course?

Check your thoughts. Reflect on your desire. Put your thoughts into action. Experts say we think more than eighty thousand thoughts per day. For the most part, this is an automatic process. If you were to examine your thoughts, would they be mostly negative or positive? What's your perspective on the obstacles in your life? Are they lemons or the raw materials to make a great lemonade?

We've accepted the judgments and criticisms of society, the media, childhood experiences, and so on, and that taints our thinking. For most of us, if we think one positive thought in five, we're having a good day—and that's bad. To claim our good, we've got to remember to be grateful throughout the day. Oprah Winfrey suggests that at the end of the day we list in a journal the things for which we are grateful, to become mindful of our blessings. Get into that habit, and you'll find it difficult to think negative thoughts all the time.

Let the truth stand over the facts. Resist believing something without knowing the higher truth about the matter. The facts can deceive you into believing that your claimed dream is unrealistic, does not meet the bottom line, is impossible. Slavery was a fact in the lives of millions of Africans, but the truth is that all men and women are free, and in 1865 the truth worked itself into the lives, minds, and laws of the land. The Great Depression was a fact during the 1920s, yet some people became wealthy, despite the "fact" that the money supply was severely depressed. Do not let the facts deceive you. Do not let the facts cloud your claim to your true desire. Study the facts if you must, but if they conflict with the pursuit of success, put the facts down! People will think you are out of your mind. The "facts" tell them so. But that's okay. You know the truth. You discovered it in your secret closet.

Let's say you've claimed a pretty big goal, the biggest ever, and you've been listening to others tell you the "facts." You've been hearing things like "that's never been done before" and "you're taking a big risk" and "the numbers just aren't working." Your friends may be well meaning, jealous, or just plain ornery. Maybe they can't see your dream because they are steeped in their knowledge of the facts. Regardless, listening to them is trapping you in a state of fear, and you need to separate.

Ignore the naysayers. In fact, don't even talk to them about the good you've claimed for your life.

Resist temptation. You've just taken the plunge and claimed your dream. One of the obstacles that has thrown many a wanna-be bootstrapper off the noble path is a delicious, tempting, seductive, beautiful distraction—excessive food, TV, alcohol, socializing when you should be working, gossiping, casual sex—any of them can cloud your thinking and undermine your prayers and best efforts. If you are spellbound by seduction, you have no mental energy to give to the claiming and affirmation of your dream. When your mind is consumed with irrelevant nonsense, you will probably miss the many blessings that will cross your path.

Follow the tenets of right intention and the ethics of claiming. Do not covet thy neighbor's wife—or anything else. Claim your desire, claim it with passion, but make sure that your prayer isn't intended to steal, deceive, or hurt anyone else. You may get what you ask for even in this case, but in the end, you will pay. Pray that all involved will mutually benefit from your success. Stick to the commandment of the Master: "Love your neighbor as yourself."

Do not claim irresponsibly. I know of men and women who have laid claim to other people's spouses or soul mates, usually with disastrous results. Just because you have a desire is no justification for working against the will of another.

Make it physical. Say you desire a new car, and you've always dreamed of owning a Mercedes. Take yourself and your camera to a dealer and test-drive one. Get the feel of it, the way the car expertly handles the road, the feel of the soft leather seats, the new-car smell, the hum of the motor. Next, have the dealer take your picture in the car of your dreams—big smile! Now, post that picture where you'll see it every day, and when you look at it, remember that you've claimed it and thank God for it. Find out how much the car of your dreams costs, how much of a down payment you'll need, how much you'll have to pay per month, and whether you should lease it or buy. Get ready, because it's coming!

Claim it and set off a chain reaction. You have no idea how much power has been unleashed by your staking your claim. There are the laws of physics, and then there's prayer. There are economics and the science of money, and then there's prayer. Man's laws don't stand a chance against the will of God.

That's what we learned in South East Queens, New York, when we decided to turn our community around. The difference between South East Queens and many other communities that are plagued by high unemployment, gangs, drugs, and violence is perspective. We perceive our community not as a ghetto but as paradise. Like many communities, South East Queens had a depressed economy and all the trials and tribulations of modern-day urban communities. We could have kept on going down, but we claimed our desire: we hungered for a safer community for ourselves and our children. We decided to change our minds about what we had and what could be done. Instead of grumbling, we took our destiny into our own hands.

We claimed peace in the streets. We claimed the total elimination of drug dealers. We claimed highly educated children. We claimed home ownership. We claimed high employment. We claimed renewal.

Allen A.M.E. Church has been a major player in the renovation of South East Queens. We've bought and developed or rehabilitated fifty million dollars in land and property, and we've created businesses. We take care of our elders and the unemployed, mentally ill, abused, hungry, and homeless; and we employ more than eight hundred people.

The first step in making it all happen was deciding to change our perspective. We had to see our community as a fertile field of opportunity, a paradise, not a violent, drug-infested ghetto. We took responsibility for our own lives, and then we got to claiming and planning, which you will begin to do in the next section. We set our sights high, and we're still growing. When one person harnesses a desire and claims a good, he or she is a force to be reckoned with. And when entire communities begin to come together to claim their good, no force can come against them.

Pull Yourself Up by Your Bootstraps . . .

I often hear people say that they have so many interests that they don't know where to start. In the meantime, the person who has few skills but applies a laserlike focus to his tasks goes on to experience success. In the next section, you will learn how to prioritize and plan for your dreams, but for now, let's start out with discovering what your dreams are.

It is very important to write down your dreams. There is something about the act of writing that makes things more tangible. Writing down your dreams takes them out of your imagination and into the concrete. Writing will take you one step closer to your goals.

The following exercises will prepare you for the next section on planning. You cannot begin to plan if you do not know what to plan for.

Brainstorming

1. This first exercise will take about five minutes, but if you need more time, feel free to take it. I want you to write down the wildest, craziest dreams you've ever had. Don't hold back. Do not edit your thoughts. Provide details. For example, if your biggest dream is to become a multimillionaire, explain how you would spend the money. Create a budget with line items detailing expenditures and dollar amounts. (Don't forget to include a 10 percent line item for tithing.) Remember your childhood dreams. We were so idealistic then. Some of us wanted to be president of the United States. We wanted to stop all wars and bring an end to world hunger. Even if you no longer have the same desires, even if you don't think your old dreams are possible, write them down. Whether your dreams are politically incorrect, good or bad, big or small, write them down. Write with abandon. Be free. Let your mind soar. Have fun with this exercise.

2. When you have finished, read over your list. What are your thoughts? How did you feel when you wrote certain ideas? Negative, positive? Did you hear the voice of criticism say, "You could never achieve that"? Or did you hear the voice of hope say, "That's a possibility"? As you were writing, did you recall the excitement you used to feel as a child when embarking on a new adventure? Or did the writing of certain dreams leave you feeling a sense of dread? Believe it or not, we can hold two or more conflicting feelings and thoughts within our hearts and minds. Moreover, negative self-concepts will override positive desires. That's one reason why so many good, talented people have failed to realize their dreams. Their subconscious insecurities have undermined their best efforts. These conflicts in consciousness can drive you crazy if you don't get a grasp on them right away. In the long run, conflicting feelings can become a major obstacle to success.

Because you were doing a freestyle brainstorm, you may have some ideas on your list that would be harmful to others if manifested. Cross them off. If you're not sure, check your ideas against the Golden Rule. If you wouldn't want them done to you, then don't do them to other people.

Now, rate your ideas from one to ten, with one being "absolutely impossible, no way" and ten being "definitely can do this." Highlight those ideas that elicited a strong emotional reaction within you. Write about it. For example, if you rated any of your dreams as "definitely can do this," why do you feel so strongly about your ability to succeed? Why haven't you done so up until now? If you rated any of your dreams as "absolutely impossible, no way," why do you feel incapable of making this dream a reality?

Again, read over your list. If there are any dreams that elicited strong emotional conflicts, try to get to the root of them. Explore in your journal how the conflicts could be resolved. This may take some time, especially if the conflicts have been brewing for years. Whatever you do, don't ignore them, hoping against hope that they'll disappear. They won't.

3. Now, highlight those dreams you rated highly. These are the dreams you feel confident about being able to achieve. Prioritize the top two or three dreams. These are the dreams that you will begin to plan for and take action on, so choose only what you can realistically handle given already existing time constraints. If you can handle only one dream right now, that's fine.

Goal Setting

Now take your top-rated dreams and convert them into goal statements. Your goal statements should reveal exactly *what* you want and *when* you want to achieve it. Your goal statements will be written in the positive and will reflect your intentions and commitment to achieving the goal. For example, if one of your top-rated dreams was to become an entrepreneur, your goal statement might read, "I intend to quit my job and start a company by the end of the year."

If one of your top-rated dreams was to slim down, your goal statement might read, "I intend to lose thirty pounds in six months."

How do you feel about your goals? Will you be able to live with them over time? If not, go back over your list and rethink your priorities. In the next section, you will begin the exciting and all-important process of planning. Your plan will help you think through action steps and time lines, anticipate possible obstacles, and identify helpful resources.

ACTION STEP 3:
PLAN YOUR DESTINY

Planning is a self-creating success prophecy.

It's fun to dream your dreams, claim what is yours, and even set goals. But the one action step in the bootstrapping process that stops people cold in their tracks is planning, and that's what this section is all about. People fail to realize the value of planning; therefore, they run from it as if it were a tidal wave chasing them. The idea of creating a blueprint for future actions can seem overwhelming at the beginning; however, it is a vital necessity. How else can you possibly project into the future? There is no way you can know every eventuality that will arise, but with proper planning you can make adjustments and keep on going.

Planning commits you to acting on your dreams. Planning forces you to assume responsibility for your life in areas that have previously eluded, confounded, and disappointed you. There is something scary about the act of writing down commitments into doable action steps with timelines. But bootstrappers have learned from experience that planning is essential to success.

In 1991, I presented a plan to the Allen Church for the remainder of the century. The plan included the building of the cathedral, reorganizing management, attending to staff and personnel needs, and upgrading equipment. It also identified new ministries that we wanted to implement by the year 2000. In December 1998, it was my privilege to report to the congregation that everything that we planned to accomplish by 2000 was already done. I introduced a new plan to cover the year 1999, which carries us into the new millennium. Without a plan, our adjustments to the new cathedral would have been chaotic.

During the course of construction of the cathedral, there were many problems that could have stopped our progress without a plan that included time lines. Any delays would have been costly. Therefore, we had to make wise decisions as quickly as possible. Our financing came from a consortium of eight banks, and walking them through the process with their differing and often conflicting policies was not easy. But we knew for sure that the plan would come to fruition, because of our faith, prayers, and hard work.

Early in the development, we hit water at a level of thirteen feet underground. The architect had designed the building to sit at that level. With all of the money we had invested at that point, we did not want to start all over. Yet, we were aware that building at the level of the water table would be disastrous later on. So we were able to get approval from the building department to raise the building five feet above the originally planned level. Without a plan, we would have been neck deep in water. But with one, we were able to make adjustments and keep on building.

There are times in all of our lives when we are forced to deviate from our plans. Without a plan, you have nothing to deviate from and thus nothing to guide you in reaching your ultimate goal. You don't travel to a place where you've never been before without a map. Life is an ongoing trip that requires a plan, which is the map that guides you on a successful journey.

Planning compresses time and space. It makes us come face-to-face with our dreams, up close and personal. It takes our fantasies and hopes out of the distant, potential *future* and brings them into the up-close and certain *now*. Planning takes dreams out of the clouds and brings them into the realm of physical manifestation. And guess who's got to do the manifesting? That's right—*you*.

Dreaming keeps us in a nice, pleasant, romantic state of mind. We think that if we share our big dreams with others, our prestige will be raised. The bigger the dream, the better our image, or at least that's what we'd like to think. But if you don't act on your dreams, and are still talking about them years later, it becomes clear to everyone that you're just a talker.

Ask Eva what she wants to be when she grows up, and she'll promptly say that she wants to be a lawyer. Ever since she was a little kid watching old Perry Mason reruns on television, she visualized herself as a defender of the downtrodden, and making a lot of money. Eva is a high school senior now, and when people hear of her big career dream, they smile and give her encouragement. She receives a lot of positive attention because of her dream.

Whether Eva will achieve her goal is questionable. At least once a month Eva gets called into the principal's office for fighting or cursing out one of her teachers. Although she always scores above average on all the national tests, she's failing English and math. Eva has the mental ability to become a lawyer, but whether or not she has the self-control and persistence to matriculate through a college program is doubtful. When her parents admonish her for not doing what it takes to achieve her goal in the long run, she tells them to stay out of her business. She says she knows what she's doing.

Carl is Eva thirty-five years later. Carl is in his early fifties, and ever since his twenties, he has proclaimed to anyone who would listen that he wanted to start his own business. And not just any business, but a multi-national corporation. He's a computer programmer and wants to take on Michael Dell. He longs for a mansion, an antique car collection, and a jet-setting life. Anything is possible, but the fact that Carl has not been able to hold down a job longer than six months at a time says a great deal about his ability to stick to anything, much less start up and operate his own company. Many people who don't fit well into the corporate structure go on to make millions by starting and running their own companies. But Carl is a classic example of a person who *won't*. He has the skills and the big dreams, but he won't get up and get busy. Carl has never gotten beyond setting goals. He stays stuck in that netherworld between goal setting and planning, and as long as he continues in this way, Carl will stay stuck in his dreams until he dies.

During my tenure as a college dean, I met countless students who had the intelligence and academic capability to succeed. They entered the university with big dreams of success in their chosen profession. But they didn't have a realistic plan. They wasted valuable time at parties, playing card games, or just hanging out. Many times they transferred to liberal arts programs because they thought them to be easier. There is nothing wrong with choosing liberal arts, but it doesn't matter what you choose if you lack the discipline to plan. Sadly, a number of them left the institution as dropouts. A lack of planning is a certain recipe for failure.

Dreaming and claiming your good is the "inner child" part of the bootstrapping process, but planning forces you to grow up and become an adult. Planning disciplines you. Planning requires of us a high level of maturity, because it makes us commit to the process.

Individuals, communities, and institutions that plan are guaranteed some measure of success. Since planning usually *ensures* success, it is essential that you plan *for* success. The renewal of South East Queens, New York, could not have occurred without a plan—several, in fact. Can you imagine AT&T, Microsoft, Coca Cola, McDonald's, or any billion-dollar multinational corporation not having a plan of operation, a marketing plan, a profit plan, a sales plan, and more? Can you imagine executives, officers, and board members saying, "I sure hope we get good profits in the future" or "Wouldn't it be great if we won the lottery?" Without planning, those companies would have quickly failed. In fact, they might never have gotten started.

Nations plan *centuries* into the future. The looming Y2K problem doesn't stop companies from planning ahead, because they know that even before the advent of computers, God determined how the century would end and how the next one would begin. After all, it's been done many times before. Why do nations plan? Because there is a desire to survive beyond today. Planning provides for social continuity *and* progress. Yet, today's prophets and soothsayers tell us to live for today. There is no past or future, only an ever-present now. Our government and institutions plan far into the future, but individually, we don't plan beyond next week! We live hand to mouth and from one paycheck to another. These practices subtly but effectively discourage us from planning for the future. If there is only now, then why bother?

So we continue to dream our dreams and hope for a better future. We trust chance, fate, whatever to get us there. We pray to God to please, please help us; and God will, but that does not mean God will chart our course for us. God gave you a mind and free will so that you can chart your own course, and your deep soul desires are pointing you in the right direction. What more do you want? God is not going to do it for you. In the creation story, after God creates Adam and places him in the Garden of Eden, he charges him with the responsibility to "work and take care of it" (Genesis 2:15).

I want you to think about your resistance, if any, to planning. Many readers will probably be tempted to skip this section, but you must come to terms with the necessity of planning.

If the idea of planning sounds about as much fun as a trip to the dentist, there could be several reasons for your resistance:

1. *You do not realize the importance of planning.* Even if, after reading this section, you still don't get it, at least do this: keep an open mind. Suspend disbelief. Just say, "I'll do it. I don't know why I'm doing this, but I'll try." Planning is not a waste of time; in fact, it will help you save time. The planning process I'll take you through in this section will tell you volumes about yourself, your ability to maneuver through society, and your belief in your own ability to get a job done. The process is simple and the end result is an organic, evolving blueprint of your success that is flexible enough to accommodate life changes and personal growth.

    Most important, your plan will help you stay on track. Our days get so busy that often we lose focus and forget to stay on track with our goals. Your plan, which has built-in time lines, will help you prioritize your day's events. It will also help you assess which of your current projects are truly worth your time.

2. *In the past, you created a plan to manifest dreams that were unrealistic.* You may have even tried to implement your plan. But in the end, the plan was not workable, and you became discouraged with the entire process.

    Even when things don't work out as planned, planning is never a waste of time because the process teaches you new and wonderful things about yourself. Isn't self-knowledge worth the price of gold? Besides, not achieving success on this go-round doesn't mean that you'll never reach your goal. Go back and brainstorm. Scale back. Try something a bit more manageable.

During the course of your life you'll make many plans. As your needs and vision evolve, so will your plans.

3. *You are spending more than you are making.* When you were a child your parents may not have shared with you information about the household budget, their salaries, and the general costs of raising a family. Many children are told that household finance is grown-up business and that they'll have to deal with mortgages, insurance, and debt soon enough. "Enjoy your childhood!" the adults say. Although your parents mean well when they say this, they miss a golden opportunity to teach you not only about money but about the principle of *stewardship*—taking care of yourself, your possessions, your loved ones, and even the environment.

No knight in shining armor is going to save you or manage your life. You must plan now to save yourself from grief and misery in the future. You need to go back into your closet and honestly assess the root causes of your fear. Often, fear of a task is caused by a lack of information, education, or skills, and it is human nature to be afraid of and avoid what we don't know. For example, if you're in massive debt and are living from paycheck to paycheck, you need to reeducate yourself about the realities of money and credit—how they work and how you are allowing yourself to be abused by the system. Perhaps you buy what you see, even if you don't need it, and soon you are overcome by debt. Ignorance is not bliss. How blissful are you going to feel in bankruptcy court? Knowledge is powerful, and the more you know, the more intelligent your decisions about money and relationships will be.

There was a time in my life when I was overburdened by debt. It started my last year in college, when unsolicited credit cards began arriving in my mail. The monthly brochures that were included with the bill provided an opportunity to purchase things that I wanted but could not afford. For just a few dollars a month, I could have almost anything my heart desired. Since I had a job, I was given credit to buy a car. American Express sent a card, and I bought at least one suit per pay period. I thought I was living well until reality hit.

Imagine how embarrassing it was when I went to purchase some clothes, presented my card, and was told by the merchant that he had orders to cut it up. Later in the same year, I parked my car in the university parking lot, only to discover that it was missing when I finished work. I thought it was stolen, but when I called the police, they informed me that it had been picked up for lack of payments. A finance company gave me a consolidation loan, which paid off my small bills, allowed me to clear up my arrearages on the car, and provided a few dollars to spare. Now that I had some excess cash on payday, do you think I saved some of it? No—I went back to the same old habits and before long was in financial straits again. Soon, I was going from one finance company to another to consolidate the consolidated loan. It took a while, but with Elaine's help, I learned how to save by not consistently investing in depreciating assets. You have the power to do the same thing. Getting out of debt is consistent with the way of a bootstrapper.

4. *You want to go with the flow.* You want to live your life like a jazz musician and improvise as you go along. You don't want to be tied down by "to do" lists and timelines.

There's a secret that all great jazz musicians share: before they improvise, they first practice the basic themes of a song. They become familiar with the structure of the music, so that improvisation comes easily. In the same way, planning provides some structure and discipline for your pursuit of success. There will be many occasions during your bootstrapping journey when you'll have to think quickly on your feet or make detours along the way. Spontaneity has its place. But improvisation as a way of life? The bootstrappers I know even plan their spontaneous moments!

Even the maintenance of your relationships requires planning. Do you have a problem with intimacy? Have you been able to maintain a close relationship for more than a few months? Are you committed to a spiritual walk? Do you attend to anything beyond yourself?

If you have a problem with making commitments, you need to do some serious soul-searching. This problem can affect every aspect of your life. You can't do the bootstrapping program without a serious commitment of your time, energy, and resources. Successful bootstrappers are secure enough in themselves to be unselfish in their relationships:

1. *You believe that your life has been preordained by God anyway, so why bother planning?* It's the age-old question of free will versus predestination. While I believe that God does have a plan for our lives, I also believe that we have the authority, power, and responsibility to chart our own course as much as we are able. We must use our deep soul desires as a compass and our plan as a map. God's broad strokes provide structure and map the major landmarks of our lives, but throughout our journey, we always have choices to make and our own personal dreams to strive for and achieve. That's what is meant by the oft-used phrase "The Lord helps those who help themselves."

2. *You have a fear of failure.* The planning process requires that you think about things like time lines, financial resources, relationships, and more. These are the tools of manifestation. As you work with these tools, you realize, perhaps for the first time, the potential for failure. Fear of failure might be the number-one reason that so many people never go beyond the goal-setting stage. Wishes and dreams never fail, but they never act.

To a certain extent we all have this fear. The difference between bootstrappers and the rest of the world is that bootstrappers do not allow fear to paralyze them. They work through their fears and succeed in spite of them. You too must develop this courage. It is one of the spiritual gifts that we all have. Courage works not in the absence of fear but in the presence of fear. Richard Carlson, author of the best-selling *Don't Sweat the Small Stuff,* says, "We rise in spite of our fears, not because of them."

3. *Your immediate appetites are clouding your long-term vision.* Name your addiction: sex, food, drugs, alcohol, television, partying. Addictions are loud. They scream for attention, often to the exclusion of everything else. If you are serious about achieving your goals, then you will have to address your appetites at the beginning of the process. Nothing can derail the pursuit of success more quickly than a fall from grace due to an inability to manage out-of-control desires and passions.

I can hear your protests now. "Planning is too much work!" you say. "I've got too much to do." "Not enough time!" Even as you protest, you are wasting time. That's a good way to ensure your failure. It's as simple as that.

How important is success to you? Are you willing to leave your hunger and desire festering in your soul? Remember the old saying "If you fail to plan, you plan to fail." The failure to plan triggers a default plan in which you have to accept whatever life throws at you. Even worse, schemers who have taken the time to develop their agenda will see you coming a mile away. They have a plan to take what you have. If you have no agenda of your own, you'll become susceptible to every con artist and smooth talker. If, on the other hand, you have your own course charted, and your actions are navigated by your desires and values, the schemers may come your way, but they won't stand a chance against you. To quote another true cliché, "If you don't stand for something you'll fall for anything."

Planning helps you avoid having to manage crises on a continuous basis. That's not to say that crises won't occur—they will. But some people live in a perpetual state of crisis. Why? Because they don't take the time to plan. They say that they have too much work to do. They don't understand that planning takes less time than managing crises.

Lora Wesley's body was in a state of crisis. She had consumed way too many high-calorie foods and put on a few too many pounds. When Lora got serious about losing weight, she realized that the one thing that had derailed her efforts in the past was that she never planned what to eat! It seems so painfully obvious now, but Lora is no different from many of us who want success but are unwilling to commit to the details of manifestation through planning. To change her habits, several times throughout the week, Lora would sit down and think about what she wanted to eat. She started with some basic dietary rules. She knew that she needed to cut down on the fat and that she needed to up her intake of fruits, vegetables, and water. Keeping those simple rules in mind, she planned and wrote down her grocery list whenever she needed to shop. She would take her list to the store and then—and this is important—she'd buy only what was on her list. She'd stick to the plan.

Planning helped Lora lose weight, and by sticking to her list, she also saved money. Whenever she did not plan, she found she wasted time trying to figure out what to eat. Sometimes she'd get so frustrated that she would go for the quick-and-easy solution to hunger, which was usually a high-fat, high-calorie fast-food meal.

Some people who have succeeded in losing weight devise entire menus on a daily basis. At the beginning of the day or the night before, they decide what they're going to eat for breakfast, lunch, and dinner, as well as the snacks in between. They write it all down and then they stick to it. Some plan for the week. Planning is a tool that can be individualized to meet your needs.

Bootstrappers are generally good planners. When I was with Xerox Corporation, I never went home without knowing my itinerary for sales visits the next day. As a pastor, even during my years in Congress, my schedule included time allocations for family, helping with homework, writing two sermons each week, and generally having food cooking in the oven and clothes in the washer at the same time. I even plan what I am going to wear the next day, hang the clothes on the bathroom door, and shine my shoes before going to bed.

Plan Your Destiny!

Planning is necessary for many different reasons—to start up new ventures, manage crises, or to recoup from failure, to name only a few. The depth, breadth, and scope of your plan will depend on what you are trying to accomplish. Obviously, a military invasion strategy is going to look a lot different from a dietary list. However, there are basic, simple planning principles and techniques that can be used no matter what your goal is to point you in the direction of success.

Whether you're starting a new venture or planning a magnificent comeback, you need a plan. You cannot go forward with confidence or make intelligent decisions if you have only a vague, hazy idea of where you're going. Inspiration, sweat, and gut instincts might get you started, but planning will take you to the next level.

We are always looking for help in managing life's challenges. When I became a father for the first time, I wished that an instruction manual had come with my baby. Since it didn't, we had to learn as we went along. But the experience was valuable when the other three children were born. Of course, each child had a different personality, but we made the necessary adjustments. Now I realize why it was impossible to create a manual that was specific to all of the unexpected adjustments that one makes in child rearing. Any plan that is successful must be flexible so that adjustments can be made.

We don't know how the stock market is going to perform far into the future. Neither do we know what jobs will be in demand before we declare a major in college. What we do know is that the more options we create for ourselves, the greater are the possibilities that we will be able to make the appropriate adjustments.

You can't possibly know exactly what's going to happen and when and where, but the exercises that follow will help you to create your own self-fulfilling prophecy. They will give you the tools to anticipate some of the challenges that are sure to come, as well as help you to see the opportunities that exist all around you. In this section you'll be doing two sets of planning activities: big-picture planning and planning on the run.

Big-Picture Planning

Pull out your goal statements, which you wrote in the last section. This is a good place for you to start a journal or get a pocket organizer. You'll also need a calendar to use as a reference and an appointment book or scheduling software.

1. *Tweak your goal statements.* In addition to what you wrote, I'd like to offer one more (yes, you can do more): "Starting today, I will schedule time for stress relief on a daily basis." Many bootstrappers run the risk of stress-related illnesses, such as hypertension and strokes. For your health's sake, include a daily activity, be it a few minutes of quiet prayer or some form of exercise, that will help you manage your stress and give you energy. Otherwise, you're not going to be healthy enough to implement your plan. I discussed earlier the benefits of exercise. Plan an exercise program today and continue it.

    Now, take your goal statements and categorize them according to the following time frames: immediate, short-term, long-term, and ongoing. Immediate goals were due to be done yesterday. These are the things that you've been procrastinating about and that cannot wait one more day. Short-term goals take anywhere from a day to six months to implement. Long-term goals take from six months to a year, or perhaps five or ten years or even longer, to implement. Ongoing goals (for example, your daily stress relief activity) are implemented on a regular basis. The purpose of the time frames is to help you prioritize the order of your goals. Make sure to also include under a "Due Dates" column an educated guess as to when you feel you should achieve your goal. Due dates will help you stay on track at all times. For you couch potatoes, the dates should give you the sense of urgency you need to get yourself moving. Set up your journal with goals, time frames, due dates, and objectives.

2. *Brainstorm action steps.* In order for you to achieve your goals, you'll need a clear idea of your first and next steps. For instance, if you want to become a doctor, then you know that there are certain course requirements that must be met before you enter medical school. Ideally, you started planning even while you were still in

high school and made the right college selection. Since tuition for medical school is extremely expensive, you should explore grant, fellowship, and other financial aid possibilities. You may even need a part-time job. Once on campus, you may need to seek out a study partner to help you in the learning process. You can't possibly anticipate every goal, but try to include as many "to do's" as you can.

Also, when you're setting due dates for your action steps, take into consideration existing priorities at work and at home. Now, record the due dates in your appointment book. Even if you could think of only one step to do, that's okay. That one step will lead to another and another. Trust the process.

3. *Identify available resources.* As I stated earlier, people often ask me how I've been able to get so much done in my life. A big part of my success is due to knowing what resources are available to me and then capitalizing on that knowledge. For example, the library is a tremendous resource that is free, yet how many of us take advantage of it? If you want to start your own business, the Small Business Administration is available to assist you with information and maybe even money. They also have a site on the Internet. Your school probably has a career planning and placement office to help you get a job. Your family and friends can be a great resource. Is there anyone at work whom you respect and admire? Would that person be available as a mentor? You have more tools at your disposal than you may realize, so in this exercise, you're going to prove it to yourself. Simply write down all the resources that are available to help you meet your goal—*to help you help yourself*—that exist on your job, at your school, in your community, in your home. Include the resources that you have within yourself, such as intelligence, maturity, faith, and skills.

Next, I want you to think about all the *information* resources that you can access. Let's say that your goal is to get married. (Don't laugh—many of you reading this book have been secretly hoping and wishing for years to get married. If that's what you want, stop fantasizing and start planning!) The problem is, you haven't a clue about how to meet good, quality people with similar interests. You need information. There are many books on the market about relationships, and that's surely one way to get information. But if I were you, I'd learn to start asking good questions, such as, "Where can I find out about singles events that are being held in my community or city?" I'd start interviewing people who don't seem to have any problem meeting quality folks. There are all kinds of appropriate venues out there. Two ministers on my staff, Elliott and Eleanor Hobbs, met at the church, got married within a year, and have now been married for the past fourteen years. He was chairing a church event when he noticed Eleanor sitting near one of the matrons of the church, Mrs. Elizabeth Miller. During the service, Mrs. Miller noticed Elliott repeatedly looking at Eleanor, and she told her. After the service was over, as he was at the door asking Mrs. Miller about the young lady, Eleanor exited the building. Sister Miller introduced them and told them that the rest was up to them. A number of other couples have also found the church to be an excellent meeting place for eligible single men and women.

Without a doubt, your goal will determine the types of questions and sources of information (people, books, media, etc.) that will help you on your journey. First, write down your questions, and then do the research to find the answers you need. Keep these lists in your daily appointment book for quick-and-easy reference.

4. *Brainstorm possible obstacles.* I can hear you positive thinkers now: "Obstacles, Rev.? That's so negative!" No, that's being proactive. Roadblocks will happen—that's a given. If you don't plan for them, you will end up in crisis mode. If they don't happen, great! But having lived half a century, I do know this much: anytime you try to do something to better yourself, I guarantee you, you'll hit resistance. You can count on it. Obstacles are a fact of life, and you

cannot wish them away. As long as there are people in the world who do not want you to get ahead, you can count on having to deal with obstacles. As long as nature has her way, there will be something blocking your way. The purpose of obstacles is not to detour you or depress you but to make you stronger, wiser, and more capable.

One more thing you need to know: the bigger your dreams, the bigger the obstacles. Or, as Betty Shabazz said to me after my election to Congress, "The higher you rise, the thinner the oxygen gets." The wise man or woman learns how to anticipate problems and prepare for them, not run away from them. And when you get really good at this planning stuff, you might even be able to predict with precision who or what might impede your progress.

First, think about all the obstacles that you might have to deal with to achieve your goal. A lack of money? The jealousy of a co-worker? Racism? Sexism? Whatever they are, write them down.

Read over what you just wrote. Now consider, if those obstacles were to really happen, how you would deal with them? Get to writing.

In addition to anticipating possible problems down the road, I also want you to start understanding that no obstacle can stand in your way if you are truly determined to succeed. Yes, sexism and racism exist, obstacles will come, *but they are irrelevant when it comes to the manifestation of your dreams.* You should feel empowered by the knowledge that you can deal with whatever comes your way.

5. *Brainstorm opportunities.* Cutthroat opportunists have given opportunism a bad name. Bootstrappers take advantage of opportunities in ways that do not compromise their integrity. Let the Golden Rule ("Do unto others as you would have them do unto you") be your guide to righteous action. Once you've determined that a particular course of action would help you achieve your goal and that it will not hurt anyone for you to take

advantage of it, then go for it. Opportunities are the gifts that the process offers.

First, think back over the past few years and write down all the opportunities you missed. Do not get bogged down in regret! The purpose of this exercise is to prove to you that opportunities surround you every day, every moment.

Next, with your goals and action steps in mind, write down all the opportunities that exist today—on your job, in your neighborhood, in your family, and so on. Write down how you might capitalize on them.

Are you beginning to see the light? Getting some great ideas? Hallelujah!

Planning on the Run

It's necessary to concentrate on each day's goals as well as on the big picture. Focus on the details that will help you keep track of your action steps. Many of you might already be doing this kind of quick-and-easy preparation. Remember Lora's weekly food list and daily menu planning? Simple "to do" lists will do. If you want to use your appointment book, feel free. The best part is when you finish your task, you get to cross it off your list. That means you're closer to achieving your goal!

A word of caution: Don't get too bogged down in planning, whether doing big-picture planning or planning on the run. Although planning is vitally important, many get stuck there, and that defeats the whole purpose of our action-oriented style of bootstrapping. I've heard of corporations taking years to put a plan together. In my opinion, that's way too long. If you're on a planning team in your company or community organization, suggest getting away on a weekend retreat, away from the phones and daily demands, and getting the planning done. If you're planning for yourself, which will be the case for most of you, the same advice applies. Give yourself a deadline. I recommend taking no more than one or two days, tops. This plan isn't written in stone, anyway. As new situations lead to new opportunities and new information leads to new directions, you'll be making revisions to your plan as you proceed along your journey.

Master Plans

Planning to Win

I remember my first political campaign. Once I agreed to run for the congressional seat, it became apparent that I needed a good plan, not only to win but also to manage my life when the campaign was over. The first problem that I faced was that other than running for delegate to the Democratic Convention in 1984, I had never run for a major political office. I was told that it is virtually impossible to run against the Democratic machine and win an election in the City of New York. You don't even think about running without having a strategy. I needed some campaign direction and found a valuable resource in an elderly gentleman, Nat Singleton, who believed in me and felt that I could beat the machine. He decided to mentor me. Next, Edwin Reed, a young Harvard graduate with an MBA, volunteered to take a leave of absence from his job as an investment banker to run my campaign. Although he had never run a campaign, he was such a quick study that I did not have to trouble myself with issues of media, voter registration, poll watchers, or election day operations. My job was to be the candidate. Once the lines of responsibility were determined, we brought in experienced political and media consultants. We put a plan together and everybody stuck with it. The outline we created included timetables for rallies, a schedule of press conferences, locations that were imperative for me to visit, other areas that campaign staff could handle, and the biggest thing of all, my message. We decided that, because of my track record in the community as a builder and deliverer of promises, the campaign theme would be "Turning Dreams into Reality." It was a formidable undertaking, because I was a novice running against a state senator, two assembly people, and a judge, all of whom had campaign experience. We soon realized we were not aware of all the variances and nuances of party politics. But we followed the plan and stayed on the point with our message of community and economic development. The strength of the message was that it was not mere words but was supported by the visible community projects that the Allen A.M.E. congregation had successfully completed under my leadership.

The other part of planning dealt with my own family issues. Since Elaine was educational director for the school that our children were attending, we decided that we would not uproot them. I committed to commuting between New York and Washington daily, because it was in the best interest of my family and the church. The plane rides became an extension of my office when I needed to work, or my bedroom when I needed sleep. A bootstrapper learns to make use of whatever resources are available to meet his needs. I committed to the church that I would take a maximum of only six Sundays a year of outside engagements. In the eleven years that I served in the U.S. House of Representatives, I honored those commitments. I never had a residence in Washington, D.C.; instead, I commuted daily from New York, prepared two sermons weekly, and preached two of the three Sunday morning services at my church in accordance with that preplanned schedule. The family, the church, and the constituents were all happy, because I did not become a Washington insider. Therefore, I was available to them and able to meet their needs. Without a plan, and the discipline to follow such a rigorous schedule, there is no way that I could have succeeded.

A Master Plan to Beautify Women

Owen and Minerva Breedlove were sharecroppers who lived on a plantation in Delta, Louisiana. Soon after they won their freedom they gave birth to a daughter, Sara. But it was a time of national transition, and life was difficult. Sara's parents were poor and uneducated. Sharecropping was barely a step up from slavery and was designed to keep laborers from progressing. When Sara was six, her parents died, never having received their forty acres and a mule as promised by the U.S. government. Her sister, who lived in Vicksburg, Mississippi, took her in. When she was fourteen, Sara married Mr. McWilliams. The couple had one daughter, A'Lelia, in 1885. Two years later, Mr. McWilliams was murdered by a lynch mob. At the tender age of sixteen, Sara Breedlove had experienced life and death at its harshest. She and A'Lelia left the South and moved to St. Louis.

If ever there was a woman who could truly say she had no boots, it was Sara Breedlove. She had no money, no husband, no education—nothing. She was living in an age when violence against African Americans was commonplace. Yet, for the next eighteen years, she survived and supported herself and her daughter as a washerwoman.

That she managed to make a living at all is a testimony to her tenacity, but her story doesn't end there. As the story goes, one day in 1905, Sara noticed that she was beginning to lose her hair. She prayed to God for a healing, and that night she dreamed that a "big African man" came to her and gave her a formula for a hair care product. Later in her kitchen, she mixed all kinds of soaps and ointments in her washtubs until she came up with a formula for her own hair grower.

Around this same time, Sara got a job selling hair care products, which sent her to Denver. There she met and married Charles Joseph Walker, and by 1906, she and her husband had formed a company to sell her Wonderful Hair Grower. She renamed herself "Madame C. J. Walker," and they took their act on the road.

Madame had a genius for marketing. She sold her products door-to-door. She went to homes, churches, and lodges to demonstrate how her hair care treatments were to be used. She hired women and trained them as "hair culturists," and her empire grew. Her products were well packaged and featured her picture on the front of each tin. She placed advertisements in Black newspapers and magazines. She even convinced a major Black celebrity, Josephine Baker, to promote and use her products as she danced on the stages of Europe. By the 1920s, Madame C. J. Walker was rich and famous.

Inspiration got Walker started, but marketing, sales planning, and personal initiative took her to the next level. She became the first American woman of any color to make a million dollars through her own labor. And she often said, "I got my start by giving myself a start."

Designing Men

I know four wonderful young men who periodically attend the Allen Church. They grew up in the greater Jamaica community and attended high school together. All of them had a love for clothes, so they began sewing in the basement of one of their homes. After a while, other young men were asking them to make outfits for them. Soon, their orders exceeded their capacity to produce with their limited equipment. One of their mothers got a home equity loan and purchased new, more powerful equipment for them.

They called their clothing line FUBU (For Us By Us) and marketed it at studios where hip-hop artists were recording. They convinced the artists to wear their designs in videos, movies, and live stage performances. They also convinced several professional basketball players to wear their line. Before long, they had moved from the basement and their product was selling in major sporting goods stores and top department stores, including Nordstrom. They have become a top name in men's sports fashion. The mother who got the loan is a bootstrapper because she was willing to invest in them, and they are bootstrappers because they had a brilliant idea and made the sacrifices to bring it to fruition.

Pull Yourself Up by Your Bootstraps . . .

Take action today. Take one opportunity that you listed in your plan, and pursue it. That's called implementation. We'll be talking more about this important step in part 3, because implementing your action plans is what bootstrapping is all about. Implementation is the heart and soul of the bootstrapping journey. After all, bootstrappers don't just sit around and dream all day. They take their plans in hand and get busy!

Create Opportunities

If you have not been able to identify any opportunities, don't slip into the whining and blaming mentality. Where there are no opportunities, bootstrappers create them. In your plan are action steps that you designed to help you accomplish your goals. If you are stuck and have not been able to easily complete the action step because of a lack of opportunity, ask yourself what's missing. What person do you need to talk to, what needs to happen for you to take action? Now, how can you aggressively create the circumstances in which opportunity can occur?

For example, do you need the support of an influential person but have no idea how to get in touch with him or her? Start with the obvious. Call her up. Be nice to the secretary and be clear about your reason for wanting to meet with the boss. Don't take no for an answer. If you can't get past the secretary, write a letter. Make sure it is clean, neatly typed, and free of grammatical and proofing errors. Fax it, e-mail it, snail mail it, or hand-deliver it—or do all of the above. Too often people let the word *no* derail them, but you must be persistent.

Do you need money? This is the one excuse I hear most often for not pursuing a goal. Community groups and schools often make this complaint. However, if you are truly committed to your goals, you will not let the lack of money stop you. Are there other ways to implement your action steps? For example, if to achieve your goal you must take a refresher course in your field, how can you get the money for the course if you have none? Can you test out of the course for less money? Is a scholarship available? Can your family help? Can you barter with the school—your office labor for a free course? Back in the good old days, when folks couldn't come up with the rent money, they'd throw a rent party. If there's no other way around it and you must have the money, throw a fund-raiser. Bake cookies and sell them. As long as it's legal and won't harm anyone, do whatever it takes.

Go the Extra Mile

Remember extra-credit work in school? Extra credit was not required, but it created the positive opportunity to get an outstanding grade. You may have to do some extra-credit work to create your own opportunities. For example, let's say that you've set your sights on a job at a particular company. Sending your résumé would be a start, but that's what everyone does. You need to take action in a way that will set you apart from the crowd. Be creative. What could you do to attract the positive attention of influential decision makers? Do you know someone who knows someone who would be willing to make a recommendation on your behalf? Volunteer to work in the position for a limited amount of time. Make a deal. If they like you after that time, they hire you. If not, no hard feelings. Create a project that would add value to the business of the company. Write a summary of the idea. If you have gotten to the interview stage, propose your idea to the person in charge (anyone else might steal your idea). If it's a good idea, you might get a job. Even if the position is temporary, it could lead to something permanent. One step at a time.

Promote Yourself

Self-promotion is an excellent way to create opportunities. How will people know about you if you don't tell them? The more people know about your skills, talents, good character, and track record, the more they will want to help you achieve your goals. People often feel that self-promotion is bragging, but when it comes to success, there's no room for false modesty. If you don't "toot your own horn," no one will. Elected officials are masters of self-promotion. Study them and see how you might apply their techniques to your quest for success. Here is my formula, which worked every time I ran for office:

1. *Be honest.* False advertising will eventually catch up with you and cause people to lose trust in you. No one wants to live or work with people they cannot trust.
2. *Record your successes.* If possible, show how your successes added value to a project or helped people. Then send your document to influential decision makers. While in office, I produced and mailed to my constituents and the media a newsletter that served to keep track of my voting record, my stand on the issues, successful legislation I'd helped to pass in Congress, and more. While campaigning, I produced simple flyers that highlighted my past accomplishments, ideological platform, and future goals for my district.

3. *Don't tear others down to build yourself up.* When you talk about your track record, don't compare yourself to others. Stand on your own merits. You do not need to use the defeats of others to make yourself look better.

4. *Be humble.* Being humble while promoting yourself might sound like an oxymoron, but it is not. Know the difference between false modesty and humility. False modesty creates the appearance of humility while masking possible issues of low self-esteem. To know your worth is to build self-confidence, but to know that God is the source of your gifts will keep you humble.

PART 3

EXECUTE!

Faith without actions is dead.
James 2:26

I can think of no better metaphor for the next phase of your journey to success than the incredible performance of the late Florence "FloJo" Griffith Joyner during the 1988 Olympics in Seoul, Korea. My family and I enjoyed watching the flamboyant FloJo run like the wind. Self-confident and in the best shape of her life, FloJo set new world records in the one-hundred- and two-hundred-meter races, and no one has been able to best her yet. FloJo won three gold medals and one silver that year. During her brief time in the Olympic spotlight, she changed women's sports forever.

While training hard was critical to her success, FloJo could not have won those races had she not taken that first running leap onto the track and kept on running with all her might. If she had tarried one second after the gun was shot, she would have lost.

The heart and soul of the bootstrapping journey is *action*. Not mindless busywork, but intelligent, goal-oriented, timely action that will eventually lead to the creation of something great of lasting value.

You have everything you need to get started, so pick yourself up, make that call, knock on that door, take the emotional risk, take your first step.

Don't make any excuses. I don't want to hear that you have no self-confidence or that you suffered in your childhood. I don't want to hear that you've failed before. Dig down deep and you'll come up with your hand full of confidence and strength. Combine that with your wits, and you'll have all you need.

When I was growing up, the old folks used to tell us, "Get some backbone!" They didn't want to hear any whining about why we couldn't do something. They loved us so much that they would not allow us to succumb to fear. Sometimes they'd physically push us out of the house to make us do the thing we didn't want to do but had to do. Some of us were thrown in the river to learn how to swim. We had to face the bullies who taunted us on the way to school. Those wise ones knew how hard it was to face your fears, but face them we did. Back then we had the benefit of their tough love. Today, you must give yourself a push and a shove.

There was one thing that the old folks hated with a passion, and that was laziness. They just would not tolerate it. "The devil finds work for idle hands to do," our elders would say. Let's be honest. What we call procrastination is really laziness, and we've all been guilty of it. Sometimes we don't do what we know we should be doing because we're lazy. We may not want to admit it. We'll come up with every excuse in the book, but the fact remains that we're lazy. As the dictionary says, we are "averse or disinclined to work." If you're unemployed and aren't even trying to look for a job, you're lazy.

Let's say that since developing your plan, you've taken a couple of steps. You went and got some information. Then, paralyzed, you decided to sit on what you know. You just stopped. You allowed yourself to get distracted. Is it fear or is it laziness? Only you know for sure, but regardless, neither is a valid excuse for not taking action.

I was pretty industrious as a child, but every once in a while, I wouldn't move fast enough for my father. Not moving fast enough was almost as bad as not moving at all. Sluggishness was seen as disrespect, and it was liable to get you a stern lecture.

My father's thesis was simple: you may be moving, but if you're moving too slowly, you're lazy. The old folks knew that if you moved too slowly, you would miss out on opportunities. You'd lose momentum. The race could be lost.

Being a typical boy, I suffered my share of bumps and bruises. Still, no adult would let me get out of doing my chores or my homework because of a scrape. Many of our parents and grandparents understood victimization better than anyone, but they never let life's hard knocks stop them from doing what they had to do.

Every day you live offers you another chance. You've got one more chance. Are you going to take action this time? Are you going to keep your promise to yourself? Did you even write down your plan?

Don't you want to feel fulfilled in your work and personal life? Don't you want your needs to be met? Don't you want abundance—or do you want to continue to run on empty?

Before you know it, the future will be here. As a matter of fact, the future is now. How are you going to meet it? Are you going to take action today to ensure that tomorrow will be different? Think about it. Ten years ago, you made certain decisions and did certain things that led to your current life circumstances—for better or worse. If you long for a different future, then you must take action today, right now. Don't let the excitement of dreaming and planning fade away. From now on, you must assume the responsibility of motivating yourself to act. The actions you take today will determine the quality of your tomorrows.

Making the decision to go after your dreams was good, but it was not enough. A decision is merely unrealized potential; action is that potential manifested. When you make a true decision, there is no turning back. Don't even think of looking back. When you make a decision to change your life, a steel door slams shut, sealing away your past, your old conditioning, your negative beliefs, your failures, and your fears, where they can have no relevance to what you need to do today.

In part 3, we're going to talk about executing your plan. This is the moment of truth in the bootstrapper's journey, the moment in which the people who *do* are sorted out from the people who *won't*. You've searched your soul. You know everything you need to know to get started. So, go for it.

The "Can-Do" Spirit of Youth

When I was about ten years old, the children at my church decided that we needed a bus to attend youth meetings, go to the beach, and provide transportation for people to get to church. There was only one problem: money. It cost one thousand dollars to buy a bus in those days. That might as well have been a million dollars as far as we were concerned.

Yet, the high figure did not deter us from our deep desire, and that deep desire caused us to focus on our goal. We developed a plan. We would create a product, then sell it door-to-door. We got our mothers to make popcorn balls, homemade ice cream, and cookies. Loaded with product, we took to the streets and also sold at the church after services. We ultimately raised the money we needed, and our pastor bought the bus.

At our home, money was always needed, which is why my father worked two or three jobs at a time. By the time I was eight years old, I

also worked. I had a paper route, did domestic work, and sold magazines and newspapers door-to-door. At the time I had the barest of survival skills—I could cook, sew, and clean house, and I could talk. I
didn't have a plan, but I had a need, which was to make money for
myself and my family.

Without ever considering the potential for failure, I took first steps
all the time. Some paid off, some didn't. But in every case, I learned
important lessons about myself, other people, and my world. My early
steps taught me how to maneuver in society, manage a business, treat
my customers, and be punctual with my deliveries regardless of the
weather or any other type of crisis.

When toddlers first begin to walk, they fall down a lot. They get
back up, waddle around, and then fall down again. They keep trying
until they get it right. In fact, they have no choice. They must learn to
walk because, after a while, they'll be too big to carry, and somehow
they must know this instinctively!

Jesus tells us that if we want to inherit the kingdom of God, we must
act like little children. This does not mean reverting back to immaturity
but reclaiming that youthful exuberance you had when you anticipated
trying out something new. When you made a decision, you would stick
to it. New challenges excited you. Life was truly an adventure. This is the
spirit you must reclaim.

Be a man or woman of your word. This is what it means to have
character. It is as important for you to trust yourself as it is for others to
trust you.

Remember the Terrible Twos? As a child, your stubbornness constantly got you in trouble. Believe it or not, that stubbornness you had
as a child is still in you. Make use of it! Time, life experiences, and maturity wear many people down and they lose their power. Their will to do
becomes atrophied.

But it is still there. You must reach down deep and reclaim your will,
and, like a muscle, you must exercise it daily to make it strong. Once you
begin to understand your purpose and soul desires, you must use your
will to take that first step—and then the next and the next, until your
goal is achieved.

There is no magic formula to success—just soul-searching, goal setting, planning, and taking action. Stay true to your course, and you will have help along the way. Be grateful for those moments of support, because they can be few and far between.

First Steps

The journey of a thousand miles begins with a single step.

By now you know that I don't want to hear any more excuses. It doesn't matter if you don't have much. Use what you've got and take your first step.

Call that prospective employer for an interview. Call the Small Business Administration and schedule an appointment with an expert who can give you advice about starting your own business. Make baby-sitting arrangements and plan to attend an event to expand your network of friends and associates. Call that worthy organization that you admire and tell them you want to volunteer your time to help out.

Reginald Lewis, the African American business genius who bought Beatrice Foods for one billion dollars, came from humble beginnings and was always taking first and next steps. What separated him from all the others who merely fantasize about making money was that he took what he had—a strong will and a gift of gab—and took action, consistently. He never let the word *no* or failure deter him. This man, who spearheaded one of the most complex financial deals of the decade, failed math three times in college before barely passing with a D in his junior year. Einstein wasn't much good at math, either.

Phil Knight loved to run, and his great ambition in life was to find a quality running shoe. In 1964, athletes depended on expensive German-made shoes that Knight felt were not good enough. He contacted his former college track coach, Bill Barrowman, put up five hundred dollars, and created the Blue Ribbon Sports company. The young company placed its first order for running shoes with the Onitsuka Tiger Shoe Company in Japan, and sold them in America. They sold so fast that the company soon placed another order for more. Lacking a retail outlet, Knight used what he had and sold his running shoes from the trunk of his car at track meets. The shoes sold well, but the partners still weren't satisfied.

As the story goes, Barrowman, lacking a manufacturing plant, took to his kitchen. He poured melted rubber into a waffle iron, and Nike's distinctive-looking running shoe was born.

Don't be surprised if your first steps threaten others. When I first came to Allen Church, my vision was to energize the place and redevelop the community of South East Queens. While many caught the vision, there were a few people who opposed our first steps. Resistance from others is a common obstacle that bootstrappers have to deal with. However, you cannot let that stop you.

Understand Beginner's "Luck"

You may have the fortunate experience of early successes. These moments motivate you to keep on going, but don't depend on beginner's luck. That's how gamblers get in trouble. The memory of that first win is like an addictive drug that keeps them trying to win again, against the odds and despite their empty pockets.

Salespeople often experience beginner's luck. The first cold call is successful, only to be followed by a succession of failures.

What many call beginner's "luck" is really God's way of helping you to stay encouraged, to keep on doing what you're doing, despite the setbacks and failures that are sure to come. The first-time-out success creates a positive memory for you to hold on to even when things are not working out so well. Don't depend on it, but understand it and appreciate it for the gift that it is.

Know Your Action Style

Bootstrappers come in many different temperaments, and they take action in a variety of ways. Some begin their quest for success with a flurry of activity, doing this and that until they hit on something that works. Others focus on one task at a time and plod doggedly through until it is done.

There are positives and negatives to both styles. The busy one sees more opportunities than the plodder but may not have enough focus to capitalize on them. The plodder may achieve his one task, while his tunnel vision keeps him from seeing the many other opportunities that surround him every day.

Build on your strengths, and stretch beyond your self-imposed limits. At any given moment, I'll have at least ten family, church, and business projects going at one time. It helps to have a brilliant staff and an efficient executive assistant, but I too have to be organized to manage it all. All of my interests are important to me, and I don't want to run the risk of letting any one slip my attention.

Bootstrappers usually will have more than one project going at a time, but if you're a plodder, that's okay. Doing one thing and doing it well is better than doing nothing at all.

Don't Despair in the Wilderness

In the last section, you brainstormed about some obstacles that might arise in your journey. The wilderness is one such obstacle that everyone will face at least once in their life. It is a time of waiting for the success you have been working toward. Wilderness times can make you doubt yourself, but paradoxically, they occur precisely when you are on the right track.

Your commitment to success will lead to significant allocations of your time, energy, money, and resources. As you become invested in the journey, it is natural and correct to expect a return. What you cannot predict, however, is how quickly your investments will begin to pay off. It may happen tomorrow, or it could take much longer.

Nothing distresses a bootstrapper more than having to wait for success. God's time is truly different from our time, and we cannot fathom it. All we can do is trust in the process and wait. This time of waiting is indeed a wilderness. The children of Israel knew it well. In between the extremes of Egyptian slavery and living the good life in the Promised

Land, they waited forty long years in a true wilderness. No conveniences, no comfort. Yet, God fed them and took care of them.

Time spent in the wilderness matures us, but it is also a time of great danger. You can get lost in the wilderness. During their time in the desert, the children of Israel lost their spiritual focus and allowed themselves to be tempted by all kinds of sin. They were out of control. Even though God fed them and took care of them, their impatience got the best of them. Many who started on the journey never made it to the Promised Land.

Beware the temptations and distractions of the wilderness. Don't allow yourself to get distracted, depressed, or disheartened. When you've done all that you can do and are waiting for your dream to manifest, you can still take action in other arenas. Waiting for your success does not mean that you get to sit around and watch television all day until it happens.

One of the most common problems people face during wilderness times is a crisis of faith. Because nothing seems to be happening, they begin to doubt God's love for them. Some may be far along in their journey and getting tired. They've been taking action, but they don't seem to be getting anywhere. They're no longer sure of themselves. I hear this so often in my ministry. People tell me that they've followed the rules; they've worked hard and tried to be good. Yet, they just can't seem to get ahead. It's taking too long to achieve success.

Faith is a spiritual muscle, and you must exercise it, sometimes every minute and every hour, to strengthen it. Even when you don't feel faith that you will succeed, affirm your good. Reclaim it. Reacting to feelings will lead you astray. Know that all of heaven and the universe is conspiring to manifest your dreams. Know that God is taking care of you.

Don't let confusion or temptations detour you. Now more than ever you must stay focused on your goals. If you matriculate through the wilderness time successfully, you will become stronger and more spiritually attuned. Read inspirational stories that describe other people's journeys through the wilderness. Take hope from the lessons they provide and know that there is an end. It will not go on forever.

Be encouraged! You're doing the right things. There is no easy way out, no shortcut. Instead of being detoured, use the time to deepen your focus. Reflect on your goals and chosen path. Pray for guidance. Learn to listen to the still, small voice within and then heed that voice.

Do not allow desperation to creep in and corrupt your purpose. Desperation will make you do stupid things. Don't go there. How many men and women have gotten into bad relationships because they got tired of waiting for the spouse God chose for them? How many of you accepted the first bad deal that came along because you got tired of waiting?

The wilderness experience exists for a purpose. You are being prepared for your success. You are being strengthened. You are being matured. This preparation will enable you to truly enjoy the fruits of your labor when they come. Honor the experience.

My greatest wilderness experience was during my four years between marriages. Over time I realized that many of my relationship problems were born out of fear—the fear of being hurt or rejected. A few years later, when I met Elaine, ours was exclusively a platonic relationship. She became my best friend. I was comfortable in sharing things with her that I could not share with others. I talked about my previous marriage, my feelings, and my hopes and dreams for the future without having to worry about making any commitment. She was such a good friend that I could even talk to her about some of the women that I was dating. She did more to bring me out of the wilderness by just listening than any counselor could have ever done. The best thing you can have when you are going through the wilderness is a good friend.

Be Persistent

If FloJo had stopped halfway through the race, she would have lost. The race is won by the person who endures to the end. I've noticed that during workshops, people will get very excited about making change in their lives and in their communities, but I often wonder what happens when the workshop is over. Does the momentum continue or, as so often happens, will one person end up doing all the work?

The only way to achieve success is to keep at it until you get it. Often, runners talk about getting a "second wind," but to get that extra burst of energy, you have to persist through the pain, fatigue, and disappointments.

People quit too soon. Breakthroughs occur just when things are getting really difficult, and it is worth waiting for this to happen.

Don't Talk—Act!

Don't you just love it when people have to come and tell you every little thing that they're doing to achieve success? To be honest, I don't have the time to hear it all, because I've got too much to do myself.

Better to keep your plans between you and God for as long as possible. God is the ultimate confidant. He will not react with jealousy, and He'll give you encouragement. He'll help you along the way.

Some people don't want you to succeed. They may try to discourage you from even trying. They may even actively work or pray against you. If you're working with a group, you have no choice but to talk about the project. Still, keep the details among a select few. Don't broadcast your activities until the time is right. There may very well come a time when you have to promote your ideas to others, but until then, keep quiet.

Expect the Unexpected

Here's another obstacle to include in your plan: the unexpected. Keep your focus and learn how to think quickly on your feet. There's no way to anticipate surprises. After my first electoral victory, the unexpected happened and the sweet smell of victory almost became the agony of defeat. I went to bed victorious and woke up with my victory in jeopardy.

We got busy, investigating what could have happened to change the entire outcome of the election overnight. We discovered that wild card called absentee ballots. It is the responsibility of each candidate to track absentee ballots, but being new to the game, I didn't know this. I'll elaborate more fully on what happened to me and how I dealt with it in action step 6.

In politics and in life, anything can and will happen. That's part of the game. Don't get mad, but trust in your own ability to resolve whatever comes your way. You can handle it.

Love Your Enemies and Watch Your Back

Jesus said to love your enemies, which was a revolutionary concept in a time when the conventional wisdom was "an eye for an eye, a tooth for a tooth." Many believed in the law of retribution, which allows for punishment and revenge. In Matthew 10:16, Jesus states, "I send you out as sheep in the midst of wolves, be ye therefore wise as serpents and harmless as doves."

My faith dictates that I love everyone, including my enemies, and to the best of my ability, I do. Like you, I am human and have experienced normal emotions of anger and rage when people have tried to block the work that I'm doing. Yet, in the end, I have hugged those who would be my enemies. This simple gesture makes it impossible for me to hate them. Granted, I cannot control the feelings and words of the other person, but it's hard for hatred to thrive in the middle of a good hug.

Now, I'm a practical man. Even though I try to love everyone, I know that I must choose my closest friends wisely. There's a fine line between paranoia and wisdom. If you're constantly looking over your shoulder for evil, eventually you will find it, but you won't get much joy out of life either. Just stick to the basics—choose your friends wisely, write memos documenting your actions and intentions, tell the truth at all times, and ask God for the ability to discern the truth from a lie. Most important, trust your instincts. If something feels wrong, check it out. Don't practice ostrich behavior—in other words, don't go into denial. It's better to put out a lit match than a brush fire.

Practice the Golden Rule

"Do unto others as you would have them do unto you" should be your guide as you're making your moves in the world. It's such a simple directive, but apparently it's a difficult one to follow. Folks want what they want and will sometimes do anything to get it.

If everyone, regardless of faith or belief, practiced this simple creed, the world would be a better place. Before you take your next step, ask yourself, "Will this hurt anyone? Would I want this done to me?" Within us is a built-in Golden Rule detector, and it is called the conscience. In the last section we discussed desires that are out of control; whatever your desires, you cannot let them override the Golden Rule.

You indeed reap what you sow, whether the seeds are negative or positive. It sounds simple, but it is true: if you do good to others, good will return to you, and the opposite is true too. Let the Golden Rule guide all your steps to success.

Motivate Yourself Daily

You're an adult now, and no parent is going to throw you into the river to teach you to swim. You're going to have to do that for yourself. Books have been written on motivation. Inspirational stories encourage us. But when the book is closed and the tape is turned off, no one but you can make you take that first step out into the unknown.

I'll share what gets me going. Every morning when I get up I pray, and then I work out. Many people depend on me, so I don't have the luxury of not being motivated. The fact that I take my role seriously keeps me motivated.

The main thing that keeps me going throughout the day is my inner conviction that I'm doing what I'm supposed to do. I'm helping others, and I love what I do. When you love your work, you'll never feel the need for an outside motivating source. Your love will motivate you. If you love your family and friends, you'll always be motivated to spend time with them. If you love your job, you won't spend your time watching the clock. If you love living, you believe that every day is the best day of your life.

If you are not motivated in some area of your life, perhaps it is time for a change—or at the very least, a vacation.

Take the Initiative

Look around you—at your job, in your home, in your community. There is so much work to be done. Bootstrappers know that needs are opportunities in disguise. I don't understand people who say they're bored. There's too much to do!

Taking the initiative to meet a need, right a wrong, or fix a problem is a great way to take a first step. There is nothing wrong with developing a controlled aggressiveness in pursuit of the things you want. I know a man who was never able to recover from having lost out when he did not take the initiative to tell a certain woman he was attracted to her. She married someone else and he is still having relationship problems. When you fail to take the initiative, you guarantee that someone else will fill the void, which could lead to much suffering and heartache.

Don't Rest on Your Laurels

You're only as good as your last success, and you'll be remembered for your last failure. That's the nature of the journey. It tickles me when, after some mishap or problem in school, a child will try to escape punishment by reaching way back to a time when he or she was successful. "I got an A two years ago, remember?" You build on your successes, and you are strengthened by each one of them, but you cannot depend on them to take you to where you ultimately want to go. The achievement of a goal is preceded by many successes and a few failures.

Political life taught me this truth: You can be a good public servant for most of your career, but make just one mistake and your entire history of good work is forgotten. You cannot rest on your laurels, because your constituency won't let you. Most important, as a self-respecting, decent person, *you* won't let you.

Always strive to do your best.

Don't Take Help for Granted

Into every bootstrapper's journey, a little help will fall. You can't make it in this life without support from other people every now and again. Be grateful. Help can lead to either dependency or self-sufficiency, so choose and accept your support wisely. And as you've been helped, you have a responsibility to help others along the way.

There are many people who think that they have gotten to their places of success all by themselves. We must continually remind ourselves that we are standing on someone's shoulders. Others have gone this way before us and have made life easier because of their sacrifices. We should honor those who help us. That is the reason I placed into the Congressional Record the names of Mrs. Gladys Grice and Mrs. Jewel Houston, teachers who helped to nurture and develop my latent gifts.

Stay on the Task

Keep your plan within reach. Check it from time to time. Continue to do your daily planning. At the end of every day, scratch off your accomplishments and check to see what's on the agenda for tomorrow. Make this a habit.

It is easy to get off focus, given the myriad choices and decisions that most of us must make each day. The many pulls and tugs on our time and energy require us to separate our major and minor tasks from one another. Since leaving Congress, I have had the greatest challenge of having to say no to a number of boards, engagements, and appointments. If I took all of them, it would be impossible to complete any of the things that are important to me. My reasons for leaving Congress, to spend more time with my church and family, would be totally obviated.

Develop Good Work Habits

Develop good work habits, and all your steps will be efficient. Punctuality and respect for the policies of the job will carry you a long way toward climbing the ladder to promotions. There are many people who do not realize that a job is more than a payday. There is an expectancy of a certain level of measurable performance and productivity. Disrespect for your job jeopardizes your career goals and aspirations. It pays to call if you're going to be late. Always look your best. Be a team player and an initiative taker. I personally love workers who take initiative rather than having to be told what to do all the time. It shows that they are interested in the success of the organization. It also provides an opportunity to examine the depth of their capability to assume responsibility without direct management or supervision.

Claim Your Successes, and Accept Responsibility for Your Failures

People love to receive accolades when they do well, but they seek to blame others when things go wrong. This attitude is prevalent in corporations and organizations in which a mistake can result in job loss.

To be truly a responsible person, however, you must accept responsibility for your successes and failures. The ability to say "I did it" is the sign of a strong, mature person who is destined for success.

An editor of a small publishing house was assigned the manuscript of a well-known author. This manuscript would be critiqued by top literary reviewers, so it was very important to do a good job.

This editor was chosen for this important assignment because of her excellent skills, but anyone can have a bad day. The manuscript was produced into a book with more than twenty errors in spelling and grammar.

Now, the editor could have blamed the system. The publishing company was a small one and could not afford to hire the necessary editorial staff. One editor was required to do the work of five people, from substantive editing to proofing for typographical errors. Mistakes were common in most of the company's books. Still, the editor accepted responsibility for the mistakes. She even offered her resignation over the incident. Because of the way she handled it, she kept her job, despite the extra time and money that were required to correct the problem.

Mistakes will happen. Face up to them and learn from them. Then keep stepping.

Learn from Others

In the not-so-distant past, young people learned valuable life lessons and skills through apprenticeships. They learned on the job from a master.

Today, we go to school, but you can learn only so much in school. The best place to learn is in the real world, and the best way to learn is directly from others.

Many studies have documented the positive effects of one-on-one mentoring for young people. Adults can also benefit from this powerful relationship. Seek out a mentor who has done what you are trying to do. Whether you are trying to become a good student, find a mate, or start a business, someone somewhere in your community has done it and has done it well. Seek that person out and develop a relationship with him or her. Watch that person in action. Find out how they achieved success.

If you can't find a mentor, read about people who have achieved success. Don't read just to be inspired, but learn the steps that they took. Use what you can, and throw the rest away.

Anchor Yourself in Sanity

I guarantee that when you begin to move, everything around you will get stirred up. Are you going to let yourself get swept away by the storm? You've got to develop a strong constitution for success, because there will be some challenging times. I keep my sanity by fasting and praying. The love of family and friends keeps me anchored. And of course, my belief and faith in God give me the inner peace I need to weather any storm.

Develop your anchors early on in your success journey. Develop a reliable network of friendships. Pray daily and learn to listen to God.

Do It Well

Mediocrity is out; excellence is in. My generation was taught that we had to be twice as good as everyone else to succeed in life. There's been a backlash against excellence recently, but if you are to stand out from the rest, you will have to strive to be the best in everything you do. If you know that you need further training in some areas, get it. If you know that you've been lazy on the job, change your ways.

The difference between mediocrity and excellence is in your approach and your intention. If my children come home with a B in their worst subject, I'll reward their efforts because I know that they've done the best that they could do. But if they show me a B in their best subject, we're going to have a long talk, because I know they can do better.

You can always do better. As you take your first steps to success, remember that how you start out determines how you will end up. If you start out sloppily, your end result will be sloppy. But if you embark on your quest with excellence in mind, you will be assured of an outstanding result.

Stagger Your Deadlines

They say that if you want to get something done, give it to a busy person. Bootstrappers often make the big mistake of taking on too much and not pacing themselves. When all the deadlines come at once, you'll feel panic. If you can, stagger your deadlines ahead of time. This is good planning. What's the point of taking on five projects that are all due at once and not being able to do any of them well?

Because I want you to succeed, I'm going to pass on the one secret that will save you time, trouble, and crisis management in the future: There will be many times when you must *just say no*.

It's Time to Execute Your Plans

The best plans in the world are of no value if you do not know how to execute them. The way you do this may differ depending upon your individual flair and taste. However, these are only external manifestations. You'll need to use all of your talents, skills, and abilities to effect change for yourself and others. There are many people who have great ideas but suffer because they do not follow through with their dreams. A lesson that I learned as a marketing analyst with Xerox is that some people are more effective at executing a plan than others. We had guys who could develop a marketing strategy but could not close the deal. Fortunately, the company also employed people who had demonstrated the ability to do effective closings and were called in to wrap up the deal. As a marketing representative, college dean, congressman, and pastor, my résumé reflects an ability not merely to make promises but to successfully execute my plans.

The next three action steps are designed to assist you in learning to execute your plan successfully.

ACTION STEP 4: WORK TOGETHER, BUILD TOGETHER

There is power in numbers.

Many authors and experts have written extensively about human relationships, but I can save you the time and trouble of reading through all those books and papers. I have discovered the source of many of our troubles, and in short, it is our inability to accept and respect one another's differences.

I have witnessed firsthand what happens when people disrespect one another based exclusively on ideological differences. When I entered the House of Representatives in 1986, there was a lot of comity among members of the two political parties. The president was the venerable Ronald Reagan, a Republican, and both the House and the Senate were controlled by Democratic majorities. Although the legislative and executive branches were controlled by different parties, they generally found ways to agree on matters important to the American people. It was possible to shape bipartisan consensus because Democrats and Republicans socialized in the gym, in restaurants, or on the golf course. There was a level of maturity among the members and a belief that the House could accomplish its goals in spite of political differences. Personal attacks were at a minimum; therefore, disagreements were manageable because they occurred almost exclusively in the political realm.

This type of practice continued for the most part during the Bush administration. Since he had once served as a member of Congress, he understood the nuances of how the legislative process worked. The

House did begin to change as the levels of comity and respect for one another disintegrated; however, both sides were able to drop their party labels during the Desert Storm debates. The unity of the Congress and the president gave confidence to generals Norman Schwarzkopf and Colin Powell, who led the American forces. It is amazing how effective people can be when they work together in unity toward a common goal.

In 1992, William Jefferson Clinton was elected as a new-age Democrat. He has extraordinary political skills that are so exceptional that he has been able to extrapolate ideas from both parties and make them his own. This approach has generated high levels of support from the American people. On the other hand, it has created difficulty within the parties, who prefer to be identified by the differences that distinguish them. The Democrats are not always certain that the president is one of them, while Republicans have felt that they have lost ground, and they are constantly looking for ways to regain or retain high ground within the political spectrum. The parties clashed in 1995 after the elections of 1994, when Republicans won control of the House and Senate with an agenda called the "Contract with America." The comity that had already started eroding dissipated rather quickly. People who had been friends for years suddenly were not speaking to each other. Decisions were made almost exclusively along party lines, which led to the disastrous shutting down of the government in December 1995. The words of Abraham Lincoln ring true: "A nation divided against itself cannot stand."

I managed to succeed in spite of the party differences by working with members of the Republican Party. Because of our mutual respect, I was able to win for my district two regional federal facilities that are now under construction. These facilities for the Federal Drug Administration (FDA) and Federal Aviation Administration (FAA) will generate fourteen hundred jobs for the people in the area. Working with the president, I was also able to establish the first One Stop Capital Shop in the nation. This Small Business Administration (SBA) program provides technical support and financial access to start-up businesses. The One Stop Capital Shop concept differs from many other government programs by focusing on investment rather than subsidies. It provides total support for an individual in turning a dream into a business plan. Once the plan has been developed, the One Stop Capital Shop assists the individual in processing incorporation status and securing financing.

A successful bootstrapper must be able to navigate the political and economic minefields, looking beyond differences in search of common ground. The strength and effectiveness of a family, community, or nation is often determined by the ability of its members to respect one another's differing viewpoints.

We may share culture, religion, nationality, gender, and race—but we are all different in spirit. Each one of us has a spirit that is unique and as special as a snowflake. That's why two children who grow up in the same environment may turn out differently. They are of the same family, but they manifest different personalities. We humans may share the externals, but each of us has our own individual thoughts, feelings, dreams, and hopes for the future. We can talk about them, but we can't live one another's lives. As close as Elaine and I are, there are some things we'll never know about each other. This is because we are constantly growing and evolving both individually and collectively. But many couples find it difficult to manage their relationship because of a lack of respect for their differences.

Without order in our lives, there would be a complete breakdown in society. We would allow our differences to govern us, and the world would have probably been blown up by now. Every day in the news we read about nations that, for any number of reasons, cannot or will not resolve their differences. Religion, race, and ethnicity are the usual scapegoats, but if those issues didn't exist, people would find something else to fight about.

In this section we're going to talk about developing relationship skills. The way of bootstrapping is to use what you have to get what you want, and good relationships are all-important to the process. Sometimes all you have are your relationships, and if they are built on mutual respect, that's enough. Opportunity often comes through other people, even those with whom we disagree. I have seen it happen so often in politics. If it can happen within such a charged atmosphere, in which people choose to be different, it can happen anywhere. The old saying is "Politics makes strange bedfellows." Working together and building together is about allying with people of like minds and also people who are different to build for the future.

Family Bootstrapping

Families usually provide us with our first set of relationships. There is so much fragmentation and brokenness in America because of the breakdown in the family structure. Families are the backbone of the community and the nation, which is why it is so important to heal families today.

There are too many contradictions: too many babies born out of wedlock to children who are not mature enough to be good parents; too many teenagers having abortions and thus losing a sense of the value of life; too many children being killed because of the proliferation of guns in homes and on the streets; too many divorces leaving families destitute; too many moral conflicts causing confusion about values.

Back in the old days, the coming together of a man and a woman was not always about romance but about building a family legacy that would last for generations. It was a planned arrangement that started while the couple were still children. People were pragmatic about love. All the members of the family would be involved in the decision, because when two people marry, it also represents a marriage of families. Today, too many marriages happen for the convenience of the moment. Although it is more common for people now to plan parenthood than it was in the past, there are still too many marriages where no planning has taken place. Interestingly, we do strategic planning for companies and other ventures in life, but when it comes to some of the most important relationships in our lives, we improvise as we go along. "Till death do us part" is a very long time, so planning is more essential to and within marriage than any other aspect of your life if you sincerely intend to honor and keep your vows.

We should be much more systematic in how we approach family relationships, or divorce, blended families, and single-family homes will continue to prevail. No matter how we try to rationalize our decisions to divorce, live common-law, or have out-of-wedlock children, the truth is we have abdicated our thrones of personal responsibility.

I'm not talking about extraordinary situations, such as rape, incest, or abuse. I'm talking about letting boredom, casual sex, and other relationship issues interfere with commitment, when these issues could be resolved. You already know that Elaine is my second wife. What makes this marriage work is that she is also my best friend. We communicate without setting preconditions that can get in the way of honest discourse. Commitments to the family must be taken more seriously if we are to become the great nation that our foreparents envisioned.

Couples in my parents' day rarely divorced, no matter what the problems were. Only death did indeed part them. There were problems with many of those unions, I grant you that, but they persevered in spite of them. Today, we have more information and support than was available to them. Why, then, are there so many divorces and separations? What we lack is the will and the commitment to make our marriages work. The same intensity of thought and devotion that goes into a relationship prior to marriage must begin in earnest after the honeymoon. This is the beginning of a process that requires love, nurturance, care, intimacy, and respect to survive.

Recently, *Sports Illustrated* published a controversial article about certain well-paid athletes whose sexual affairs have led to a number of children born out of wedlock. To make matters worse, many of these guys have not assumed responsibility for their children, financially, emotionally, or otherwise. Paternity tests, court battles, and national media attention have made an already difficult situation worse—for the parents and especially for the children. Even with rich fathers, many of them will wind up falling through the social safety net. These athletes should follow the lead of Karl Malone, the all-star forward of the Utah Jazz. The article motivated him to reconnect with his two children in Louisiana and adopt them. That's the way of a bootstrapper.

Getting your family relationships in order should be high on your list of priorities. Not only does it make good emotional and moral sense to get our households in order; it also makes good financial sense. Strong, intact families are generally more prosperous than broken ones. According to Thomas Stanley and William Danko, authors of *The Millionaire Next Door: The Surprising Secrets of America's Wealthy*, the typical millionaire marries once and remains married: "Nearly 95 percent of millionaire households are composed of married couples." Which leads me to believe that the opposite is also true, that poor households are most often single-headed or blended.

Not only do divorce and breakups cause pain and suffering for everyone involved, but broken families lose in time, energy, resources, and money. All of the sacrifices that the family has made and goals that they have worked for can be lost in an instant. Poverty is a reality for many individuals because they have not gotten their family relationships in order. When animosity occurs between husband and wife and they break up, money is drained from the family coffers. Money starts leaking everywhere—the father, often with limited income, has to pay child support and/or alimony. The mother, whose income helped to support, or carried, the household is now barely making it on her salary. A centralized pool of money provides great leverage to build wealth. Financial fragmentation may not provide enough to pay the bills, let alone provide extra income for investments.

With the divorce rate as high as 50 percent, and higher in some communities, with the single-parent rate even higher, it is our responsibility to reclaim the sanctity of marriage and the family. We have a duty to ourselves and especially to our children to get our emotions and desires under control. The cost of being guided by or acting on our carnal instincts and urges is too high.

Bootstrapping can be used to build a strong, healthy, loving, and financially viable family. Have each member follow the basic formula: search your soul and pray together, set individual and family goals, develop a plan together, and then, as a family, execute it. Each member will have his or her own duties and responsibilities to ensure that the plan leads to success. Weekly family meetings can be convened to make sure everyone is on task. We have always eaten dinner together on Sundays for this purpose.

Let me share with you a family plan that has been successful for me and Elaine. As you take note of some of the adjustments that we have had to make, be mindful that your plan must be flexible enough to accommodate unexpected situations. The following is a brief outline of how our family plans progressed.

We agreed that our money would be kept in a central account so that we could pay bills in a timely manner. Since Elaine is more detail-oriented and had not brought as many debts into the relationship as I, we determined that she should manage the account. I know that there are many men who have problems with having the woman manage the money; however, the real issue ought to be who can best do the job.

We assumed in December 1975, when we married, that we would live in the home provided me by the university in Brookline, Massachusetts. We decided to rent out the home on the Cape.

We agreed that we would wait three years to have children. However, in April 1976, we received the good news that Elaine was pregnant. This was not a time to get upset or to blame—rather we rejoiced and made the necessary preparations for the birth of our first child. Elaine discovered that she had a fibroid cyst in her uterus, which meant that we needed a doctor in whom we had great confidence. We chose a great doctor in Boston and expected him to be with us throughout the process.

In August 1976, I received the invitation to pastor Allen Church in Jamaica, New York. This was an unexpected occurrence, but we made the decision to accept the invitation and move to New York.

Once we left Boston, the renters stopped sending payments, yet we were saddled with a mortgage and expecting a child. Fortunately, Dr. John Silber, who was president of Boston University at the time, provided us with a decent severance package, so we managed to keep our heads above water.

In November 1976, our first child, a beautiful, healthy daughter, was born. We named her Aliya (blessing) Mariama (gift of God).

In New York, we were living in the church parsonage rent-free, which meant that we were building no equity. We had to sell the house on the Cape because the tenants were not paying their rent on a regular basis. We realized that although I was in my thirties and healthy, if something happened to me the family would have no place to live. Elaine's mom and dad were nearing retirement, but they were considering purchasing a new home in Memphis, where they lived. Since Elaine is an only child, she felt that if something were to happen to me she would want to return to

Memphis. So we decided that rather than having her parents assume a mortgage at that stage in their life, we would begin saving and buy them a home in Memphis. We saved Christmas gifts, vacation money, and love offerings (honorariums) and purchased a home for them in 1992. This deal has worked extremely well for all of us. Mom and Dad are the greatest; they treat me as if I were the son they never had.

In addition to Aliya (blessing) we had three additional children: Nailah (one who succeeds), Rasheed (righteous), and Hasan (handsome). So, when I was elected to Congress, it was necessary to develop a plan that would allow me to spend quality time with them. As I indicated earlier, we worked it out with an agreement that I would commute to Washington. We applied for social security cards for the children and started educational savings accounts for them soon after they were born.

After living in the parsonage for seventeen years, we decided that we needed to purchase a permanent home in New York. The congregation sold us the parsonage.

After Aliya had spent two years in Atlanta at Spelman College, Nailah decided to join her. We realized that it would be more economical to purchase a home in Atlanta than to pay room and board on campus. Now, the girls live in the house, and Rasheed, who is a freshman at Morehouse College in Atlanta, will join them in the house next year. This has proven to be a good plan now that three children are living in the same city.

You, too, can claim financial prosperity—and a wealth of spirit—for your family. That is the way of a bootstrapper.

Networking

Networking is an art, and bootstrappers happen to be masters at it. For bootstrappers, there are at least three primary reasons to network: to further one's own goals, to invest in the success of others, and to contribute to the building of the community and a greater society. Networking takes place in business, politics, education, and almost every other area of life. Many conferences and social gatherings provide great opportunities for networking. Golf outings and other sporting events are also good times to network.

The power of networking was demonstrated by groups who immigrated to America at the turn of the century. As soon as they were established, they sent for other relatives to come to the land of liberty. African Americans followed this pattern by migrating from the South to the Midwest or North, where jobs were more plentiful. This was especially true during the thirties and forties, when jobs were prevalent in the steel mills and auto factories. Today the trend continues with the immigrants who come to America in hope of making their dreams of prosperity a reality.

People network for a variety of reasons. Professional organizations provide opportunities for members to discuss industry trends and jobs. Some meetings may turn into social events, but as long as you are focused on your purpose for participating in the event, you can still get business done. You can still make strong contacts, regardless of what the occasion is.

The Internet

The Internet is causing a revolution in how we conduct our personal and professional relationships. Communities have sprung up on the Internet.

John and Mearys Greene use the networking capability of the Internet in several ways. John is a computer consultant who works from home. During the day, he interacts with numerous companies who utilize his services to assist them in solving their computer problems. In the evenings, he and Mearys use the Internet to build their Amway business. They are able to gain access to more than twelve hundred suppliers who are in a joint venture with Amway. They network with other distribution organizations and are positioned to supply thousands of products from various entities at the touch of a button.

They also network in the people arena through the Britt-Worldwide Association, which provides them with training materials, seminars, and tapes and also organizes conventions. The entire Amway construct is built on networking. People invite others to join the organization if they are interested in earning extra income. The meetings become instant groups out of which organizations are built. Those who do not join the group become a part of the client base.

Now, Amway is building a virtual mall on the Internet where people will be able to access joint venture groups and order products from the company. John feels that through networking they are better able to meet the financial needs of the family while also meeting lots of new friends. Necessity is the mother of invention, and often, networking inspires ways to resolve a variety of problems.

Social Groups

Sororities, fraternities, and social clubs provide an excellent way to meet and network with other like-minded people. Their party reputation is only part of the truth; many do good works for their communities, such as offering after-school counseling, mentoring programs, breast-cancer awareness classes, community clean-up days, health fairs, tutoring programs, and rites of passage classes. Some of them have built housing for the elderly and day care centers for children.

Faith Communities

The best way to network is to join a faith community. Christians call it fellowshiping, but whatever you call it, there is no more powerful relationship than one that has as its purpose and focus the worship of God and service to humanity.

Allen A.M.E. Church offers an array of ministries that provide great opportunities for networking. Look at the following list and you will see how a faith-based institution interacts with its parishioners and networks for community needs.

Discipleship Ministry
Street Ministry

Single Parents Ministry
Communications Ministry (audio/video)
Marriage Enrichment Ministry
Security Ministry
Educator's Ministry
Cancer Support Ministry
Music Ministry
Dance Ministry
Missionary Outreach Ministry
AIDS/HIV Ministry
Seniors Ministry
Substance Abuse Ministry
Counseling Ministry
Investment Ministry
Parish Health Ministry
Shepherd's Ministry
Men's Ministry
Intercessory Prayer Ministry
Women's Ministry
Drama Ministry
Elder-Care Support Ministry
Youth Ministry
Singles Ministry
Young Adult Ministry
Prison Ministry
Hands in Praise Sign Language Ministry
Unemployment Ministry
Bereavement Ministry
Ministry to the Homeless
Feeding of the 5,000 Ministry

The Allen ministries have been very effective as networking vehicles. The interaction of church staff, high school students, senior citizens, retired workers, and others created vast opportunities for networking. This experience was especially good for the high school volunteers, who developed relationships that can be helpful to them when they apply for college or for jobs.

Those who serve the homeless on site in the church are able to assess the needs of many of them and make agency referrals.

The "God's Love We Deliver" group, which delivers meals to home-bound HIV/AIDS patients, is able to assist in networking on behalf of many of the people they serve, to get better responses from social service agencies and providers.

Here are some other networking examples:

- The Feeding of the 5,000 Ministry involved over three hundred volunteers this past Thanksgiving, preparing meals for 7,600 people.
- The Ministry to the Homeless serves free meals each week.
- The Unemployment Ministry has a weekly networking session and has been successful in making many job placements since employers have become aware that the ministry exists.

Networking Tools

Effective networking requires having the proper tools. Sign up with an online service company, such as America Online or CompuServe, or an Internet service provider, such as MindSpring or EarthLink. That will provide easy access to the Internet and allow you to send and receive e-mail. Print up calling or business cards so that when you meet interesting and influential people, you can present a professional image.

Another important element of networking is learning how to make a good first impression. When I was a dean at Lincoln University in Pennsylvania, I would have many of my male students come see me before going for job interviews. Some of them would be going to interviews with Fortune 500 companies wearing jeans, combat boots, T-shirts, and caps. I would send them back to the dorm, insisting that they wear suits and ties. Oftentimes they would argue that it didn't matter what they wore. Since I had been with Xerox, I knew that was not true. I perceived my role to be one of educating them to dress for success.

You will need to work at feeling comfortable in social situations to be an effective networker. Try to remember and then use people's names. Learn to greet everyone that you encounter by name, from the security guard to the chairman of the board. I assure you, from my own personal experience, it works.

Networking, or "pressing the flesh," is the main tool in a politician's campaign. The best politicians and clergypersons truly love to interact, and people can sense that. I always enjoyed getting out to meet and greet the residents of my community. When I enter the church, I embrace everyone that I encounter.

When I agreed to run for Congress back in 1986, my organization had only about seventy thousand dollars to spend in comparison to the two hundred and fifty thousand dollars of one of my main competitors. Mostly, I used that money to design and print flyers. I bought no advertising spots on television. My strategy was simple: shake as many hands as possible. I stood on street corners, walked door-to-door, went to the senior citizens' centers, talked to parents and students. Fortunately, I had a ready-made campaign army of church volunteers who were willing to help me succeed, and we did so on a shoestring budget. What we didn't have in money was more than made up for by the proactive spirit of the people. We were all political bootstrappers focused on one agenda: getting our message across to the public, networking on a grassroots level.

Teamwork

Whether it is Amway, Mary Kay, a faith community, or children working to buy a church bus, it is team spirit that really counts. When everyone fulfills his or her responsibility, an organization is strengthened, productivity increases, and the results are astounding. An effective teamwork concept is one in which all the people work together rather than placing the lion's share of responsibility on any one individual.

People like to single out individual stars on athletic teams, but in reality none of them can succeed by themselves. Some sports, like boxing, golf, and tennis, are individual sports. But in the majority of sports, a team effort is required for victory.

In my work at Allen Church and in Congress, I have seen phenomenal examples of effective teamwork put to the test time and again. Prior to running my first political campaign, I had been a very hands-on type of manager. When I won the election, my schedule became extremely hectic. Every day I'd make the commute to Washington and come back late in the evening. I simply did not have the time to pay attention to the day-to-day church details anymore. Fortunately, I had an excellent management team in place, and the church and community development projects continued to run like clockwork.

What was the secret to my success with team building? We all agreed on the vision. We were, and still are, excited about the work we're doing. Because I had to leave so many projects in the hands of my staff, they became better managers themselves. Officers of the corporation assumed greater leadership roles when they realized that I would not always be available to them. I put my trust in them, and they have consistently risen to the occasion. This is the essence of team spirit.

If you are fired up about your vision, you will excite others also. The true test of a visionary is whether he or she can get others to participate on a project even if it is on a volunteer basis! Tight budgets are a reality, especially in the early stages of a project, and I have heard of projects failing because of lack of money more than for any other reason. Inherent in many of those failures is the rampant desire for immediate gratification. People couldn't get paid, or they couldn't get the glory, so they quit. My mother would have said that they were just lazy or had "big heads" (egos). Whatever the case, don't start a project unless you and the team know what the objectives are and intend to finish it. If you are the only one left standing on the team, go back out and recruit new members.

Recruiting team members should be done in a thoughtful, systematic fashion. Sometimes we get so desperate to solicit help that we wind up recruiting anybody, and we end up being disappointed and doing more work in the end. You want people who have:

- A reputation for getting things done.
- An extensive network of friends and associates.
- Respect among their peers.
- A common vision.
- The ability to work well with others.
- Lots of confidence, but limited ego.
- Clout and influence.
- A strong desire to help.
- Integrity.
- A bootstrapping approach to life.

The goal in team building is to get people emotionally invested in the project and in the process of executing the plan. People are busy, so make sure that your meetings are run efficiently. Start on time. Preplan an agenda and stick to it.

During planning sessions, many debates will come up. Congress uses parliamentary procedures to manage a process that can get downright crazy. All it takes is one member to start filibustering to rob people of their enthusiasm for and commitment to a project. Establish in writing how the meetings are going to be conducted. Take a few minutes and make sure everyone gets a copy.

If you're leading the committee effort, then you will probably have to be the taskmaster. Establish time frames and who's accountable for meeting them. Take minutes so everything is in writing. Compile a list of everyone's name, address, and home and work telephone numbers; make sure every person on the team gets a copy. If emergencies arise and it's difficult to get people together, use the telephone to conference.

Many experts believe that it's important to have a diversity of representation on a team. In the beginning this is absolutely essential to ensure that all voices are heard. But when it gets down to planning and execution, a wide diversity of opinions is going to slow down the process. Bootstrapping teams don't want to stay stuck in planning. Your goal should be to get the project done as quickly as possible. Keep the planning and execution team a lean, mean bootstrapping machine.

Conflict

When two or more people get together, inevitably, conflict will arise. Some folks thrive on conflict, and others, like me, avoid it like the plague. Whenever conflict arises, remember the words of the Master: "Blessed are the peacemakers." I know how difficult it is to assume the role of peacemaker. But an objective peacemaker is essential in resolving conflict.

Relationships provide mirrors to our own strengths and weaknesses. We tend to attract people into our lives who mirror the parts of us that need fixing. These are the people who really know how to push our buttons. Conflicts have a way of generating a life all their own. If not quickly resolved, they will escalate.

Let's say that you just received a ten-thousand-dollar bonus from your job. You and your spouse are excited about the money, but you disagree on what to do with it. You want to go to China, but your spouse wants to invest it in a money market fund. The following is how the disagreement, if not resolved quickly and to the mutual benefit of both, could escalate along the conflict continuum:

1. Difference: You are not your spouse, and your spouse is not you. Yes, I'm stating the obvious, but how often have you made comments like "He just should have known how I felt" or "If she loved me she would do thus and so"? Because we are all different, we perceive the world—and a ten-thousand-dollar bonus—in different ways.

2. Disagreement: You both perceive the ten-thousand-dollar bonus as an opportunity—but an opportunity to do what? You want to explore an exotic new culture. Your spouse wants to begin planning for retirement. Your desires are both valid, and you both feel strongly about your points of view. You're still in the discussion phase, and you both secretly feel that you'll change the other's mind.

3. Problem: You're both still speaking to each other, but the tension level is starting to rise. You have not changed each other's opinion about what to do with the money. You're starting to feel that if you

don't get what you want, there will be some negative consequences.

4. Conflict: You're both beginning to feel that there can be no fair resolution to this problem. Now you're starting to get mad, and the kids are wondering what's going on.

5. Violence: Violence does not have to be physical to do real damage, although it sometimes gets that bad. In this case, you try to damage your spouse's self-esteem. You remind your spouse about that risky investment in which you lost all of your savings. You know it's not right, but you remind your spouse that it's your money and that technically you should make the decision about how it's spent. Your spouse fires back with a threat to take a sizable sum of money from the joint account and start an independent one. There's so much shouting going on that the kids are covering their ears.

6. War: The kids are crying. They're scared that they're going to end up like their friends who have to go visit their fathers every other weekend. You threaten to call a lawyer, and your spouse says to go ahead. All of this over a ten-thousand-dollar bonus. It ain't worth it!

At almost any point along the continuum, conflict can be resolved. But once it gets to war, you'll probably have to hire a lawyer, counselor, or some other type of mediator, which will cause a deep drain on your energy and resources.

You have a responsibility to get your own emotions in check. You cannot control another person, but you can control yourself. The tribal wars in Eastern Europe and Africa are caused by men who refuse to get a grip on their greed, lust for power, and unruly emotions.

Conflict resolution is all about negotiation and effective communication. Use "I" language instead of "you" language. Really listen. When the arguments get hot, it is hard to hear the other person because of your own shouting and strong emotions. But you are not at the mercy of your emotions or the other person's contrary point of view. You are a thinking person, and it is your responsibility to use your mind to recall the high spiritual values that you profess to believe in.

Learn how to argue well. The point of a debate should not be to tear the other person down and get into all kinds of personality attacks, but to get to the truth. By getting to the truth, you have a chance at a peaceful win-win resolution. Learn how to pick your battles. If the issue in question really isn't all that important to you, state your position clearly, and then let it go. Save your excellent argumentative skills for something that's really important. Use your mind, not your emotions, to deal with conflict. Aim to get to the truth; forget about having to be right.

Pull Yourself Up by Your Bootstraps . . .

Building stronger, more fulfilling, productive relationships does not require any outlay of cash—just your time, energy, and willingness to work to enhance them. Today I want you to work on resolving any conflicts that may be brewing in your family. If you are in the middle of the conflict, practice active listening. Really listen to what's being said, and then repeat it back to ensure that you've heard it right. Many times, conflicts arise because people are not listening. They unconsciously omit tiny parts when they do, or read into the conversation things that were not said.

Relinquish your need to be right, and resolve to get to the truth of the matter. When a family conflict is resolved there are no winners or losers, so stop thinking in those terms. Peace is always preferable to war, but if you cannot figure out how to negotiate a peaceful settlement, see if you can at least agree to a cease-fire. Separate for a while, and promise to get back together when tempers have cooled.

Networking Activity

Resolve to attend an upcoming event that will put you in touch with the kinds of people you want to meet. When you go, try your best to overcome any residual shyness. Introduce yourself to as many people as possible. Exchange business or calling cards. Make sure that you've got, at the very least, their name, telephone number, and address. Record physical details that will help you to remember them. Write down one sentence that summarizes their interests.

As soon as you get home (no procrastination!), file your cards away in your Rolodex or your system of choice. Include them on your Christmas card mailing list. If you clicked with one or two of them, call and ask them out for a non-threatening date (coffee, tea, whatever).

Many of your opportunities will come through other people. A strong network will create your opportunities for you. Capitalizing on opportunities is of such critical importance to the bootstrapper that it warrants a deeper look. In the next section, we'll further explore and attempt to dispel the myth that opportunism is a bad thing. Regrets occur when you do not take advantage of the opportunities that are presented to you. Don't procrastinate, or some day in the distant future you'll be crying, "I could have been a contender." Keep reading, put the ideas into practice, and you'll be singing, "I am a contender!"

ACTION STEP 5:
SEIZE OPPORTUNITIES

Positive opportunism is a win-win situation for everyone.

America is the land of opportunity. I say that knowing full well that our country has a checkered reputation when it comes to granting equal access to opportunities. I know that racism, sexism, and all kinds of injustice and intolerance exist. As a pastor and former congressman, I have had to deal with bigotry in the media, the financial sector, and Congress. I have even stood in front of the Capitol and watched taxis pass me by and pick up white customers on the next block. It's one of those bumps on the road, but I refuse to internalize such stupidity.

I remember reading sometime ago an interview with actor Denzel Washington. He had just finished filming Spike Lee's movie *Malcolm X* and was being asked about racism and discrimination in Hollywood. I truly appreciated his answer. In essence he said, "Sure, there is racism, but so what? I'm not going to let that stop me from working." Sure enough, Denzel is one of the busiest and best-paid actors of any race in Hollywood.

My bootstrapper attitude is similar to that of Denzel's. When not given a chance, I've created one for myself. Wherever doors have been locked, I have not become despondent but merely knocked on other doors. I tell young people in my speeches that whenever a door opens ever so slightly, they should go in and prove that their talents and gifts are equal to anyone else's. My challenge to them is to never allow themselves to be held back because they are Black, a man, a woman, Christian, Muslim, or Jewish. Nor should they be limited by their accent, where they were born, or whatever the cup of bigotry is. You must find a way around, under, over, or through it, so that you never become bound or limited by other people's ignorance. We should refuse to stay in boxes that racism and bigotry have built for us, and we should refuse to embrace the attitude of victimization. Someone with the victim mind-set stays stuck thinking, "There's racism, classism, sexism, ageism, ethnicism, schoolism. How am I going to fight that? I'm only one person."

Perception is reality, and if you don't think that you stand a chance against society's challenges, then you won't. Oppression may be evil, but that fact alone will not stop it. The immovable object of evil will be destroyed only when it comes against an unstoppable force—and that's you. In the sixties, the answer was to protest. In the nineties, the answer is better planning, quality education, political participation, and economic and community development. That takes more work than a protest, but the benefits are greater in the long run.

An Unstoppable Force

What happens when an unstoppable force meets an immovable object? When *you* are that unstoppable force and one of the "isms" is the immovable object, then a collision will occur. It will take courage, persistence, and determination to overcome it. Out of that collision, opportunity is born.

Martin Luther King, Jr., and the civil rights movement were an unstoppable force; racism and discrimination were the immovable objects. Activists of all races, ages, genders, religions, and political ideologies moved nonviolently against a power that had been entrenched in the institutions and social norms of America for centuries. Those courageous men and women were beaten and spat upon, and some were even killed. It was a bloody revolution, but it was absolutely essential for the progress of all people.

Out of that collision, opportunity was born. Civil rights legislation was passed, social norms gradually began to change, and slowly but surely, opportunities, at least on paper, were made equally available to all.

Some of the civil rights legislation from the sixties is on the respirator today. Be aware of it, become politically active, but don't let injustice stop you from pursuing your goals. Ultimately, the success of the civil rights movement will be measured not by a legislative yardstick but by the success of those who benefit from it. Their success validates its reason for being.

Bootstrappers must know who they are if they intend to succeed. They must also have a sense of their own self-worth in order to freely give of themselves to others.

Discrimination is nothing new. Descendants of African slaves and Native Americans still encounter it. Descendants of European, Asian, and Hispanic indentured servants have had their share. Women confront it, and so do the physically challenged. We must fight against oppression, but in the meantime, we cannot let it stop us.

The banking and real estate industries are notorious for their unfair lending and selling practices. During my tenure in Congress, I worked with these industries and authored the Bank Enterprise Act (BEA), which, in its own right and along with the Community Development Financial Institutions (CDFI), has become a major vehicle for community and economic development. Rather than the traditional "whippings" that the banks received from the Community Reinvestment Act (CRA) advocates, my method was viewed as a "carrot," and it is working. The BEA and CDFI allow banks to receive credit for CRA investments while getting a reduction on their insurance premiums. The CDFI/BEA funds are allocated through the Department of the Treasury to individual banks through a competitive bidding process. The banks, in turn, award the money to community development groups for housing, commercial development, and other ventures that benefit areas that have been historically undercapitalized.

Buying a house for the first time can be an overwhelming process, especially if you're self-employed and a member of a so-called minority. These were the obstacles Maria Sanchez faced, although she didn't know it in the beginning. All she knew was that she wanted to move. The neighborhood she lived in was unsafe, and the school her children were attending did not meet her high standards. Researching various suburbs outside the city, she finally settled on a small, middle-income community whose school system was reputed to be among the best in the country. On the weekends and sometimes after work, she and her two children would drive around the community, looking for a reasonably priced home to buy that was in good condition. Most of the homes that she looked into were beyond her price range, but she kept looking.

Then one Saturday, she drove down a quiet street that ended in a cul-de-sac. At the end of the street was a small yellow house with brown trim, and it had a FOR SALE sign on the front lawn. The owners had landscaped the yard with roses and evergreens. There was a big weeping willow tree in the backyard. Her heart leapt, and the kids sensed her interest. "How about this one, Mommy?" they asked. She didn't have an answer for them yet, but she had a strong feeling. Excited, Sanchez wrote down the telephone number of the realtor, called her up, and scheduled an appointment to view the house.

She and her children inspected the house from top to bottom. It was everything she had wanted in a house and more. There was even a fireplace in the living room. Sanchez asked the realtor the price, and although it was slightly above what she was willing to pay, she had a strong intuition that she could negotiate the price down.

Then the hard work began. She contacted a loan officer and went through the extensive paperwork. The bank turned her down. Shaken but not stopped, she contacted another agent, and again she was turned down. Her credit was excellent, and she had the down payment. What was the problem? In the meantime, as an incentive to hurry the process, the seller came down on the price. She knew she could meet the monthly mortgage, and her credit history proved it. She still could not understand what the problem was. The last loan officer took pity on her and told her confidentially that technically there was no reason to turn down the loan, but the reality was that Sanchez was Latino, a single parent, and self-employed. That she had been supporting herself and her children well as a systems consultant for three years didn't seem to matter.

Her first reaction was anger, but her desire to move and provide a better life for herself and her children overrode her anger. She decided to be more selective about her choice of a mortgage company. She interviewed a young man who said he believed he could get her approved for the loan. He told her about his track record, which included some cases that were much more difficult than hers. She chose him, and they went to work.

For six months they maneuvered through a bewildering maze of red tape. Again she was turned down, but the young loan officer resubmitted her paperwork. His persistence paid off when she finally received the call stating that her FHA (Federal Housing Administration) loan had been approved. Fortunately for her, the house had not sold. She closed and had a big housewarming party, and today, she's enjoying decorating her house.

Maria Sanchez was an unstoppable force that came against the immovable object of red tape, bigotry, and antiquated policies. But she did not let any of that stop her. She created her own opportunity, and today, she's living in the home of her dreams.

Opportunity Defined

According to the Webster's Comprehensive Dictionary, opportunity is "a favorable position or chance." When the situations or positions that you need are not available, you must create them. Even though real estate policies hadn't caught up with the realities of the market, Maria didn't let that stop her. She found a loan officer who was committed to making the loan happen and who therefore stuck with it. He argued her case with such persuasion that he created a condition that was favorable to her. The Allen Church experienced the same type of condition when it applied for a fifteen-million-dollar loan to build a cathedral. Chase, which was the lead bank, was determined that the loan would be made. They persuaded the other bankers in the consortium that this was a good loan. The process took over three years, but in the end the project was financed. Chase had now developed a faith-based community initiative that makes it easier for religious institutions to borrow.

How you perceive opportunities is a subjective process, and your mind-set is critical. To say that you need to be positive, however, does not fully take into account the complexity of the process. How is it that two people looking at the same abandoned building can see two different things? One sees an eyesore—broken windows, rotted wood, and litter covering the grounds. The other sees its *potential*—splash on some paint, clean up the yard, fix the windows, and the building will look almost new. Nonperforming properties like these represent your fertile field of opportunity. The opportunity can be there for you, but you must go for it.

To be able to see the potential that surrounds you, you must develop an opportunity mind-set. Positive thinking and affirmations are a start, but alone, they are not good enough. Refer back to your goals and your plan. Now, open your eyes and look around you. What do you see?

Walk around your neighborhood. Those guys hanging out on the corner—do you see their potential, or do you see them as problems? Some of them have skills and abilities they have developed in the streets that are transferable from negative to positive activities. It may be hard to imagine at first, but when you consider the business acumen of a drug dealer running a complex marketing enterprise, you realize that it entails many of the skills required in running a large company. The problem is that no one has talked to the drug dealer about how he could more effectively use his marketing abilities to help rather than hurt people and communities. Talk to people like him, and you will be surprised at how many of them will listen.

The playground that has broken glass scattered all around, vandalized play equipment—opportunity or problem? Organize teams to help clean and fix it up. There are many people in your block who would volunteer if you shared your vision for providing a safe and wholesome environment for the children.

The vacant lots and boarded-up houses—these may be eyesores, but they also may be your opportunities. Many of those houses are foreclosures, from either HUD (Housing and Urban Development) or the bank. Check the city registry and you may find that this is a great opportunity to become a homeowner. If there is no planned development for a vacant lot, at least keep it clean so that it does not become a junkyard that depreciates the value of other properties in the community. Consider Charles Jenkins, a retired social worker now working as a receptionist at Allen Church, who rather than allowing a vacant lot in his neighborhood to become an eyesore, decided to make it a garden. In the fall, he plants tulips to bloom in the spring. Once the tulips begin to fade, he then plants vegetables, which are enjoyed by other members of the neighborhood.

Freddie Dill is a classic bootstrapper who realized more than twenty years ago that there were profits to be made from repairing tires damaged by potholes in New York. He started a tire company and named it Pooor Freddie's Mud Hole. He placed billboards at every major intersection bordering the Southeast Queens community. His theme, "We love to fix tires," was so prevalent on the boards that people soon found their way to his establishment. Even as other franchise dealers have opened up in the area, Pooor Freddie's Mud Hole has continued to prosper.

Freddie likes to testify that he has only a sixth-grade education and could not read or write when he left the farm in Georgia. Now, not only does Freddie read, but he has become a major investor in the stock market and does his own analyses on his personal computer. He is also quite well versed in current events. I often stop at Pooor Freddie's Mud Hole just to share in inspirational conversation with him.

His ever-expanding business empire, which includes a barbecue restaurant, wheel alignment center, and many landholdings, proves that opportunities can be found anywhere.

Any situation that you've ever thought negatively about has an opportunity buried in there somewhere. With an opportunity mindset, you do not wait for opportunities to knock on your door. You seek ways to create the situations and circumstances that can make something positive happen. This is demonstrated in a very vivid way through Colin Powell's campaign for volunteerism. For a man of Powell's popularity and stature to devote himself to such a cause helped create a climate of heightened awareness, impressing on people that it is everyone's responsibility to invest their time and energy in worthy causes. The heightened awareness created the possibility for many nonprofit organizations to increase their people power, which in turn created the opportunity to get more work done.

One of the best ways of helping people to take advantage of opportunities is through education. I told you earlier about Mrs. Jewell H.

Houston's influence on my life. Now I'd like to share some of the things that she taught me. She was my history teacher, and she came from a family of teachers and ministers. Although she is only five feet tall, she has never been afraid to stand up for the things that she believes in. When my co-author and I visited Houston recently, we had an opportunity to visit with her. She stated, "I always wanted to be a teacher. Money was never my object. I wasn't born with a lot of money, but I knew I wanted to help people."

Mrs. Houston's classes provided an exciting learning experience. She'd tell us to reach for the stars and to always keep our principles and goals in mind. She also admonished us that we could achieve our goals without stepping on somebody else's toes. During this recent visit, she expressed regrets that schools no longer allow prayer or discussions about God. Back when I was in her class, our memory verse each morning was "In all your ways acknowledge Him, and He will direct your paths" (Proverbs 3:6).

The books we received at school were passed along to us after being used by the white students. Mrs. Houston told me and my co-author, "We had old material and no information whatsoever about African Americans; so, we teachers had to be very inventive to make our young people feel like we were reaping the benefits of this America."

She bequeathed to us this definition of the American Dream: "Every man, woman, boy, and girl should be equal." She was determined to do her share, and that was to produce doctors, lawyers, ministers, good parents, leaders, and entrepreneurs. She knew that the way the American Dream was being played out was nowhere near perfect, but she taught us that it was our responsibility to do what we could to make it better. She blessed us with an opportunity-seeking mind-set. She would say, "Don't leave your community. Go get your education; then come back and build it into what you want it to be." And she practiced what she preached. She was raised in Houston and she taught there. In fact, she and her husband still live on the family homestead left to her by her mother.

Mrs. Houston was an educational bootstrapper whose concern for her students was primary. She said, "Every child that came to my room was special because I'd look beyond their little mischief. I knew they needed some guidance. They needed some love." Mrs. Houston didn't have many discipline problems in her classroom. She'd never send her students to the principal's office. Her motto was "I'll handle it." She had a way of looking at you that let you know she meant business. Even when she chastised or criticized us, we knew it was done with love.

We were constantly kept busy with in-class projects in Mrs. Houston's classroom. She managed to make history relevant to our lives. Often, she'd have us talk about the news of the day, which meant we had to read the newspapers or listen to the radio. She took a special interest in me and allowed me to work in the room where books were stored and disseminated to the classrooms. She'd go and have her cup of coffee and leave me in charge. By her actions she let me know that she trusted me, and that had more of an effect on me than anything. I didn't want to let her down. Mrs. Houston was a bootstrapper because she would not allow herself to be defined by the limitations of her situation. She gave her best to her students, and they in return gave their best in her classes.

She *made* me accept the position of president of the Young People's Division of the Women's Missionary Society. This is a denominational organization that trains youth in every facet of Christian life and also provides meaningful programs to enable them to develop strong leadership potential. In government classes, Mrs. Houston instituted parliamentary procedures and taught us Robert's Rules of Order. Little did I know that this was the initial stage of my preparation for Congress. This reinforces the idea that we should always learn as much as possible, even if we don't know how we will use it in the future.

It was a different era, and Mrs. Houston was one of the great educators of her time. Yet the principles of good education remain constant across time. The goal is to create a classroom and community environment conducive for learning opportunities. Now retired, Mrs. Houston offers these words of wisdom: "If you are truly committed to making a difference in the lives of young people, you're going to have to deal with yourself first in order to reach a child. Ask yourself, 'How can I make a difference?'"

Opportunities come in all shapes and sizes and from places where we least expect them. Often they have your name and your name alone on them. While I was serving as dean of students and chaplain at Boston University, I was making 29,500 dollars. My denomination offered me the pastorate at Allen Church. Elaine and I prayed about it and decided that Allen was where God wanted us to go. I accepted the offer and took a 14,500-dollar cut in pay. At the time, I'm sure some people questioned my sanity, since Elaine was in her fifth month of pregnancy, expecting our first child. My job at Boston was secure, but only God knew what would happen at Allen. But we just felt that we had to go. This "career move" may have looked like a step back, but we believed that it was God's will and that it would pay off in the end. I am certain that the opportunities that I have had in New York would not have been available to me in Boston. Bootstrapping means going into unknown places and making the most of everything that comes your way.

What may look like a dead-end situation to one person may seem filled with the potential of a lifetime to another. When making a decision that involves enhancing your future, you must be very careful whom you talk to. People who are not aware of your goals and plans may try to dissuade you. Sometimes the high-paying job is not the right way to go. I have found that it is better to do something that you enjoy and that gives you a sense of fulfillment and satisfaction. The good-looking man with the nice car may not be good husband material. The woman who is the class queen may not be the best wife for you. Deep down, you know what's best for you. Honor your intuition. If you've been praying for guidance, trust that if there is any discomfort in your spirit, it is God's way of telling you "no."

The old saying "All that glitters is not gold" is a good guide when trying to make up your mind about an opportunity. Don't make decisions based on superficial appearances.

Seizing Opportunities

How did the word *opportunism* develop such negative connotations when *opportunity* has no such taint? This is one of the deep mysteries of the English language.

Let us rethink this word *opportunism*. If an opportunity is a "situation or condition favorable for attainment of a goal," then how did *opportunism* become "the policy or practice of adapting actions, decisions, etc., to expediency or effectiveness *without regard to principles or consequences*"?

With all due respect to Webster's, for the purposes of our discussion, I'd like to propose a new understanding of this much-maligned word. There are two kinds of opportunists: bad ones and good ones. Let's call the bad kind "immediate gratification opportunists" (IGOs) and the good kind "positive opportunists" (POs).

IGOs want what they want, and they want it right now. When an opportunity presents itself, IGOs step over people, stab folks in the back, and undercut and undermine others to get what they want. POs take advantage of opportunities, but not at the expense of others. They'll compete hard and fight fair, but they won't try to destroy another person in the process.

If they don't get what they want, IGOs often employ a "scorch the earth" policy: if they can't seize the day, then no one can. POs practice good fellowship. They'll shake hands all around, even when they lose, because they know that there are other battles to be fought. They may retreat, but they will never give up because of a defeat.

Boostrappers are POs. Being in tune with their goals and plans enables them to see possibilities all around them. They have a gift for recognizing and then capitalizing on the potential in any situation. In the old, outdated myth of the self-made man, immediate gratification opportunism was promoted as the way to get ahead. It was a dog-eat-dog philosophy, a jungle mind-set that dictated that only the strong survive. Positive opportunism promotes enlightened self-interest with social responsibility. The old myth also promoted the erroneous and destructive idea that nice guys finish last. If you practice positive opportunism, you too can finish first while having right behavior on your side. You won't be sowing any bad seeds that will come back to haunt you later on.

Seizing the moment is an art, especially with so many IGOs out there. Still, I truly believe that it can be done. Here's how:

1. *Claim your good.* Aggressively pray for guidance on how to proceed when opportunity knocks.
2. *Practice the Golden Rule.* Love for others is the principle that POs live by.
3. When you hear of an opportunity that seems tailor-made for you, *act decisively.* Then work hard. Go the extra mile.
4. Take action in a *timely* fashion. If you've ever played chess, you know how it parallels real life. Chess is a game of strategy, and so is life. One element to consider in strategy is *timing.* When should you make your move? There are no hard-and-fast rules: you'll have to feel your way through this one.
5. *Deal with every obstacle that comes your way.* Opportunities are often embedded in obstacles. To flinch from an obstacle might cause you to miss your blessing.

Opportunity Magnets

How do you attract opportunities?

Remember Midas, the guy in mythology who turned everything he touched to gold? That's you. You're Midas, only everything you see will be a golden opportunity to help yourself and others. We're talking mind-set.

For some strange reason, the busier you are, the more opportunities will come your way. As I mentioned earlier, they say that if you want to get something done, you should give it to a busy person. Busy people rarely complain of having too much to do, and if they take the project on, they'll not only get it done but they'll do it in a timely fashion. Busy bootstrappers are magnets. They attract opportunities on a daily basis.

Phil Fisher is a case in point. His company, On Line Productions, produces festivals, expositions, and concerts around the world. He has produced Sinbad's Caribbean concerts since their inception. Fisher, who always has a full schedule of activities planned, says that not a day goes by when he doesn't receive a call from some radio station, the tourism department of some country, or a community-based organization asking him to set up an event or to run the entire show. And even though his schedule is packed, somehow, he always figures out a way to do more.

Make sure you're prepared to capitalize on opportunities when they come. Ever since she was a little girl, Laura Williams had wanted to be a stage actress. For many years, she studied hard and went on auditions. Then one day, after years of hard work, she became an "overnight" sensation in Chicago theater. She worked every season, and she'd often capture the lead. If she hadn't done her homework and taken the time to master her craft, Williams would not have been prepared at audition time when the right part came her way.

Check your mind-set. To be an opportunity magnet, you'll not want to think things like, "I'm too young," "I'm not pretty enough," or "I'm not the right race." You must believe in yourself, your ability to get the work done, and your ability to achieve. If you don't believe it, no one will, and opportunity will knock on your neighbor's door.

Impatience leads to desperation, and desperation attracts bad opportunities. Charlatans and con artists prey on desperate people. They come in sheep's clothing, bearing gifts—but beware. Too many people lose their entire savings because they trust in the wrong person offering them a get-rich-quick scheme. Others end up in bad relationships because they believe someone else will provide them with the self-esteem they lack. Stay focused and don't let impatience creep in.

Some level of self-promotion may be required to help you achieve your goals. Although self-promotion is often frowned upon, it helps to influence people and let them know you exist. It is important to balance self-promotion in such a way that it is done with finesse.

Muhammad Ali often proclaimed himself "the greatest." He was a master self-promoter and entertainer. What made him so effective as a self-promoter was his ability to back up his claims in the ring. In his day, he *was* the greatest. To be an effective self-promoter you must have self-confidence, a strong belief in yourself, and the ability to produce.

If you are shy and have an aversion to tooting your own horn, get over it. Just don't become obnoxious, or your good works may become overshadowed. The best of all worlds is obviously to get others speaking about the good that you do. Can you imagine going on a job interview and saying, "Well, I guess I'm okay at some things"? I can attest that you will not get the job. Employers are looking for people who have self-confidence. It is not wrong, illegal, or unethical to promote yourself. Study the masters—actors, athletes, high-profile entrepreneurs, politicians. They each have different styles. Some toot their horns loudly; others just smile a lot. Still others have other people toot their horns for them. Even when you have not been able to amass an impressive résumé, there is still a way to sell yourself. To be a good bootstrapper you must learn the value of knowledge and be willing to study and work hard to improve yourself, so you can put yourself in the most advantageous position possible.

Take a Chance

The Chinese word for crisis is represented with two symbols: one for danger and one for opportunity. Sometimes, capitalizing on opportunities is risky. The bigger the goal, the greater the danger. Some love to live on the edge—Donald Trump, Michael Milken, Reginald Lewis, and the big deal makers of the 1980s are excellent examples.

Remember the daredevil Evil Knievel? This man took risk taking to the extreme. He ended up in the hospital countless times, and he broke more bones than I even knew a body had. I think the last stunt he tried was jumping over the Grand Canyon or some other big hole in the ground with his motorcycle. Knievel's stunts were thrilling to watch, but they were also more than a little crazy. For him, the danger and the risk of dying were far outweighed by the media attention. For him, taking risks was what it was all about. I suspect that he just liked the danger. He was not that different from the eighties deal makers. I am by no means advocating that you take risks that are extreme and unmanageable. However, capitalizing on most opportunities will require some risks.

You don't have to push billions of dollars around or take crazy chances to experience this two-sided coin, however. Maybe buying a house seems dangerous to you. Maybe proposing marriage is a frightening proposition. The point is, you'll never achieve success if you don't take a chance.

Creating Opportunity

People usually see an opportunity as one event, and it can be. However, achieving your goal may require following through on a series of events. A job fair is an opportunity—and so is the interview, the second interview, the offer, the hiring, and the promotion.

What you need to be on the lookout for is a favorable situation or condition that will help you achieve your goal. If you cannot create an event, you can create the conditions—mental, physical, spiritual, social, emotional, financial—that will most likely help it to occur. Creating the conditions is just as powerful. When I was a boy, my mother had a vegetable garden next to our house. We children did all the work of cultivating the soil in the garden and looked forward to the day when the seeds we were planting would produce food. We learned lessons in gardening that are applicable to life. There is a season for planting, another for watering, and then comes the harvest. Through the sunshine and the rain of life, we must still persevere. There are times when we carry heavy loads that pull us down, as a tomato does its vine, yet we also realize that there are people who will help us to remain standing. Just as we took pieces of wood and tied them to the vines to hold up the tomatoes, God gives us the support of others as we make this sojourn through life.

Bootstrappers know that all results are not immediate, that there is a time of waiting for the results to come. But as we wait, we get new energy knowing that at some point there will be a reaping of the harvest.

Pull Yourself Up by Your Bootstraps . . .

What is your goal, and what would be the best conditions—spiritual, emotional, physical, financial, mental—for that goal to be achieved? Today, I want you to work on creating favorable conditions in your life that will lead to goal-producing opportunities.

1.   Do one act of self-promotion. Regardless of what your goal is, some self-promotion will help attract opportunity to you. Have calling cards printed. If you have a computer, this can be done

cheaply. Think of a brief, personal motto to put on the card that says something positive about your skills, abilities, philosophy of life, intelligence, compassion, or beauty. Now give it to someone.

Sometimes, it may seem as if your persistence is not paying off. However, if you stick with it, often you will get the results you want. I recall that of the number of contractors who were interested in working on the Allen Cathedral, some of those who wound up with jobs were those who had been the most persistent. Even when informed that contracts had already been "let," they kept calling, writing, or dropping by the job site until they got someone's attention. Because they were vigilant in their self-promotion, they were able to convince us to give them the job.

2. Clean out the clutter in your home—in your drawers and closets, under your bed. Organize your files and important papers. Cleaning out the clutter will help organize your home, your thoughts, and your life. How you're thinking and feeling on the inside is reflected in your home. Cleaning out your home is one way to achieve the clarity of thought that you'll need in order to see opportunities and make good decisions. I don't go to bed with dirty dishes in the sink. Just as I did growing up, I clean the toilets almost daily. When Elaine is away on a trip, she knows that if I am home on the night before she returns, she will enter a clean house, a meal will be cooked, and the clothes will be washed, even if the housekeeper did not come. She calls me the best husband and wife a woman could have.

A real bootstrapper does not manifest characteristics outside of the home that are not evident in the home. The same spirit that drives one to be a "go-getter" at work and in pursuit of opportunities should be operative at home. Imagine what a wonderful world we would live in if bootstrapping businesspeople used the same success plans in their marriages, with their children, and at home in general. A true bootstrapper values the family as much as the other areas of his or her life.

ACTION STEP 6:
DEAL WITH CRISIS

Into every life, some rain will fall.

I don't know anyone who has escaped having crises and setbacks in their life. Everyone must face them, yet many self-help books gloss over this subject. Their theory is that if you just chant a few affirmations, all the pain will go away and your circumstances will magically change. However, most of us who have lived through difficulty will attest that there are some things that just will not go away or change with chanting or positive thinking. The message in this action step is that your difficult circumstances do change and you *will* get through them, but you have to deal with the crises.

The first thing to remember is that when trouble comes, one cannot give in to feelings of despair and hopelessness. The goal should always be to move through the difficult situations knowing that trouble and adversity will make you stronger, wiser, and ready for greater opportunities.

Crisis should not be confused with the *wilderness experience* that we discussed earlier. The wilderness is like a void, the place of God's silence. It is the time of life when you feel that you are going in circles and the thing that you've wanted and been working for seems to elude you. Often you are bewildered by your circumstances and you know that precious time is being wasted, but the way of escape is hidden from you.

Crisis is also different from *challenges*. When you accept a challenge, you know that it is going to be difficult. You understand the terms and nature of the contest, and you willingly use your skills, wits, and resources to rise to the occasion. Opportunities are often embedded in challenges, and it is up to us to discover them.

A crisis may be a part of a wilderness experience or a challenge, but what distinguishes it is that it feels like an attack. You don't willingly seek a crisis; in fact, you sometimes don't even see it coming. Without warning, you're in the proverbial "back against the wall" position. You want to fight back, but you cannot clearly define the opposition, and even when you do, the target keeps moving. The key to living through crises appropriately is to maintain integrity and self-control. Dealing with adversity is bad enough, but trouble is only exacerbated when one reacts with rage and recklessness.

A crisis or setback can be as benign as being passed over for a promotion or as life-threatening as being diagnosed with cancer. It can be as intangible as a serious crisis in faith or as tangible as the loss of wealth. A crisis is the huge mountain that blocks our view of our goals. It causes fear and trembling, depression, and feelings of defeat. Adversity can make a self-reliant woman fall to her knees or a strong man cry. But it is a reality from which you cannot escape. If you are not careful, a crisis can make you lose your self-confidence, especially if you've been doing everything by the book—soul-searching, goal setting, planning, and executing. It is even more dramatic if you have tried to live your life on high moral ground and your character is attacked. You can lose your faith and begin to doubt that God loves you and is moving on your behalf.

Those who try to stir up the world and reach beyond their limitations often find themselves under attack. You can be assured that if in the midst of your work you are experiencing unreasonable assaults, it is because you are on the right track. The bigger the goal and the grander the dream, the more formidable the foe. Undoubtedly, those who do not disturb the status quo and live within the confines of safety and/or mediocrity will never provoke attacks. But for those whose goal is to make a difference, "safety" is rarely achievable. They take the road the poet Robert Frost calls "the one less traveled," and that makes all the difference.

Despite the setbacks, adversities, and failures, you must focus on achieving your goal. The presence of adversity in your journey forces one to ask the questions, "How badly do I want to achieve this goal?" "Am I willing to abandon the vision to keep peace?" These are the make-or-break questions that will be asked of every person at some point in his or her journey. If you are a high achiever, as is the case with most bootstrappers, you will not give in to feelings of self-doubt and fear. Your focus must be the implementation of your plan. Go into prayer and reach deep down into your pocket of determination, because you're going to need it.

Without a doubt, the most important factor during your entire period of crisis will be your attitude. It will determine whether you will emerge from the ordeal a victim or a victor. Your attitude will shape your perception of the entire journey to success, because perception is indeed reality. The best way to move through a crisis is with courage and faith, knowing that God will work in all things for our good.

Career Crises

The dreams that I have had for myself and my family, church, and community have always been big, so I should not have been surprised when the tidal wave of attack came against me. I should have seen it coming, but I was blinded by the belief that my hard work would be rewarded with exemption from trouble. Unfortunately, this is never the case. There comes a time in all of our lives when we must come face-to-face with crisis. Maintaining integrity and spiritual demeanor in the midst of personal attacks was indeed a challenge for me. In the following pages, I will explore exactly what happened. Throughout the ordeal, I did not engage in negative counterattacks, and when others wanted to go on the offensive on my behalf, I did not allow them to do so. I assumed a defensive, prayerful posture. My time of testing was at hand. I had preached so often about my faith in Jesus' approach to trials, and now this was being tested. Would my faith prove to be real, or nothing more than lip service? I was being forced to practice what I had been preaching since I was a child.

My first six years at Allen Church were not only productive, but void of any major dissension. On the whole, the membership was warm, receptive, and encouraging, and most were supportive of my ideas for the future development of the church. Although I was only thirty-one, I had already had several part-time pastoral positions, but this was my first full-time assignment. My career goal had always been to become a president of a major college or university, and my position as dean and interim chaplain at Boston University had positioned me well to achieve that goal. When the pulpit at Allen Church was vacated, the presiding bishop of the district offered me the pastorate, which I accepted in spite of the cut in salary. Prayer and introspection led me to know that this was God's purpose for my life.

When Elaine and I arrived at Allen in 1976, the church had a thriving ministry. There were fourteen hundred members, eight hundred of whom were active, an annual budget of approximately 250,000 dollars, and two other full-time and two part-time employees. By definition, this was one of the leading churches in the denomination, but I saw the need and potential for massive growth and expansion. No real bootstrapper is content with prior successes; there is always a vision for new and innovative undertakings. Upon my arrival at Allen, I immediately began to identify new ministries and programs for the church.

Located in Jamaica, New York, Allen was basically a middle-class church, which placed it in a good position to deal with the problems of the community. South East Queens was suffering the decay that is, unfortunately, typical of many urban communities that transitioned from a predominantly white to largely African American population in the late sixties and early seventies. Drugs, vacant lots, business flight, low-performing schools, abandoned buildings, and high unemployment were sending the community on a downward spiral. My perspective on the community was that this represented a fertile field of opportunity for new ministries, both spiritual and social. As is often the case with a middle-class congregation, everyone did not fully share my vision, but they worked with me and rejoiced at the successes that came rather rapidly during my first few years as pastor.

Since its beginning in 1787, my denomination, the African Methodist Episcopal Church, has subscribed to a spiritual, educational, social, economic, and self-help interpretation of the gospel. We are called to minister to the human spirit and help meet the physical needs of people. My approach to ministry is similar to that of our founder, Richard Allen, who was a former slave and who purchased his own freedom. He started the denomination after being thrown out of St. George's Methodist Church in Philadelphia because Africans were not permitted to worship in the main sanctuary. To me, he exemplifies the true spirit of a bootstrapper. I've always believed that God helps those who help themselves and that my role is to help facilitate this holy transaction within people. With this in mind, Elaine and I prayed for guidance, and then we got busy.

Because of our educational backgrounds, we felt that building a school was essential to uplifting our church and community. Elaine began to visit private schools and worked with state and city agencies to determine how best to set up the curriculum and program for the school. We recently celebrated the sixteenth anniversary of the Allen Christian School. The current student enrollment is 482, in grades pre-kindergarten through eight. Our home became a processing center, as we clipped from newspapers requests for proposals for city, state, and federal funds. We wrote grant proposals seeking funds for various programs including the Allen A.M.E. Neighborhood Preservation and Development Corporation and the Allen Women's Resource Center.

I reasoned that one way to get rid of the drug addicts and drug dealers on the streets was to buy up every square foot of land and property that we could afford. After restructuring and centralizing a fragmented internal accounting system, the church was positioned to buy property in preparation for the building of the school. This restructuring was no doubt the beginning of my trouble, because for some church leaders, it meant a loss of power and control. I was so certain of the vision God had given me, however, that I made this unpopular move and was willing to risk their short-term anger for the long-term strengthening of the church. As we developed the land and rehabilitated the abandoned buildings, educated children, created social programs, and provided senior housing, we put people to work, kicked out the drug element, and changed the aesthetics of the community. The trouble that would eventually come was worth the good that we were accomplishing through the ministry.

In 1978 we organized an Education Committee and began aggressively planning for the school. The members of Allen raised 1.5 million dollars in tithes, offerings, and various fund-raising programs for the construction of this educational facility. Over the next few years, Elaine structured the Women's Ministry so that the programs generated a great deal of these funds. In September 1982, Allen Christian School opened its doors to 234 children in pre-kindergarten to grade three. Because the new building had not been completed on schedule, the first days of the school were spent in the lower level of the church. But by January 1983, the children walked into their beautiful new facility. My own four children attended Allen Christian School and graduated from there. Today, in spite of the success of the Allen Christian School, I am still painfully aware of the many students in public schools who have not had the opportunity to receive a quality education. It is my belief that charter schools (public schools with local control) and voucher initiatives (public or private funds for poor children who are denied equal educational opportunities) are the means by which a great number of young children can be given educational opportunities.

Between 1976 and 1982, the church was growing extremely fast, in its membership and outreach to the community. I became aware of some rumblings of discontent from some of the leadership, which reached a crescendo by 1985. My greatest opposition, one would think, should have come from the drug dealers we displaced, but trouble had been brewing right on the board of officers of Allen Church. Some disapproved of the fast pace and the new direction that the church had taken. We had several tense meetings about the moves the church was making; the officers even went so far as to complain to my predecessor and invoked his disapproval in our discussions. I was shocked and disappointed, but I felt even more determined to continue leading the church in higher levels of achievement through ministries that improved the quality of life within the community. Fortunately, the majority of the officers were solid in their support of these initiatives, despite the vocal minority that let their feelings be known.

Ignoring their disapproval, I moved forward. An opportunity to purchase a group of eleven run-down stores was made available to us, and I felt that it was in the church's interest to capitalize on it. The stores were located across the street from the school and one and a half blocks from the church. They were a haven for winos, drug addicts, and illegal after-hours clubs. They also represented a fire hazard because of their state of disrepair. The sellers wanted 50,000 dollars down in thirty days; the entire purchase price was 250,000 dollars. I initially spoke to some church officers who did not agree with the purchase. In spite of their response, the next Sunday I told the entire congregation about the opportunity and the terms. Their approval was apparent, and the response was overwhelmingly in favor of a move to buy the property. As it happened, Elaine was in the midst of planning activities for the Women's Ministry, and in just thirty days, they raised the money for the down payment. Six months later, they had raised the balance and we paid cash for the property. It was incredible.

In the meantime these same officers did not cease to voice their opposition to the church's continued expansion. Insulted that I had ignored their disapproval and taken my case to the congregation, they became more determined than ever to derail the church's new endeavors. They felt that after having built a school and purchasing numerous properties, our attention should be turned solely to paying off the mortgage on the school. They felt that community outreach could be left to other churches. "You have led us into too much debt," they protested. I thought it interesting that so many people complain when their church is doing nothing, but they also complain when they feel their church is doing too much too fast. Educating others to become bootstrappers is an extremely difficult task because risk taking does not appeal to everyone. It was my belief, however, that since we already had made a four-million-dollar investment in the community development project, it would be ludicrous to allow the community that surrounds the church and school to continue its decline because of deterioration. Also, I knew that the stronger our portfolio was, the more leverage we would have in dealing with lenders, foundations, and government agencies.

One night, while Elaine and I were in Bermuda, where I was doing a revival, I had a strong feeling that I needed to go back to New York. It was as if God was telling me that all was not well on the home front. When we got back, I was informed that a group of officers wanted to have a meeting to discuss some "concerns." The community renewal projects were coming along nicely, and church membership and income had risen significantly. My thinking, even as I went to the meeting, was that their disagreements had to be minor since I was providing progressive leadership to the congregation. After praying and fasting, I had the reaffirmation from God that no evil could destroy me. My faith made me feel that God had found pleasure in what we were doing, and that was all that mattered to me. More important, the work we were doing, in my opinion, was reflective of God's revelation, vision, and plan for Allen Church. The scripture "No weapon formed against me shall prosper" kept playing itself over and over in my mind.

Lee Iacocca probably felt the same way. Car manufacturing and ministering to souls are as different as night is from day, yet he too had to deal with the realities of human politics. Whether you're building a family, church, company, or nation, you'll have to consider human desires and idiosyncrasies. This will be the source of many of your conflicts.

Before Iacocca saved Chrysler, he served as president of the Ford Motor Company. His boss was none other than Henry Ford II, chairman of the board and grandson of the founder of the company.

Iacocca had worked his way up the ranks at Ford. He started in 1946 as a student engineer, and over the years he worked in various sales, managerial, and executive-level positions. He had many successes along the way, but his major claim to fame was that he spearheaded the design and development of the Mustang, which became Ford's best-selling car.

On December 10, 1970, he achieved his ultimate career goal. He was promoted to the presidency of Ford, overseeing 432,000 employees worldwide and 14.9 billion dollars in sales. The profit margin was 515 million dollars, which was respectable, but only 3.5 percent of total sales. They could do better. He decided to boost the profit margin by cutting the fat.

His first initiatives as president involved cutting costs in operations and shipping and boosting productivity. He cut loose twenty major departments and subsidiaries that were not showing enough of a profit.

Iacocca was on a roll, and he had to answer only to Henry Ford II. Herein was the problem. Ford's power in the company was absolute, and according to Iacocca, he wielded his power capriciously. Once Ford insisted that Iacocca fire a man because his pants were too tight—which in Ford's mind meant the guy was gay. Iacocca says that Ford's management philosophy was to not let any employee get "too comfortable." He believed in keeping people "anxious and off-balance."

Iacocca also says that Ford drank too much. He was paranoid and saw conspiracies everywhere. He didn't keep files for fear they would fall into the wrong hands, nor would he sign documents. Iacocca says that for the eight years he served as president, he had virtually no documentation that carried Ford's signature.

Ford was also a racist whose bigotry guided his business policies. When the oil crisis of 1973 hit, and suddenly people wanted small, fuel-efficient cars, Iacocca struck a deal with the Honda company in Japan to buy packages containing a transmission and an engine for 711 dollars each. It was a great deal, but Ford was not pleased. According to Iacocca, Ford said, "No car with my name on the hood is going to have a Jap engine inside!"

Iacocca's successes and Ford's paranoia led to trouble. Ford began to undermine Iacocca's authority in countless ways. As president, Iacocca was responsible for making the big decisions and overseeing the daily operations of the company's interests worldwide. In 1975, Ford began making decisions without consulting Iacocca. In fact, he made many decisions while Iacocca was overseas, and once when he was home with the flu. Ford began giving directives to people who reported directly to Iacocca. He cut spending in Iacocca's programs that were allocated to address trends in the market. Then, in the spirit of Watergate, Ford spent 2 million dollars bugging phones and rooms to investigate top-level executives, particularly Iacocca, to determine if they had Mafia ties.

Although everyone came up clean, it was quite an ordeal. During this troubling time, Iacocca says that his wife, Mary, "wanted to punch Henry out."

By 1977, it was all-out war. Henry had top management reorganized, which cut into Iacocca's authority. Instead of the president running the show, outside consultants, hired by Ford, recommended that the company be headed by three people. Iacocca became the number-three man.

Ford's firing of Iacocca was inevitable, brutal, and painful. Iacocca says, "I was fired for being a threat to the boss. Henry was infamous for dropping his number-two men under unpleasant circumstances. To him, it was always the uprising of the peasants against their lord and master. Still, I had always clung to the idea that I was different, that somehow I was smarter or luckier than the rest. I didn't think it would ever happen to me."

Eventually, Iacocca went on to bigger and better things, but those last few months at Ford left a deep scar that would last for many years.

Emotional Setbacks

Back to the brewing crisis at Allen. The meeting began with them telling me how much they appreciated how, under my leadership, membership had grown from one thousand to over three thousand and offerings had increased from two thousand dollars per Sunday to more than fifteen thousand dollars. Nevertheless, they felt that Allen had expanded too quickly into the real estate business. They were not educators, but they had many complaints about the operation of the school. They indicated that my personal expenses were too great, even though they had previously stated that the many trips that were now required to HUD and city and state agencies should not be personal expenses but rather should be reimbursed, because I was taking care of church business. Now the charge was that all of these funded programs did not constitute church business. They also felt that Allen was getting too big, and I was getting too popular. The bottom line: they wanted me to know that they were in charge.

Respectfully, I listened to what they had to say, and then I stated my position, which was, "The reality is that there is only one name on pastoral appointments, and the bishop placed my name on this one." Although I had delegated a great deal of responsibility to them, it now

became apparent that some changes had to be made. I needed to surround myself with those who had a vision for community expansion
and church growth. The church needed leaders who were committed to
outreach ministry and economic development. This group had been my
closest confidants and friends since my arrival. I was totally shocked by
the sudden change in attitude.

The meeting ended with them insisting that because I was stretching myself too thin, I must hire an administrative assistant to help me
get my work done. In the spirit of compromise, I hired the person that
they recommended for the job. This turned out to be a big mistake.
Although she was extremely talented, her loyalty rested with those who
had become my opposition within and without the church. It was
inevitable that conflict would arise.

This already bad situation soon turned disastrous as I realized that
my dissenters' goal was to control the church. I know many pastors who
have found this type of crisis and were either removed from the church
or chose to leave rather than fight. This same type of problem occurs in
many businesses.

Before Sam Walton's tremendous multibillion-dollar success with
Wal-Mart, he cut his teeth in retail by buying a Ben Franklin store in
Newport, Arkansas. The former owner hadn't been able to make it
work, so Walton took it on. He set a goal for his little store: to be the
most profitable store in all of Arkansas in five years.

At the end of the five years, he had more than met his goal. He was
a success. There was only one problem: "In all my excitement at becoming Sam Walton, merchant, I had neglected to include a clause in my
lease which gave me an option to renew after the first five years." As a
result, he and his family had to move from the little town they had
grown to love.

Walton says, "It was the low point of my business life. I felt sick to
my stomach. I couldn't believe it was happening to me. It really was like
a nightmare. I had built the best variety store in the whole region and
worked hard in the community—done everything right—and now I
was being kicked out of town. It didn't seem fair. I blamed myself for

ever getting suckered into such an awful lease, and I was furious at the landlord. Helen, just settling in with a brand-new family of four, was heartsick at the prospect of leaving Newport. But that's what we were going to do."

Physical Setbacks

At this time in my own career at Allen Church, I entertained thoughts of leaving, but I felt compelled to stay. I had to be true to my calling and my responsibilities, and I had to weather this storm. Arnett Pack, Sr., one friend who was an officer in the church, realized what was happening and encouraged me not to quit but to take a stand. I shall never forget him telling me, "You were assigned to this church to pastor. We are happy with your work. So don't let anybody run you away. Do what you have to do and the majority of us will support you."

I know that you can't be friends with everybody, but I don't like being in the midst of dissension. I have spent much of my pastorate carrying out the belief that in the midst of conflict it is my role to be keeper of the peace. I must confess that the daily tension of working in an atmosphere of hostility and subversion had a negative effect on my health.

I began to experience chest pains, so severe at times that I could not stand up straight. The doctor told me to stay home and do whatever it took to relieve the stress. I followed his advice and took several weeks off. Although my body was weakening, I still fasted while I prayed, meditated, and studied my Bible. I refused to stay in bed. I would spend the days reading and preparing sermons. By the third week, though still moving slowly, I returned to work with the knowledge that I had to make some immediate decisions to create a peaceful work environment.

Good health is a blessing, and when you don't have it, everything slows down. The spirit that dwells in the heart of a bootstrapper demands excellence, and when my strength and energy began to dissipate, I saw that if I did not go on the offensive, my performance would diminish and I could easily lose the spirit that had been the defining characteristic of my life.

We had moved from the church building, which seated six hundred, into the school gymnasium/auditorium with twelve hundred seats. The congregation started growing again because of the additional space, and soon we expanded from two to three Sunday morning services. I terminated the administrative assistant and did not nominate the officers with whom I was in conflict for trustee or steward boards for the next year. The tensions subsided, and the ministry continued to flourish.

By August 1985, church membership had grown to five thousand and the annual budget was two and a half million dollars. The ministry of Allen was taking on new challenges and responsibilities while further expanding community outreach.

Legal Crises

In April 1986, some ministers from the Southeast Queens Clergy for Community Empowerment came to ask me to run for the congressional seat representing the Sixth District in Queens. At this time, the seat was held by Joseph P. Addabbo, but his health was failing and it was expected that his seat would soon be vacated. This group of preachers had organized during my first foray into politics when I made a successful run for delegate to the Democratic National Convention in 1984. I held them in high regard because they had continued to work collectively on community projects.

I had never been inclined to seek an elective political office. At first I declined, but the ministers prevailed based on their sense that there was a broader community mandate. Ironically, during the meeting, a call came in informing us that Mr. Addabbo had died. One of the ministers spoke to the reporter who made the call and announced that I was their candidate for Mr. Addabbo's seat. Grieved by the death of a friend and shocked at being suddenly thrust into the political arena, I left the office almost speechless. On the other side of the door, we saw Elaine approaching. Of course I had not had an opportunity to inform her of the day's events, so you can imagine her surprise when one of the preachers announced to her that I was about to run for Congress. Unfortunately, the way she heard it denied us the opportunity to discuss the matter privately. In the weeks that followed, my supporters and I tried to help her to see how a congressional seat would allow me to expand my ideas on economic development and community renewal to the federal level. Still, Elaine was not convinced. The tension between us built even more as the church and community began to organize for the campaign. One Sunday morning during the 8:30 A.M. worship service, I announced my withdrawal from the campaign. Elaine arrived before the 11:15 A.M. worship service and was informed that I had announced my withdrawal. She rushed to the office and stated that I could not withdraw because she did not want to spend the rest of her life feeling that she had denied me this opportunity. Both puzzled by and grateful for this shift, I announced at the next service that I was back in the race. The next day one of the newspapers headlined their story "Flake Flip Flops." If there is one thing that is characteristic of a bootstrapper it is the ability to be flexible enough to adapt to change on the spur of the moment.

A special election was held June 10, 1986, to choose someone to finish out the remaining six months of Mr. Addabbo's term. Being a novice to politics, I learned some important lessons. When you are a political outsider and take on a party apparatus that has already predetermined who should fill the seat, you must be ready for a fight. Because of the hard work and diligence of a dauntless grassroots organization, election night ended with a victory. But the absentee ballots for the primary had been mailed without my name printed on them, so when they were counted, I did not have enough votes to win. I went to bed a victor and woke up a loser. Feeling that the election had been stolen from us, my supporters, who had now become a legion of bootstrappers, prepared for the next battle. I immediately announced my candidacy for the Democratic primary to be held in September 1986. At the same time, we initiated court action to argue that the omission of my name from the absentee ballots should disqualify them. Although we did not win in court, we won overwhelming victories in the Democratic primary in September and the general election in November. I was officially seated in the U.S. Congress in January 1987.

In December 1987, trouble began to haunt me. The administrative assistant who had been terminated sent a series of letters to me, officers of the church, bishops, and other people throughout the denomination. The letters contained many threats and false accusations, including charges of sexual harassment and financial improprieties. Obviously my new prominence and political success had brought a level of public attention that made me an easy target.

In April 1988, I was told that the Justice Department was initiating a federal investigation, at which time a lawsuit was also filed on the sexual harassment charges. Additionally, the person I beat in the primary had been appointed to the State Commission on Investigation, which has the responsibility for investigating public officials! At the time, I had no idea that these three issues were related.

In the A.M.E. Church, every pastor is required to attend an annual conference for either an appointment or a reappointment to a congregation. I was expecting to be reappointed to Allen, but the swirling winds of the developing legal crisis put that in jeopardy. The bishop, in an attempt to resolve the issues before the May conference, insisted that I meet with the former employee.

I set up the meeting in a public place, a conference room in LaGuardia Airport, between the two of us and our lawyers. However, my lawyer appeared, but hers did not. Our meeting was leaked to the press, and photographers from several newspapers suddenly materialized. Realizing that this was a setup, I turned to leave, but unfortunately, a photographer had already taken my picture. It appeared on the cover of a local newspaper, which wrote that I was departing a "secret, clandestine" meeting. Of course there was nothing secret about this meeting at LaGuardia, but public figures are often the victims of press fabrications and exaggerations. Several times following that disastrous meeting, the bishop tried to get me to call my accuser, which I refused to do even though I knew the matter would now come before the conference. I refused not out of disrespect but because my new lawyer—whom I had hired to address the federal issues—and I assumed, and later confirmed that our telephones had been tapped. I believe that God was truly guiding my actions at that point. I learned quickly that in high-profile cases like this, "innocence in not necessarily your best defense."

Elaine and I share a very close relationship with our four children, and during this period, we were even more banded together trying to work our way through this crisis. My greatest challenge was to be husband, father, and pastor with my own family while also being the spiritual leader for the congregation and tending to the congressional needs of the district. Many members of the congregation wanted to declare all-out war on those they considered our adversaries, even suggesting that I remove them from the church roster. I would not heed those suggestions nor allow them to engage in internal warfare. In spite of the problems, we were still a church, and as its leader, my obligation was to hold us together. Elaine was worried most about the kids' education and how it would affect them if we got involved in a long, drawn-out trial. We were receiving death threats, and the church was receiving bomb threats. There were also threats to kidnap our children, which meant they had to be transported to ball games, dance rehearsals, and other events by the New York City Police Department. In Washington, the Capital Police met me at the gate in the airport and escorted me to my office. It was a stressful season, as I flew back and forth to Washington each day. But in the true spirit of a bootstrapper, I would not allow adversity to distract me from the work that God had given me to do. There were too many things needing to be done that could not await the outcome of the investigation or the decision of the conference.

The A.M.E. conference was held in Buffalo, New York, in May 1988. A few days before the conference, the former pastor of Allen, in what I suppose was an attempt to be helpful, called me on behalf of the former employee and stated that the case would come to an end if I paid her 125,000 dollars. He indicated that there were others who would assist him in raising the funds if I would agree to it. But I could not agree to such an arrangement for two reasons. First, I was innocent, and second, I was now aware that there was a federal probe and such an arrangement, even if the money came from other sources, would have put me in jeopardy. When I ultimately learned of the wiretaps, once again I realized that

God was guiding my actions. With that, I waited for the bishop to make his decision. He reappointed me to Allen.

Although we did not think the investigation would end in a trial, we were better off being safe than sorry. We hired Gus Newman and Theodore Wells as our lawyers. It's a good thing too, because in August 1990, we were indicted. Elaine and I were charged with an assortment of felonies stemming from the former employee's and former officers' allegations. It was hard enough that I was being charged, but it seemed impossible that Elaine, who had no dealings with the finances of the church, was charged as well. A few days before the indictment, the prosecutors, Elaine, and our lawyers met to discuss her situation. She was offered the chance to have her case dropped in exchange for convincing me to plead guilty to several felonies. Elaine is the most honest person I have ever met, and even though she dreaded the trial, she refused to accept the offer because she knew we were innocent. Elaine is a wonderful, spirit-filled woman, and when she felt that the family was being threatened, she did what was natural for her: she entered into a period of prayer, fasting, and meditation. Her resolve had never been more obvious that it was during the trial.

As the case moved forward, numerous church employees, officers, and leaders received calls from people who were being subpoenaed to testify before the grand jury. Since we were under investigation, we did not engage them in conversation on the matter but referred them directly to our lawyers. When the newspapers began reporting the details of (secret) grand jury testimony, we realized that the former employee had copied checks, memos, file reports, and other data prior to leaving her position. The newspaper accounts also named those who were testifying against us, which included the former church accountant. We were in a daily state of nervous anticipation, never knowing what would be reported in the newspaper on any given day or who else was involved in the conspiracy. Of course the harassment suit was also moving forward at the same time, which necessitated another set of lawyers, Andrew and Kenneth Fisher, who handled it. Because the congregation knew my reputation, both spiritually and morally, they continued their full support of the Allen ministry and my family. A number of prayer groups emerged, and the remaining officers closed ranks, believing that in God's own time this process would end in our favor.

During this period, I focused on work, sermon preparation, and family as I maintained an active prayer life and weekly fasting. Fasting was natural for me, because I do it once a week starting on Friday evenings and ending after the last worship service on Sunday. It allows me to stay in a meditative state while enjoying the benefit of physical cleansing. Fasting also helps me maintain a consciousness of God's presence in all aspects of my life. I recommend this practice, but if you have a medical condition, be sure that you check with your doctor before beginning a fast.

In the midst of my church and congressional duties, I was also working to complete my doctor of ministry degree at United Theological Seminary in Dayton, Ohio. As much as I believe that a large number of a bootstrapper's successes are attributable to the individual investment of time, energy, and resources, I also believe that without God none of it would be possible.

Prior to the trial's beginning, the former employee whose accusations started the investigation died in a tragic automobile accident. Therefore, our lawyers were able to subpoena records that contained information regarding the case that was not a part of the grand jury testimony. From this information we learned, to our surprise, of some other people's involvement in the case. To this day, I have not confronted them because of my resolve to get beyond this wilderness moment in my life. I did realize that if the bishop's directives had been followed, additional charges would probably have been brought against me. Further meetings with the former employee could have generated charges of harassment of a witness, obstruction of justice, or a host of others, not because of willful intent on my part but because of the weakness of the Justice Department's case. Entrapment was their only hope of winning the case. We have seen a similar thing happen in the case of President Bill Clinton. "There, but for the grace of God, go I" is a most appropriate statement. I truly believe that the spirit of the Lord was guiding me.

For three and a half weeks, we were in court every day. Throughout the trial, the prosecutors made no accusations against Elaine, although she was charged with two felonies. So, after two and a half weeks, her lawyer asked the judge to drop her from the case. The judge indicated his willingness to consider the motion and further indicated that at this point, the prosecution had made no case against either of us.

By the end of the third week, the prosecution's witnesses, both present and past officers of the church, had been called to testify. They were presented with every single check that they had written to me and verified that these were either salaries that the church paid me or gifts. The whole trial was quite an ordeal; not only were we pained and hurt, but the accusers seemed to be equally pained. I don't think that they had expected the situation to go that far. Even as they testified against me, their testimony on the witness stand did not support the charges that they had made before the grand jury. It is strange, but I could not hate them and still don't. As a matter of fact, I embrace them whenever the opportunity presents itself. One guiding principle in my life is that forgiving is helpful. It has helped me to get on with a life that has had measurable quantitative and qualitative successes since the trial has ended. The writing of this book is a means of bringing some closure to this chapter of painful experiences. I find comfort in the ability to forgive and move on. I am convinced that this whole episode was all a part of God's plan for our life and for the future growth and development of the Allen Church. The trial helped clear the air and helped to move the church into a higher spiritual realm in preparation for the subsequent work and ministry that had been revealed to us, and that we have been able to perform.

Financial Setbacks

By the end of the third week, the judge announced that he was going to dismiss the entire case out of court if the prosecutors couldn't come up with real evidence of wrongdoing. Tuesday morning of the following week, the prosecutors requested a dismissal of the case. Our relief and joy were so overwhelming that both Elaine and I broke into tears. We were so happy that the worst ordeal of our lives was finally over. Sitting in that courtroom day after day had, needless to say, been emotionally draining. The members of Allen rallied around us from beginning to end of the ordeal. We felt so loved and blessed that our hearts had no place for hate.

All total, our legal fees came to about 1.2 million dollars. Half of the fees went toward preparing for the trial. Our lawyers had to talk to every potential witness, and they hired private detectives and did everything necessary to get us ready in case we were called to testify. We still owe about four hundred thousand dollars for legal representation in a trial that should never have taken place.

Some wanted us to charge that the government had brought the case based on race or politics, but we refused to make that accusation because the issues emanated from within the church, which is predominantly African American. I personally get tired of everything that happens to a Black person being called racial, because that jeopardizes the credibility of situations where race is truly the predominant factor. Since the sixties it has been popular to claim a racial basis in an inordinate number of cases where a Black has been charged. Unfortunately, the more people scream about race in cases that are not, in fact, race based, the more difficult it becomes to adjudicate those cases where race is actually the underlying issue.

After requesting and being granted dismissal of their own case against us, the Justice Department brought civil charges, which I believe reflected their need to justify a three-year investigation using American taxpayers' money. All of the civil issues have now been resolved by payments of fines and penalties. In true bootstrapper fashion, I went back to Washington and remained in Congress until I retired in 1997. I also finished my doctor of ministry degree in 1994 and led the congregation in the construction of the twenty-three-million-dollar cathedral, which was completed in 1997.

Lessons Learned

I can't say that crisis always makes people more humble, although I know that mine made me a more compassionate pastor. But, a crisis does have a way of reminding you of your own mortality. God is no respecter of persons. Anyone can suffer defeat or get knocked down. That does not mean that you do not rise to fight another day. Anyone can suffer an emotional, financial, or spiritual death. But remember that resurrection, restoration, and reconciliation are always a possibility. It does not matter if you are the president of a bank, a corporate executive, a teacher's aide, a homemaker, or an entertainer. In every life, some rain will fall. The question is, How will you weather the storm?

My ordeal strengthened me and made me a better person, pastor, husband, and father. I now know more than I ever wanted to know about the legal system. I learned a lot, though I would not wish the experience on anybody. But, if it happens to you, don't let it take away your bootstrapper spirit.

I learned the power of forgiveness. It not only releases the person who has committed an act against you but also releases you to be free of feelings of hate that require energy that can be put to better use.

During this episode in my life, I never lost sight of my goals, my vision for Allen Church, New York, or the nation. Through it all, I kept on going and doing what I know best: working, praying, preaching, and fasting. It has paid off. The results are seen both in my personal life with my family and in the Allen Church.

During the trial, on most Sundays there would be standing room only, with crowds filling the twelve-hundred-seat church auditorium at all three services. Some of those people were inquisitive because of what they had read in the papers; but many more joined the church because amid all the negativity in the media accounts, there was always some testimony about the good works that the Allen A.M.E. Church and I were doing for the community. We've come a long way since the trial ended in 1991. Because the Lord has blessed our bootstrapping efforts so much, our twenty-five-hundred-seat cathedral cannot now contain all the people who want to attend our church—even though we've scheduled three services each Sunday. We are a spirit-filled, Bible-believing faith community who know that we are conquerors who are victorious and reigning with Jesus.

I am continually reassured that God has a purpose for my life and that I am doing God's work. Bootstrappers believe in their heart that no weapon formed against them can prevail. So come on, all you boot-strappers—pull yourselves up, forgive those who may have mistreated you, step out of your hate, and learn to love yourself even as you learn to love others. I am a witness that such forgiveness will help you to go on with your life rather than allow you to be destroyed by the pain that others inflict on you. God knows how much you can bear.

Lee Iacocca said, "It's a good thing God doesn't let you look a year or two into the future, or you might be sorely tempted to shoot yourself. But He's a charitable Lord: He only lets you see one day at a time. When times get tough, there's no choice except to take a deep breath, carry on, and do the best you can."

Pull Yourself Up by Your Bootstraps . . .

If you are going to survive your crises, you must first be willing to learn from the experiences that you gain from them. Sometimes it takes a crisis to wake us up to an inefficiency or flaw in the way we've been doing things. Ask yourself some questions:

1. What is the worst possible thing that could come from this crisis? How would this outcome affect your life? Your status in the community? Your self-esteem? Your overall plans?
2. What have you done to resolve the crisis? Did it work?
3. What are some outrageous, creative things that you could do to resolve this situation?
4. How is this crisis affecting your health? How can you maintain a healthy equilibrium in the midst of your crisis?
5. Who has been advising you in this matter? Have they been truly helpful or not? Is this the time to be talking to anyone? Would it be better for you right now to keep your business to yourself?

Revisit Your Plan

Do you still feel that you are on the right track, or did you take a wrong turn somewhere? Are your goals realistic? Do they fit in with what you believe to be your life mission? Take a hard look at your plan. Only you can decide what to do at this juncture in your journey. After some time spent in your soul's closet, you may decide to persevere through the storm. On the other hand, you may decide to retreat. If you decide to retreat, ask yourself if you've done everything that could be done in the situation. If there is absolutely no hope for a resolution to the crisis, it might be time to throw in the towel and cut your losses. You never know. Often, when you're down for the count and there's nothing left for you to do except depend on God for a miracle, that is exactly what happens.

Bootstrappers have such high levels of integrity and endurance that it often takes much pain and suffering for them to even consider giving up. But sometimes that is exactly what you must do. Even if you feel you have failed, lift up your head and get ready for the next challenge. You are still alive, so there is still much more that you can do. Take time to reflect on the lessons that you learned from your experiences. Write down what you've learned about yourself and the situation.

Most important, set aside some time to reflect on matters as you renew your faith in God. No matter how bad the crisis, do not let desperation steal your belief that even in the midst of this storm, God's helpful forces in the universe are moving on your behalf. Don't let your crisis steal your joy. Learn how to rejoice for the good things that are happening in your life even as you deal with the negative aspects of your crisis.

Help Others

Do you know someone who is in the midst of a crisis? If you've ever been in a crisis, come through it, and learned from the experience, then you're in the perfect position to help someone else through their crisis. Today, call that person and offer your assistance. Don't feel offended if your offer is not appreciated. Some people value privacy above all else, and that is their right. If that is the case, respect their privacy. But if the individual is open to assistance, ask how you can help. Let the person tell you what is needed. Be a good listener, and if they'll let you, pray. Remember, when two or more come together in God's name, God is right there with them.

PART 4

✳

ACCELERATE!

This section of the book is for the person who is moving in the slow lane and can't seem to get ahead. I love driving, but I hate taking trips during the height of the travel season. The highways seem to always be under construction, backing up the flow of traffic. The rest stops are crowded, making it impossible to duck in and out quickly. There are generally too many trucks to contend with. I set my timetable before I start, and these situations make it impossible for me to stay on schedule.

My most recent car trips have been between Atlanta and New York. I drove at night because I have discovered that the highway is pretty clear between 11:00 P.M. and 7:00 A.M. Generally, there is no radar, construction, or heavy traffic to contend with, so I can make good time. I travel along vast stretches of highway with my thoughts and CD's. I don't join in caravans because I believe it is dangerous to try following anyone or have them follow you.

In many ways, this is also how I live my life. I am constantly accelerating, trying to stay ahead of the traffic. Most often, I am the leader of the pack, looking for ways to help make life's journey easier for those who are in need. I am determined to make the road better, safer, and smoother for the generations who will follow me. I don't have time to sit in the traffic of discontent, failure, discord, and disappointment. I want others to learn the joy of moving in the fast lane; therefore, I get a little upset when people have the gifts, talents, intellect, and ability to move faster but choose to stay in the slow lane. Why can't they realize that by going so slowly, they are not only endangering themselves but also slowing down others who are trying to move forward with their lives? Why don't they move when I blow my horn or flash my lights? Don't they understand that they are retarding my progress and slowing me down? That's why I work while others sleep: I can get so much more done by driving, planning, or writing at night.

I learned the value of working at night at the Uvalde Rock and Asphalt Company, where my father worked for a number of years. He was able to get summer jobs for me for two years. We made asphalt and vinyl asbestos floor tiles. I have calluses on my hands today from grading and boxing tile for shipment. Periodically I was assigned to the graveyard shift, 11:00 P.M. to 7:00 A.M. The more senior workers hated the night shift, so the junior members had free reign of the plant during those hours. We were often told that we produced more work than the day shift, because there were fewer distractions.

As I am writing this section of the book, it is 4:00 A.M. I have discovered that one way to raise the level of my productivity is to take advantage of the time when I will not be interrupted. Whenever I am working on something big, such as my doctoral thesis or this project, I have learned to sleep fewer hours and sometimes work through the night. Acceleration requires a lot of discipline and sacrifice. It is the way of the bootstrapper.

Many people prefer to put their lives on cruise control. They feel secure keeping the same job all their life, even though they are unhappy with it. They watch the whiz kids fly past them for one promotion after another. They think that they deserve the promotion because of their seniority, but they refuse to accelerate. To get ahead in life you cannot be content to sit and wait for things to happen. You must learn to accelerate so that you can be better positioned to move forward when your big break comes. For me, staying in Congress would have been easy, but leaving Congress has allowed me to accelerate to another level and to use my mental, emotional, physical, and spiritual powers in many new and creative ways as a speaker, columnist, and author.

As a society, we stand on the threshold of a new era of human understanding and achievement. We are finally learning what the ancients knew—that we are amazing creations made by God with mental, emotional, physical, and spiritual powers. Supercomputers, which can make billions of calculations in one second, cannot compare to the ability of a fully charged mind to dream, think, create, invent, discover, and innovate. Even the greatest prodigies and geniuses humanity has ever produced didn't use their minds to their full capacity.

God gave us 100 percent brain power, but our old childhood programs and social norms straitjacket our perception so that we see only our limitations. That's why, when Marva Collins first started teaching students with her unique methods, many of the old educational order criticized her. They said that what she was doing was impossible.

Never tell a dreamer that anything is impossible, because all things are possible with God acting as a force for good in your mind, heart, body, spirit, and actions. If you walked into Marva Collins's classroom, you too would be stunned. Young children aren't supposed to be reading college-level texts, especially not African American children from the inner city. Yet, there they are, learning how to discipline themselves according to the principles of Plato's *Republic* and at the age of three learning words from a book called *Vocabulary for the College-Bound Student*.

Even though they've been branded by bigots as inferior and mentally deficient, children in Africa learn three or four languages, including English. American-born children are deprived of the joy of learning a second, third, and fourth language primarily because of the intolerance of their parents and the low expectations of society at large. To speak another language requires that you think in it, and people are terrified of opening their minds to a new way of thinking. But that is precisely how we begin to use the amazing facilities with which we've been blessed. In recognition of this problem, we introduce a second language to every child at Allen Christian School, starting at the age of three. They overcome the fear of learning a second language at such an early stage of life that it becomes natural.

Changes in Education

Undoubtedly the most controversial issue I adopted while in Congress and continue to promote is school choice. School choice includes a wide range of educational options, such as tuition vouchers, charter schools, open enrollment in public schools, magnet schools—even home schooling and paraschooling. The purpose of the school choice movement is to put the responsibility for educating children back into the hands of parents. School choice is an unstoppable force that is currently coming against the status quo of public education, and the reverberations will be felt well beyond the year 2000.

I decided to support school choice because of the millions of poor children who are being let down by public education in America. The guarantee that the Supreme Court made in its ruling in the 1954 Brown versus the Kansas City Board of Education case was "equal opportunity for all children." This guarantee has not been honored in most urban schools and many of the other areas where poorer students are not getting a quality education. The problem with public education today is that it lacks any meaningful competition. Public education has a virtual monopoly on molding the minds of our children. As a result, studies report that too many children in public schools are reading below their grade level, dropping out, and performing poorly on national tests. I submit that the problem is not with the children but with the system. Charter schools and vouchers, both public and private, may be the last hope for bringing equality to education.

School choice is a powerful way for parents to assume the responsibility for educating their own children. This is family bootstrapping at its best. In a free and democratic society, for parents to not have a choice in how and where their children are to be educated signals a serious flaw in the system that must and will be corrected.

Use Your Brain Power

As I have said, we use only a tiny portion of our brain power. Billions of people have died across the ages never having realized that they were more than what they thought they were. Nor have we used our social power to full capacity—nowhere near. We have 100 percent social power, and although from time to time we get together to use that force for the good, we've not even begun to tap into our total collective ability. This is not socialism or communism but "where two or three are gathered together in My name, I am there in the midst of them." And when God is in the midst of a group project, nothing can stop it.

If as individuals we use only, say, 10 percent of our brain power, as a society, we've used about 1 percent. In fact, given all the wars, rumors of war, weapons of war lying in wait, and even more destructive weapons on the drawing board, I'd say we're at a deficit in social power.

For all the good one church might do, wars in distant lands rage on in the name of religion. For all the good one nonprofit organization might do, global terrorism threatens to destroy everything we've built.

We are given only a short time on the earth to dream our dreams and execute our plans. That's why I feel such a sense of urgency. I am well aware of my mortality; however, I also know that God has given me everything I need to make my life meaningful, exciting, and productive. I've done a lot, but I have not reached the pinnacle of my abilities. I've not manifested all of my dreams. Nor have you.

If you've been faithfully executing your plan and have even achieved some goals, congratulations! You should feel good about your accomplishments. In this final section, I will challenge you to do more by accelerating your pace so you can run with the bootstrappers.

Overnight Delivery

Fred Smith's instructors at Harvard Business School said it couldn't be done. He believed it could. Smith had written a research paper examining the packaged delivery business and proposed the revolutionary idea that small packages could be delivered to their destination overnight. His instructors dismissed this preposterous idea with a near-failing grade. Smith, undaunted, went on to stake his inheritance on the purchase of a jet, took on none other than the entire U.S. Postal Service, and created Federal Express. Smith revolutionized not only the way mail is delivered but how we do business. He sped it up, and he was instrumental in taking us global. Most important, he raised our expectations of what's possible.

Who would have thought that Smith's dream could have been improved upon? But then fax machines and e-mail came along, and the world has not been the same since.

Innovations such as overnight delivery, fax machines, and e-mail are not just progress—they are accelerations. To accelerate means to speed up, go faster. When progress is combined with acceleration, we are required to reevaluate our old ways of doing things. We are required to change our thinking and actions. Even our vocabularies change. This is what's going on right now in every field of human endeavor. This massive change is called a *paradigm shift*. Not only is the unstoppable, combined force of progress and acceleration obliterating the old order, but our very perceptual framework is changing.

This massive change is absolutely necessary to effectively function in the new world that we see emerging before us. The year 2000 is an arbitrary number and year; the new era, however, is not. It is real. The question is, Will you keep up and master the new technologies and thought, or will you be left behind? Y2K is not the primary concern of the average person, who knows that civilization will survive. What we don't know is what form it will take or in which direction it will go.

Admittedly, I am technologically challenged. I have some residual computer fear; however, I have every intention of conquering it. Changes are coming so rapidly that I will not otherwise be able to keep up. Some of the older people I know will not go to an ATM machine to get money from the bank. They are still looking for the bank assistant or transacting business at the teller window. They don't trust machines to handle and record their money correctly, so they always deal with a human bank teller. However, there may come a day when banks will no longer use human tellers because they will no longer be necessary. In fact, some satellite bank locations already function with skeletal staffing, forerunners of things to come. We have come a long way since the Depression. Would you believe that my Depression-era parents paid all their bills with money orders because they did not trust banks?

Will you keep up, or will you get left behind? We are being challenged to access more brain power and become true multidimensional human beings. I'm talking not about parallel universes and quantum physics but about our God-given ability to creatively and expertly handle all of our powers—spiritual, mental, physical, and emotional— and all of our many responsibilities at once.

When companies engage in strategic planning and sales forecasting, they take into consideration the macroeconomic context. They analyze trends and then seek ways to anticipate and capitalize on them. Way back in 1968–69, when I was with Xerox, they had already started globalization through their Xerox-Rand Division, which covered Europe.

I recommend that you begin the practice of personal globalization. I'm no prophet—however, given the innovations, discoveries, and ideological shifts of the past two decades, we can make a good estimate of what the future will bring. Consider these trends in your own planning.

While they may appear disturbing at first, remember that change and crisis always contain within them the seeds of opportunity.

Changes in the Workforce

When some of the largest corporations in the world started slashing people off their payrolls, America panicked. This was not how it was supposed to go. We had been taught that if you attend school, work hard, and pay your dues, you'll have job security and retirement benefits for as long as you live. Then the unthinkable happened. Sears cut 50,000 from its workforce; AT&T, 40,000; IBM, 35,000; Boeing, 28,000. And it hasn't ended. No one really knows how many layoffs there have been because of downsizing. Conservative estimates say around 3.1 million since 1989; *The New York Times* says 21.2 million. Whatever you want to call it—downsizing, rightsizing, or getting fired—when it comes to corporate America, everyone is disposable and expendable.

Downsizing has hit many people hard, especially those close to retirement. In the July/August 1996 issue of *Mother Jones*, former corporate "hit man" Alan Downs admits that often downsizing campaigns are done with little care or thought to their effect on the employees—those who leave and those who stay. Many loyal employees give their lives to the company store, only to be kicked out just before retirement benefits are due to kick in. Says Downs, "Once I sat in a room at AT&T where employees' fates were decided by moving their photos—attached to small magnets—around on a large panel similar to a chessboard."

I would like to think that this is not the prevalent attitude among those who are involved in mergers and acquisitions. However, you should prepare yourself as if this were indeed the case by developing all of the innate potential that is within you. You must develop new options for yourself. Your survival requires that rather than feeling sorry for yourself, you get back in the fast lane as quickly as possible.

Also contributing to the massive change in the workforce is the elimination of "equal opportunity" initiatives and laws. Affirmative action as a social vehicle for correcting past injustices is on the respirator, as are quotas, set-asides, welfare, and other social programs. Those initiatives were designed to level a playing field that was unjust and discriminatory. The playing field is now better, as evidenced by the growing Black middle class, but there is still more that needs to be done. Although our basic mind-sets have been broadened, there is still too much discrimination to consider ourselves a "color-blind" society. We know that it's evil to enslave people and to discriminate on the basis of race, ethnic background, gender, or physical ability. So, we should all make the effort to work together to assure that this great nation accommodates the needs of all of its people regardless of any of those factors. The future affirmative action program that America must embrace is not merely a rhetorical "mend it, don't end it" but one that is based upon the principles that guide this nation. Affirmative action must also embrace competition, standards, and productivity. Now that the legal mechanisms have created a more level playing field, the final vestiges of prior discrimination can be removed only by investing in people through quality education, homeownership, commercial development, and other programs that eliminate the need for social programs.

We should not fear the changes that have occurred and the changes that are to come in the workforce. With downsizing comes the opportunity of a better job or even self-employment. What corporate America has done to create bigger profits for shareholders, God has done to create opportunity for millions. And as soon as we begin to wield our social power to advocate for such important issues as affordable health care and fairer practices in lending laws, the institutions will have to respond to the needs of the people.

We should fear bigotry, whether individual or institutional. We must continue to fight against injustice. We must move those mountains that prevent us from achieving our goals. At the same time, we must individually continue to pursue our dreams. The scriptures state, "Faith the size of a mustard seed can move mountains."

Medical Advances

If you knew you would live to be 120, how differently would you live your life? Think seriously about this, because longer life spans are on the way. Diet and exercise, stress relief, and other preventive measures have long been promoted as a way to arrest the process of aging. Also, researchers are gaining new insight into the genetic roots of aging, and as they get closer to our cellular fountains of youth, more drugs and surgical procedures will certainly be on the way. Since HMOs will be a major player in the field of health, it is hoped that they will provide a level of care that supports our desire to live as long as possible. They cannot be allowed to deny access to medical care based on cost and profits. Their primary concern must be the preservation of life.

I believe that perceptual shifts, spirituality, and fellowship will play equally critical roles in enhancing longevity and the quality of life. In my church and particularly in the senior citizens' home we operate, I am confronted with the reality of how dismally we age in this country. While we're younger we should live healthfully and do everything possible to keep ourselves strong enough to ward off senility, arthritis, hypertension, loss of hearing and eyesight, and other symptoms normally associated with aging. The best medical care in the world is preventive maintenance. We should not wait until we become old to change habits that are deleterious to our health. There are cultures around the world whose members not only live to advanced ages but do not succumb to traditional aging symptoms. So why do we?

Much has been written about the alienation and isolation that many Americans feel and how this leads to depression. Prolonged depression compromises the immune system and can lead to a whole host of stress-related diseases. Some researchers boldly state that most illnesses and diseases have their roots in stress, poor dietary habits, and a sedentary lifestyle.

We must assume responsibility for the quality of our health, because affordable health care for all may not be a reality in this country anytime soon. We must advocate for health care, but we must also take responsibility for our own health. By practicing prevention, we keep illness and disease at a minimum. By becoming proactive through daily exercise, healthy eating habits, and stress relief, we become healthier and fit. And by praying, fellowshiping with others, and changing our perception of aging, we'll probably add a few years to our lives.

A daily prayer regimen and regular fellowship with like-minded people will make you feel better. A change in your perception can truly change your life. Why do you fear old age? When you consider the alternative, you should rejoice that you have been blessed to live so long. So, start looking forward to getting older, knowing that the best is yet to come. You'll see dramatic changes in your body, mind, and outlook on life.

I've been fortunate to work and fellowship with seniors in their sixties, seventies, eighties, and nineties who are vibrant, healthy, and full of life. They are my role models. They demonstrate my belief that God would have us all be healthy and long-lived. Some of them still have the bootstrapper spirit, proving the old adage "Age is but a number."

Henry and Geneva Smith are an inspiration to me because they have not allowed age to control their activities. Henry is a retired postal worker who recently celebrated his eightieth birthday, and Geneva is a retired cosmetologist. They are an exciting couple who enjoy life by taking frequent trips together and participating in numerous community activities. They were very active in my congressional campaigns, doing every conceivable job. They marched in parades, helped coordinate fund-raisers, decorated cars and facilities, ran errands, distributed literature—anything. They do volunteer work on a daily basis at the Allen Community Senior Citizens Nutrition Program, where 250 meals are served. In addition, Geneva spends Friday mornings at the church with a group called The Busy Bees, who process the Sunday bulletins and prepare bulk mailings. The Smiths are too busy helping others to spend their time complaining about aging. Rather than slowing down, they have accelerated their pace as they move briskly through the octogenarian stage of their lives.

Personal Acceleration

The beauty of bootstrapping is that its principles and processes can be adapted to rural, urban, suburban, industrial, or high-tech economies. Whether you're raising a family on the farm or in the city, whether climbing the corporate ladder or starting a company on the World Wide Web, the bootstrapping approach described in this book will enable you to achieve your goals, regardless of the changes that are occurring in society.

In order for you to succeed, you must take bootstrapping to the next level of achievement, which is personal acceleration. This means doing for yourself rather than waiting for someone else to do for you. If anyone embodies the concept of personal acceleration, it's Oprah Winfrey. Given her troubled childhood, Winfrey should not have achieved the level of success that she has, but she continues to amaze. Born in Kosciusko, Mississippi, on January 29, 1954, she was poor and abused as a child. Yet, even at age nineteen, when she was crowned Miss Black Tennessee, she began to demonstrate the drive and determination that would later make her a household name. In 1973, she became a newscaster in Nashville, and she then moved to a Boston station.

Oprah moved to Chicago to host a TV program called *AM Chicago*. In less than a year, the show became number one. Chicago's ABC affiliate knew they had a winner. Management repositioned Winfrey against Phil Donahue and renamed her show *The Oprah Winfrey Show*. Within a brief time, she revolutionized television with her self-revealing, sympathetic style of talk.

Winfrey has matured personally and professionally. Her challenges with her weight and body image have been fully chronicled, as has her work as an actor and executive producer. Today, you can find her gracing the cover of numerous magazines, and as the chair of Harpo Entertainment Group, she is one of only a few women in television and film to own her own production studio.

Winfrey is watched by millions, and if she wanted to, she could rest on her laurels. She's worth five hundred million dollars. Some might say, What else is there to do?

Using her show as a forum, Winfrey has set out to enlighten and heal America. Signaling a major departure from the run-of-the-mill talk-show themes, in September 1996 she started Oprah's Book Club. Books featured on the Book Club *always* end up on the *New York Times* best-sellers list. Using a television format, she's gotten America reading again. Later that same year, Winfrey was named one of "America's Twenty-Five Most Influential People" by *People* magazine.

At the beginning of the following season, she announced the creation of Oprah's Angel Network, in which she encourages and spearheads Good Samaritan efforts. The Angel Network has raised more than a million dollars for worthy causes.

A renaissance is the time of renewal that follows a dark age. Oprah Winfrey is the quintessential Renaissance woman, having lifted herself up to overcome poverty and an abusive childhood. Personal acceleration is about achieving mastery and doing more. It is about taking a leadership role in helping others achieve their potential.

Virginia Stewart is another person who demonstrates daily what can happen to a person who knows the value of personal acceleration. She grew up in Manhattan in the fifties, with dreams of one day becoming an artist. While she was in junior high school, she was discouraged by teachers from pursuing art as a career. She wanted to attend the famous New York High School of Music and Art, but her counselor refused to provide her with the information for the entrance exam. That counselor made a judgment that an African American woman should be content to pursue a career as a secretary. But Virginia was determined to become an artist, so with assistance from one of her teachers, a Mrs. Blum (who felt that she had talent), she applied to and was accepted by the Washington Irving High School. She enrolled in their fine arts program. When she graduated, she received a scholarship to the National Academy of Fine Arts in New York.

Since Virginia was on a partial scholarship for the first year, she worked part time in the school's art store. The school was so impressed with her artistic abilities that she was awarded a two-year scholarship. Although fine art was her first love, Virginia made the decision to major in textile design in order to prepare herself for the job market. After graduation, she continued to pursue fine arts part time, as a freelancer. She worked for various art studios doing fabric designs for wallpaper, shower curtains, slipcovers, and so on. Some of her designs have been published in the *New York Times* and in *Women's Wear Daily*.

In 1982, Virginia's life took a dramatic turn. She learned she had breast cancer and had to have a mastectomy. But rather than slowing down, she accelerated her pace. Even while undergoing chemotherapy treatments, she kept working. In 1984, her husband passed when he was suddenly stricken by an aneurysm. She still did not slow down. She began counseling other women in the church and community who were victims of breast cancer. Although Virginia has volunteered many hours of her time working with others, she never abandoned her art work. The new cathedral of Allen A.M.E. Church is graced with a window that she designed. She is an excellent model of a bootstrapper who has achieved success because of her willingness to accelerate at times when it would have been easier to slow down or give up.

Most people who are successful have learned to accelerate to the highest level possible in their pursuit of goals that they have set for themselves. Goal-oriented bootstrappers know that intellect and talent alone are not necessarily synonymous with success. The ability to take one's God-given intelligence and talents to a higher level through personal acceleration makes the difference. If you are in life's slow lane, functioning beneath your potential, then it's time for you to accelerate. Read books that can expand your knowledge. Take on some task that is not easy but offers a challenge and requires you to perform in some area outside of your familiar turf. Look at what others have done who are successes in your profession. Don't get jealous or insecure and move further back into the slow lane, but accelerate by examining what you can do to reach the heights that you desire. Move into the fast lane, even if you periodically have to slow down. You don't want to go so fast that you crash; neither do you want to go so slow that everyone passes you by.

Institutional Acceleration

As I travel, I not only look ahead, but I constantly look in the rearview mirror to see what's behind me. In my pastorate, I examine the successful ministries of others and invite pastors whose ministries are outstanding to preach and teach at Allen. When they share their experiences with the congregation, Allen's members realize that as great as we believe our ministry is, there are so many other things that we need to add. Acceleration is essential to keeping the ministry vital, visible, and visionary. We are always looking for new means of meeting the needs of our church and community.

Businesses succeed because they analyze market trends and make adjustments. They accelerate the production of products when they know a competitor might have a new one forthcoming that could blow them out of the marketplace. The price of the refusal to accelerate is stagnation. When you stagnate, your life ceases to be active, your mind becomes dull, and your natural gifts and talents atrophy.

Your mission, should you choose to accept it, is to accelerate by moving into life's fast lane and using, to the best of your ability, every gift that God has placed at your disposal. That is the way of the bootstrapper.

ACTION STEP 7:
TAKE THE LEAD

Leadership is the art of inspiring people to achieve.

Leadership is a noble calling, but it is also a difficult one. People often aspire to leadership positions because they see the glamour but not the hard work involved. However, being in charge is not a popularity contest. Heading a family, a community, or a corporation often means shouldering the burdens alone. It's not easy taking the first few steps into the unknown: seeing what no one else sees and having the courage to act upon that vision, sacrificing immediate gratification for the greater good, and making life-and-death decisions that will affect others.

There are two types of leaders: those who protest and those who lead by taking action and building institutions. Protesters are known by their fiery rhetoric, which stirs emotion in the hearts of their listeners. Unfortunately, they seldom produce anything tangible and of lasting value. We live in the era of the million-man, million-woman, million-youth march. It would probably be of greater value to have a million-dollar march. Imagine every marcher giving a dollar to start a national investment fund to rebuild America's deteriorated urban communities! Think about it. Imagine what could be done if each person gave ten dollars or one hundred dollars! That would represent a major capital investment. That is the basic approach that has worked extremely well at Allen Church. A lot of people tithe and give offerings, and with the six million dollars raised annually, we are able to invest in community, economic, and educational development. Leaders must do more than get their followers excited. They must engage them in ways that prepare them so that when they leave the march the momentum leads to some tangible result.

Leaders who take action are bootstrappers. They challenge themselves and others to stretch beyond their limits. They are often obsessed with leaving a lasting legacy. They are consciousness raisers, institution builders, money makers, and policy changers. Action-oriented, legacy-leaving leadership is what we'll be discussing in this section.

Presiding at the head of a family, corporation, church, or organization does not automatically bestow a person with leadership abilities. Nor does the ability to garner media attention. The leader must stand boldly, even in the face of opposition, giving direction and guidance as people try to navigate their way through life's troublesome waters. True leaders must see their work as a calling.

Leaders and followers generally have a love-hate relationship. When things go wrong, it's leaders who take the punishment, but they are often taken for granted when things are going well. Leaders who are chosen by their followers can survive a crisis if they have established a good track record. On the other hand, those who have merely declared themselves to be the leader will usually cut and run at the first sign of trouble.

Are leaders made, or are they born? I believe a little of both. My high school history teacher, Mrs. Houston, and the ministers I mentioned in part 1 saw my potential for leadership, and they took great care to nurture it. Without their involvement, I might never have thought of myself as having "take charge" potential. They helped me to refine my people skills and develop confidence in my ability to make tough decisions.

There's a dearth of quality leadership today, and this vacuum is felt in every sector of our society. There's plenty of rhetoric but no institutional substance. There's glory seeking but no hard work. I believe the reason for this vacancy is that individuals, regular folks, have abdicated their responsibility to assume positions of power on a local level, whether it's running a volunteer program or running for an elective office. People always think that someone else is going to assume responsibility for getting the project done. Children are even taught to "follow the leader." Seldom are they taught how to take the lead.

Most people like to look up to their leaders and expect them to do many things that they could do for themselves. It is easier for them than assuming total responsibility for their potential successes or failures. Bootstrappers don't feel that they need someone else to chart their path for them. People who *won't* are always looking for a boss, a preacher, a mother or father figure, or the government to take care of them.

In America today, there are many people who have abdicated their personal responsibility to the government and are saying to the president and other governmental officials, "You go out and fight our battles: protect our Social Security, provide us with affordable health care, educate our children, etcetera, etcetera." Oftentimes we fail to understand the limitations of government and therefore do not take on the tasks that we charge others with doing. Even if government provides good health care, the individual still has to be prepared to take care of his or her own health. If government educates our children, parents are not absolved of the responsibility of making a major investment of time and resources in those children. We have yielded too much power to entities and agencies that are not structured to do all that we ask of them. When they cannot perform, we indicate our displeasure by not exercising our right to vote. That is evident when you read the voter turnout numbers of recent elections. Never before in the history of this country has voter turnout been so low. People say, "Why vote? There's no quality leadership." I submit that the lack of quality leadership is due to public apathy. It's a vicious circle.

Only when people begin to assume personal responsibility for their communities and country will we begin to see a significant change in the quality of government leadership. People do not have a right to complain when they don't vote. And voting is not enough. People must become politically active on local, state, and national levels. If you leave the management of your world to other people, then you've abdicated the right to speak out against how that world has turned out.

I do not know any apathetic bootstrappers. Even if they do not assume leadership positions, at the very least they invest their time, energy, and money in worthy causes. They sit on nonprofit boards, mentor children, and are inclined toward volunteerism. As you accelerate the pursuit of your goals and intensify your quest for personal mastery, you'll want to develop leadership skills, because sooner or later, you'll be called upon to take charge. It's good to know how to follow, but if you are going to take the next step in personal responsibility, you need to learn how to lead.

The Qualities of Effective Leadership

Leaders come in a variety of work styles and temperaments. Some are micromanagers with a hands-on approach to every detail. Others are visionaries who only attend to the broad strokes while delegating the details to trusted aids. In a recent case study of my ministry by the Harvard University Divinity School for its summer institute for faith-based community leaders, I was classified as a visionary leader. They interviewed a number of individuals who work with me, and the overall consensus was that it is my style to delegate responsibility and hold others accountable for their performance and success. This classification represents an evolution in my leadership style. There was a time when I had no staff to whom I could delegate, so I was in the habit of doing everything myself. Now the organization has a strong enough support staff that I need not be involved in every aspect of the operation on a daily basis.

Without a doubt, the most difficult aspect of leadership is building strong teams and persuading people to share your vision. As I've said before, the true test of a leader is his or her ability to get others to work in unity with one another. Some leaders push and some pull, while others know how to do both, depending on the situation. Some are compassion personified, while others are harsh taskmasters. Some lift up from below; others rule from on high. There are as many different styles of leadership as there are leaders in the world.

Bootstrapping and leadership often go hand-in-hand. Do you have what it takes to be a leader? You don't have to be the president of the United States, the CEO of a corporation, or the pastor of a church. You can be a leader in your home, office, church committee, and block club—but don't force it. Let the role come to you. If you have leadership skills and ability, others will notice.

What does it take to be an effective leader? In essence, it takes vision, initiative, follow-through ability, people skills, and a strong sense of duty.

Vision

The truly great leaders are visionaries. In response to their ideas, they often hear "it can't be done." Their ideas are often on the cutting edge. Einstein was a visionary, as were Martin Luther King, Jr., Gandhi, and my favorite, Jesus. Visionaries are so certain of their objectives that they will often pursue the manifestation of their ideas at great personal hardship.

The Bible states that "without a vision the people perish" (Proverbs 29:18). A visionary must be able to foresee that which is in the future and seize the moment. It may take a while for others to understand or appreciate your idea, but if it is focused and meets the needs of the people, ultimately they will gravitate to it. When I started doing community development years ago, there were many pastors who did not consider this type of work the responsibility of the church. Some of them are now trumpeting the role of the church as a vehicle for economic empowerment.

Initiative

Where followers and apathetic people see problems, leaders see opportunity. Where others will not challenge the status quo, leaders take the initiative to solve problems and make changes.

Although we employ a full-time maintenance staff at the cathedral, from time to time debris drifts onto our property. When I arrive at the church and find this has happened, I personally stop and remove it rather than calling a staffer to do so. Too many people wait for others to do simple things that they could easily do themselves.

Follow-Through Ability

Without follow-through ability, a dream will die. The worst thing a leader can do is make promises and not deliver on them. People will tolerate a lot of things, but they don't like being lied to. A strong leader needs to see a project through until the very end. Often that means working alone, staying up late, going the extra mile. When you are in a leadership position you become the setter of the agenda; therefore, you are responsible for its implementation.

People Skills

People skills is an area where many of our leaders and elected officials fall down. Some don't really care about people but just use them in their pursuit of power and glory. I have found that people generally know when they are being used. They may not have found a way out of the relationship yet, but sooner or later, they will. My basic approach is to inspire people by making them feel vested in our endeavors, rather than intimidating them. Generally, people will appreciate you more if you respect and encourage them. They will also volunteer to do additional work beyond the call of duty. When I am in the church, the staff usually knows it, because if I have the time, I visit every office to speak to and embrace each employee.

A Strong Sense of Duty

The leadership ideals of a strong sense of personal responsibility, duty, and obligation are not popular concepts today. In fact, to many they seem old-fashioned. However, there can be no continuity in societal traditions if the people have no sense of duty—to self, others, and the world they live in. Given the absence of this trait in the masses of people, leaders truly stand out from the crowd.

Are You a Leader?

The following questions were designed to get you thinking about your strengths and weaknesses as a leader. Think back to times in your life when you were drafted into a position of power or when you volunteered for the role. Perhaps you are considering such a position today. Take out your trusty notebook and answer each question honestly and to the best of your ability. If you cannot think of an actual leadership role that you've assumed, then imagine what you would do if called on to lead.

Vision

1. Is your mind bursting with ideas about how to change conditions for the better in your home, community, city, state, or nation?

2. Do people often ask for your advice or opinions? What is your listening style? Do you listen without comment, or do you share personal anecdotes? Do you feel comfortable giving advice?

3. Are you often told your idea is impossible? How do you feel when you are told this? Think of an idea that you had that met with resistance and what you did to make it a reality.

4. Do you find yourself often professing the minority opinion about an issue? Do you often stand apart from the crowd? How do you measure your own beliefs—through polls, through personal discussions, or some other way?

5. Do you have a strong desire to make a mark in this world? Have you ever thought about it? Do you know anyone who feels strongly about leaving a lasting legacy? If so, describe what that person is trying to accomplish. If you have a similar desire, describe your own personal goals. How do you feel this will positively affect future generations?

6. Do you have a strong desire to make the world a better place? What in particular would you like to see changed in the world? What will you do to make a contribution?

7. Do you have a strong political ideology? Describe it.

Initiative

1. Do you find yourself always taking the initiative to start up or volunteer on projects? Describe some projects that you started or volunteered for. Were your efforts appreciated? Was taking the initiative satisfying? Would you do it again?

2. Are you a problem solver? Describe a recent problem that had everyone stumped but that you were able to solve. How did that make you feel? Did you receive recognition for a job well done?

3. Have you ever been resented for taking the initiative? Did you care? Describe what happened. Honestly, was it the *way* you took the initiative or was it *that* you took it?

4. Do you enjoy the challenge of a new project or problem to solve? If so, why? Is there a challenge that you'd like to tackle right now? Describe it.

5. Have you been able to make commitments—personal, professional, physical, spiritual—in the past? Did you stick to them? Why or why not?

Follow-Through

1. Can you comfortably handle many tasks at once? If so, do you manage by delegating or by doing everything yourself? Can you think of more efficient ways to get everything done?

2. Long after everyone has gone home, are you still working on the project?

3. Are you known as a person who will do whatever it takes to complete a job? If so, why do you have this reputation? If not, why not?

4. Do you have the energy to constantly follow up with people who procrastinate and make excuses? If so, what are your strategies? If not, what can you do to inspire team members to stay on the task and perform to the best of their ability?

5. How would you describe your management style? Has it worked for you in the past?

People Skills

1. Do you often find yourself encouraging and inspiring people? Do people often tell you that you're an inspiration? How does it make you feel to empower people in this way?

2. Are you a team builder? Do you have an ability to persuade people of the viability of your dreams? If so, what's your strategy? If not, how do you intend to develop this ability?

3. Do you genuinely like people? Can you tolerate, accept, respect, and appreciate differences? Do you have a keen understanding of human nature?

4. How are your conflict-resolution skills? When there is sibling rivalry among your children in the home or conflict at work, what do you do? Are you effective? If not, how will you become more effective?

5. Can you keep people on the task and ensure that they meet deadlines? In the past, what were some of your challenges in this area and how did you deal with them?

6. Can you easily remember names and faces? If so, how do you do it? If this is a problem for you, how do you intend to develop this ability?

Duty

1. Do you accept praise and blame equally and accept that the buck stops with you?

2. Do you have a strong sense of responsibility and duty?

3. Do you find that you have courage that other people lack? Do you act based on the courage of your convictions?

4. Do you feel guilty when plans or projects under your direction go awry?

Service Leadership

Every religion, political party, and social ideology has its share of people in power who are merely protesters and complainers. Today's leaders, while identifying with the people and acknowledging the burdens, must speak on behalf of empowerment, not victimization. Their duty is to help set goals and raise levels of achievement.

Today, the challenges that face us require bold leaders who understand the historical burdens of their followers and can inspire them to look for the opportunities that are in their midst. There is a need for influential people who do not merely complain about problems but develop plans and strategies that allow people to have real power. The leader's purpose is not to judge or belittle but to activate the "can do" spirit that resides within each individual.

Strong leaders realize that they cannot carry the burden of the people by themselves. I have learned a lot about service leadership by studying the life of Moses. In the biblical tradition, he was called by God to confront Pharaoh to emancipate the people of God. He became frustrated as he tried to lead them in their journey from slavery to the Promised Land. They were upset because the journey was taking so long and they were in unfamiliar territory. Although the Lord provided them manna from heaven so they would not starve, they complained about the lack of variety.

Moses took their complaints personally and asked God why he had called him to lead these people. He charged that it was like leading infants, that these people had no vision for the future Promised Land, because they were still emotionally and mentally connected to the land that had enslaved them. When he registered his complaint, the Lord responded by challenging him to find other leaders to whom he could delegate some of the responsibilities. He was to choose seventy people and share his spirit with them so that they could communicate to the others God's vision for their liberation.

Moses was like many of today's leaders in that he thought he had all the answers and could carry the burden of an entire race by himself. The same plan that God gave Moses for identifying potential leaders and creating leadership teams would be helpful in building the kind of nation that we would all like to live in. Moses learned this lesson the hard way and found himself confronting God in a moment of utter frustration. We should learn from the lessons of history that delegating responsibility is the only way to truly build leaders and empower people.

Many new voices who speak to the issues must rise up from within communities across America. They must be people of vision who do not join in the complaint but lift people's aspirations beyond their complaints. They must be people who do not allow the burdens to frustrate them but rather count the burdens as a necessary evil in the journey toward achievement.

We need visionaries in every realm of human activity who will model a style of leadership that combines spirituality, integrity, and action. We need people who will have the strength to remain independent and uncompromised, even when tempted. This kind of initiative will inspire a new agenda for excellence in education, health, personal finances, family, and personal relationships.

Leaders can be born or made, but in either case, their potential must be nurtured. We must all nurture the spark of leadership in young people. Often, they don't seem to be listening to us. However, we must keep talking to them, because although they don't appear to be listening now, they will retain some of what they have heard and it will help them later in life. Thus, we must have a strong and steady hand in raising the young role models of tomorrow. In doing this, we will all be accelerated into the new era of understanding and achievement.

I have been very fortunate in identifying young talent and giving those people positions of responsibility. I appointed Marshall Mitchell as my chief of staff in Congress when he was twenty-three years of age. Sam Moon served as my district manager when he was twenty-four years old. Roderick Dwayne Belin and Anthony Lucas served as assistant pastors at Allen Church at the age of twenty-six, and Felicia Faye Long, who is twenty-one years of age, is the current youth minister. In most instances, they have performed beyond the expectations that most people set for their age group.

Pull Yourself Up by Your Bootstraps . . .

Take the initiative wherever you are. In your church or community, volunteer to develop a program that will meet a need. There is so much work to be done that it won't be difficult to find a program that needs your assistance.

There are young people in your realm of influence who have the spark of leadership potential within them. As you identify those people, commit to spending time with them as Mrs. Houston did with me. Listen to them and guide, challenge, and encourage them to fulfill their potential. If you are doing a project, allow them to work with you. Delegate tasks, making sure that your instructions are clear, and hold them accountable. Give positive reinforcement for jobs well done and correction when mistakes are made. Constructive criticism should build up self-confidence, not tear it down. And when your young charges are ready, delegate to them more work of increasing difficulty and responsibility. You are a bootstrapper when you commit to helping develop leadership for the future.

Take the initiative on the job. Want to be noticed? Want a raise or a promotion? Stretch yourself. Volunteer to take on a project that needs doing. Promote yourself. Remind your boss of your significant accomplishments. To begin, do your research and record your exploration of the issues in a report. Develop a plan of action, and don't forget to include a budget if needed. Submit the report to your boss. Once your plan is approved, implement it. Communicate your progress verbally and in periodic memorandums. Be mindful of deadlines, especially if you are still assuming your normal workload.

Your church, community, or company project may require a team effort. If so, you'll have to coordinate and manage the team. When putting together a team, don't rush to fill positions with friends or just anyone who happens to be available. Take the selection process seriously. Choose team members who have the right skills, influence, and a strong commitment to your project. Make sure meetings are run smoothly and efficiently. Be friendly but firm about tasks and deadlines.

As the team leader, you'll also serve as liaison between team members and company management or church or community leaders. Support your team members, even if they sometimes make mistakes. Assume responsibility for setbacks—remember, the buck stops with you. When a team member shines, give praise. Use setbacks as a teaching tool.

By all means, be enthusiastic about your project and team efforts. You are the official cheerleader, so promote, promote, promote. If your company, church, or community has a newsletter, make sure to let the editor know about what your team is up to. If you have staff meetings, request to be put on the agenda. Use those meetings to cheerlead and solicit help or information if needed.

ACTION STEP 8:
STRETCH!

All barriers to mastery are self-imposed.

Every day when I get on the treadmill, ride the Nordic Cycle, lift weights, and do my "abs" exercise, I stretch muscles in my body to help build endurance. I exercise whether at home or on the road. Because of this, I am in better health today than I was twenty-five years ago. Although I was younger, I was also fatter and slower, and I tired more quickly. My stretching has not only been physically beneficial but also strenghened me mentally, emotionally, and spiritually.

The attachment and commitment that I have to Elaine and the children provides me with a level of emotional stability. I would have a difficult time if they were not in my life. After my first marriage, I wondered if I would ever marry again. Now, I can't imagine life without my wife and family. We should all learn the value of emotional stretching. It helps in managing our relationships, for we learn how to be faithful in marriage, patient with our children, and positive in our outlook on life.

My mental stretching has come through ongoing educational pursuits and career changes. When I was younger, I would read the paper from the back, starting with the sports section. Now, I read the paper from the center, starting with the editorials. My endless search for answers leads me to the pages where the opinion makers help to shape people's lives. My mental stretching has brought me to the point where I cannot even sit and watch sporting events on television. There was a time when these events governed my schedule; now there is too much reading, writing, and studying to be done.

When I was in Congress, I did not even allow my staff to write speeches for me, and I don't let anyone write my sermons. I think we lose something when we don't stretch mentally by doing things for ourselves that challenge us mentally.

Spiritual stretching is an ongoing process in my life. I have already mentioned fasting, but it goes beyond that. I take time early in the morning for meditation and reflection. It is the only way that I can live within God's purpose for my life. The more I meditate and exercise, the freer I feel. It is that freedom that allows me to function at an optimum level. That is important, since my parish is not merely the Allen congregation but also includes the many thousands of people and groups that I am called upon to inspire, uplift, and assist.

My spiritual walk is a constant stretching of the muscles of my faith, hope, and love. The spiritual stretch helps me to maintain optimism through all situations. It allows me to move through the day with power and endurance. Spiritual stretching can also help you to master the challenges that you face in life. Spiritual stretching is not metaphorical. It is a real sense that there is a God-given power within you that compels you to reach beyond your human limitations.

Achieving mastery at a craft or a task is a basic human need that involves stretching the unused portions of our brain power and abilities. Mastery goes beyond mere competency to performance that is superior on a consistent basis.

We all need to feel that there is at least one thing that we can do extraordinarily well. This need is almost as basic as the need for oxygen and goes beyond the need to succeed. Success as popularly defined refers to material achievement. Mastery, however, borders on the spiritual. Without personal mastery, there may be survival, but there is no quality of life or emotional fulfillment.

For some fortunate masters, their livelihood is their passion. Others are content to develop expert skills in other arenas. I know some master chefs who never receive a dime for their kitchen creations, just the appreciation of family and friends for their delicious meals. Yet nothing makes them happier than to spend time in the kitchen and work with the tools of their "trade." I have been blessed to know great masters in education, law, the arts, ministry, sports, and government service.

Mastery redefines us and teaches us that there are no limits to what human beings can achieve—except for those limits that we impose upon ourselves, individually and collectively. In action step 2, we explored how perspective can either empower or limit us. Remember Elaine's definition: "Perspective is how we view, understand, or interpret reality." If you believe that you cannot achieve mastery, then you won't. If you believe you can, then you will. It is the spirit within you that determines whether your perspective is pessimistic or optimistic.

Barriers to personal mastery are also created by social consensus. That's why, when Olympic athletes break world records, the news is reported around the world. Athletes do not buy into limitation; competition forces them to constantly improve their performance, and in so doing, they help us all see what's possible.

Masters can be young—like the twenty-one-year-old Tiger Woods, who won the 1997 Masters golf tournament—but more often, they are older. To achieve mastery takes time and patience, which is anathema to our immediate gratification culture. Woods won because for most of his twenty-one years , his father had immersed him in the art and sport of the game. He worked with him on developing his skills from the time Tiger was a young boy.

The great artists of old would spend years not only mastering their craft, but creating a single work of art. For three years, Michelangelo chipped David out of a block of marble. Leonardo Da Vinci worked on the Mona Lisa for two years. Before classroom education became the standard teaching forum, African children would apprentice for years under a master before receiving the title and gaining the experience and expert skill of a master themselves. They understood what we have forgotten: mastery takes time.

The Truman Show

The Truman Show is a recent popular film that imaginatively depicted what happens when we attempt to stretch out of the "tight chemise of culture," as Zora Neale Hurston put it. Society creates for us a perceptual framework, and all is well until we are activated to wake up, change, and take our pursuits to a higher level. That's when we, the unstoppable force, come against the immovable object, which is anyone and any-thing that has a vested interest in keeping us at a low level of awareness.

In *The Truman Show,* Truman Burbank (Jim Carrey) makes history when he is the first baby to be adopted by a corporation. It is his mis-fortune to have been adopted by a film production company. From the time he is in the womb to the moment of his emancipation, perceptual and physical, Truman's every movement is filmed, twenty-four hours a day, seven days a week. What's more, he has no idea that his life is a tele-vision show.

As he gets older, the world created by director Christof (Ed Harris) becomes more intricate, with thousands of cameras recording Truman's every move and an army of actors and extras posing as his friends, fam-ily members, and co-workers. The set is designed to simulate in exact-ing detail Any Town, U.S.A. By the time Truman becomes an adult, the corporation has created the largest sound stage in the world.

Truman's idyllic 1950s-style world might have continued until he died, but several consciousness-raising events begin to chip away at the perceptual framework Christof has created. The first is when a televi-sion spotlight falls from the "sky." Later, "prophets" from the "outside" try to warn him that reality is not what it seems. Like John the Baptist, they are beheaded—in other words, fired.

Deep down, Truman has a hunger to know and to explore. He begins to suspect that something is wrong. He asks, but no one will tell him the truth that he needs to know. Things get interesting when he decides to find out the truth for himself. The director and actors attempt to stop his search. Clearly, they've got a vested interest (pay-checks, fame) in Truman not discovering the truth about his reality.

But Truman can't help himself. He begins to stretch out of the percep-tual barriers that others created for him. Jesus says that you cannot put new wine into old wineskins because the old wineskins will break. Truman has to literally escape his physical world in order to achieve true freedom. In a last-ditch effort to convince him to stay, Christof tells him that by stay-ing in his perceptual prison, he gives others hope. The insanity of this is obvious. With a farewell—"good afternoon, good evening, and good night"—Truman walks through the exit door and into freedom.

Mastery can be achieved only when we cease to accept the limitations that others put on us; we must get out of the box we are in. As you begin to awaken to the gifts of intelligence and ability that God has given you, you'll have to make a decision. Will you allow others' fears, doubts, and resentments to stop you, or will you pursue mastery, regardless of what others think?

A young man who has a dream of building a real estate empire is asked by relatives, "Where are you going to get the money?"

A nurse who dreams of going back to school to become a doctor is told by her boss, "Slow down. Take one step at a time."

A poor high school student who has the spark of leadership within her aspires to become a lawyer. Her guidance counselor tells her that given her low grades, she should rethink her career choice.

A senior citizen trains to run the New York Marathon. His peers and family members tell him that he's too old.

A man with one leg wants to ski again. The doctors say, "Impossible!"

Every day, someone has a dream of doing the impossible, only to have some well-meaning person provide the "voice of reason." Expect criticism and doubt, but don't let others' words and lack of support stop you.

In addition to other people's doubts, you may have perceptual limitations that you've imposed upon yourself. Name your excuses—age, race, gender, lack of skills, prior failures, lack of education, no contacts, no mentor. Change these perceptual limitations. For every excuse that you use to talk yourself out of pursuing excellence, there are thousands of people who crashed through the same perceptual barriers. The following are some of my favorite examples of individuals who ignored the naysayers and went on to become superior performers. They have stretched beyond the "limits" and declared, "There are no limits to what I can achieve! All things are possible with God who is within me!"

A Dance into New Artistic Territory

Dance has historically been viewed as too worldly to occupy a place in worship among the other art forms such as music and literature.

However, during the past twenty years, our church has experienced a renaissance in dance ministries. One of the people responsible for bringing the liturgical art form to the forefront is Kathleen Sumler.

Kathy (as she is commonly known) grew up in New York and began dancing professionally in 1972 when she was a senior at the High School of Performing Arts. She later received a bachelor of fine arts in dance from SUNY and a master of fine arts in dance from Sarah Lawrence College. She is a bootstrapper who has traveled extensively with various dance companies throughout the United States and Europe. Dancing has been her forte since she was five, when she entered the Gloria Jackson Dance Studio. She is an assistant professor in the Dance Program at Hunter College.

What makes Kathy a renaissance woman is that with her excellent background and training, she could grace any stage as a world-class artist. Instead, she has chosen to introduce liturgical dance into not only the ministry of Allen A.M.E. Church but also many others throughout America. She started the Allen Liturgical Dancers in 1978 with fifteen young people and twelve women. Today, that ministry has over three hundred dancers, featuring junior girls, junior boys, intermediates, women, teens, men, and Daughters of Wisdom—women over the age of fifty.

When asked why she made the decision to develop this type of ministry, Kathy responded that she traditionally included sacred or gospel music themes as a part of her dance repertoire and coming to Allen gave her the opportunity to expand this area of her work.

Age

To launch into orbit around the earth, the space shuttle *Discovery* required an enormous expenditure of activation, execution, and acceleration power. The shuttle cost more than 1 billion dollars to make; NASA spent an additional 450 million dollars on the mission. Each of the rocket boosters on the *Discovery* carried more than *one million pounds* of solid propellant just to launch it off the earth. To enter into and remain in earth's orbit, the shuttle had to reach and maintain a speed of 17,500 miles per hour.

The science behind this journey was amazing, but even more profound was the demonstration of men and women stretching above and beyond the ordinary to achieve extraordinary success. John Glenn going into outer space at age seventy-seven was a stretch. His participation in the mission revealed to all of us that we are limited only by the conventional wisdom of our culture. No longer can we use age as an excuse to not dream our dreams and stretch into the unknown.

Glenn's so-called victory lap into space on October 29, 1998, gives new meaning to the phrase "the sky's the limit." Many criticized NASA for allowing Glenn to participate in the mission. Given the youth orientation of our society, the criticism was no surprise. Many felt that a seventy-seven-year-old man should be put out to pasture, but Glenn was determined to stretch beyond society's limited expectations of what an older man or woman can do. For nine days, Glenn participated in ten experiments that were designed to assess the effects of space flight on aging. During the mission, he flew around the earth 144 times.

Glenn's entire professional career has consisted of one stretch into the unknown after another: war hero, pilot of the first manned mission into outer space in 1962, first senator from Ohio to be elected for four consecutive terms, oldest astronaut to go up into space.

When people stretch, they break down perceptual barriers for the rest of us. If John Glenn could go into space at age seventy-seven, imagine what *you* can do. Anything is possible. Open your mind. Dare to dream big.

Medical Mysteries

At ten years of age, Ben Carson knew he wanted to work as a doctor at Johns Hopkins Hospital. "Those guys are finding cures and new ways to help sick people," he said. At thirty-three years of age, Dr. Ben Carson was appointed chief pediatric neurosurgeon at Johns Hopkins Hospital and was internationally recognized as a leader in his specialty of brain surgery.

Dr. Carson has a gift. He performs brain surgery on children who have been written off by other doctors. He has performed several controversial surgeries that the experts said were impossible. For example, four-year-old Maranda Francisco, who was having as many as one hundred epileptic seizures per day, sometimes three minutes apart, was dying. Dr. Carson performed a very controversial surgery called a hemispherectomy, in which one of the hemispheres of the brain is removed. Previous attempts at this procedure had been largely unsuccessful. He performed this surgery on Maranda successfully, and on many more children with an extraordinarily high success rate. Another child, Bo-Bo Valentine, was in crisis after having been hit by a Good Humor truck. Her pupils were fixed and dilated, which meant trouble. Dr. Carson successfully performed a risky craniectomy, in which a portion of the skull is removed.

Many of Dr. Carson's surgeries received international attention. His ability to perform procedures that "couldn't be done" astounded the medical community. Despite the level of difficulty of his previous surgeries, however, his most challenging case was yet to come.

In 1987, a pair of twins were born to a West German couple, Josef and Theresa Binder. The twins' physicians called Dr. Carson's team and asked if they could help the boys, who were conjoined at the back of the cranium. Dr. Carson accepted the challenge, although as good as he was, this surgery would test all of his abilities and knowledge. No one had been able to successfully separate *occipital cranio pugus* twins, such as Patrick and Benjamin.

A team of seventy specialists, nurses, and technicians was formed. Prior to the surgery, they had five months of intensive study and training. A ten-page plan was developed detailing each and every step of the surgery, including possible problems. They practiced on dolls that had been attached at the head with Velcro.

The historic procedure was performed on September 5, 1987. For *twenty-two hours* the team labored to separate the boys. Dr. Carson did the actual separation. Before they were finished, there were many close calls, including one incidence of "frightening bleeding." Some sixty units of blood had to be used.

For a week, people watched and waited in eager anticipation. Finally, the boys opened their eyes, and miraculously, they could see. Blindness, among many other potential problems, had been a big fear. "God, thank You, thank You," said Dr. Carson. "I know You have had Your hand in this." We don't know why it took a week for the boys' eyes to open. But thank God, they did.

Captivity

Harriet Tubman is one of my favorite heroines from history. Her story dramatically illustrates how nothing can stand in the way of mastery, not even slavery. Born around 1820, Tubman was a slave on a plantation in Dorchester County, Maryland. When she heard rumors that the plantation owner was going to sell off all the slaves, Tubman saw this as her opportunity to free herself.

Tubman escaped from slavery to freedom following the North Star to Philadelphia. In spite of her fear of captivity, she was determined to never again be a slave. For two years, she worked as a domestic, but she never forgot her family and friends. Between 1850 and 1860, she went back to the South nineteen times and led three hundred people to freedom along an established route known as the Underground Railroad. During the Civil War, she continued to free slaves as she worked for the Union army as a nurse, spy, and military leader. After the war, until her death, she ran a home for elderly black people in Auburn, New York. She was buried with full military honors.

If you believe that mastery is out of your reach, study the story of Harriet Tubman. This woman had been born in the worst of circumstances. She could neither read nor write. The laws of the land legitimized the bondage of human beings. When she ran away, she was in contempt of the law. In fact, at one point, there was a forty-thousand-dollar bounty on her head. But she did not let any of that stop her—not attack dogs, racists, or fearful slaves who wanted to go back "home."

Harriet kept looking forward at all times. One of the more troublesome things she had to deal with was the attitude of some of the slaves. Having lived in captivity all their lives, they often were paralyzed by the fear that they were breaking the law and would pay with their lives if caught.

Tubman would not allow anyone to go back into slavery. She would threaten them at gunpoint, and given a choice, they chose to keep going. She never lost a passenger. I once lived in the house of Colonel George Young, located in Wilberforce, Ohio. It had been one of the stops on the Underground Railroad and was a great source of inspiration to me.

The story of Harriet Tubman is not just for African American school children but for anyone who is in their own captivity—a dead-end job, an abusive relationship, overwhelming debt, an addiction. Harriet teaches us that no matter what your particular prison, you can break free. This is the way of a bootstrapper.

Pull Yourself Up by Your Bootstraps . . .

Stretching beyond your perceptual barriers can be uncomfortable in the beginning, but it is a prerequisite to achieving mastery. Take the first steps. First of all, know that you can achieve whatever your mind can conceive. Take advantage of every resource that can bolster your mission. Read up on your particular area of interest. Go to the library, or subscribe to a trade publication. Fill your mind with knowledge until you are so full that you cannot help but begin to try. And keep trying. This is for you and you alone.

Can't think of anything to do? Here's a list of ideas that should stimulate more ideas and a sense of adventure. The purpose of this exercise is to challenge yourself, so choose an activity that has a high level of difficulty.

Physical
Train for a marathon

The Bible correctly states that "the race is not given to the swift, but to those who endure till the end" (Ecclesiastes 9:11). You cannot treat life as if it is a short-distance race and give up after the first setback or crisis. Nor can you stop and relish each success for more than a short period of time.

The next time you start a project, think about what you are going to do next. About the time that you are halfway through the current project, start laying the actual foundation for the next one. You will soon gain a reputation for being able to perform a number of activities well.

Start an exercise program today!

I lost a lot of money joining health clubs and spas because I would not get up, get dressed, and drive to the gym. Even when I did, I would have to come back home and dress for work. I got regimented to exercise when I began buying equipment and exercising in the basement. I don't have to dress or drive—just wash my face, brush my teeth, put on my sneakers, and away I go. I sometimes come in from work and, before going upstairs, I undress in the basement and exercise. For a good, healthy, and wholesome life, you must exercise. My mother-in-law does not have a lot of equipment, but I have seen her do sit-ups, knee-bends, and so on. So even if you cannot buy equipment, you can start with some simple sit-ups. Start by doing as many short repetitions as possible and continue to build up to a number you are comfortable with.

You can run in place and do push-ups in your bedroom. Do enough each day to begin stretching your muscles. These simple exercises might help you fight off arthritis and other ailments that come with the aging process. You will feel and look better.

Take a dance or aerobics class

A few years ago, the members of the Allen Senior Citizens Center started aerobics and dance classes. As I watched them do the "Electric Slide" as well as any young person, it was apparent that they were truly enjoying life. It didn't take long for the dance class to become a troupe in popular demand at various places around the city. My daughter Nailah started dancing at the age of two; now at twenty, she still dances. Many of her current friends are those who started dancing with her in her youth.

Learn to swim

My mother would not allow us to swim when we were young because she had witnessed a drowning in her youth. I was required to take swimming in high school, so I came to realize that you could swim without necessarily drowning. Swimming is considered a good cardiovascular workout, as well as good conditioning for the back, arms, and legs. If you have bad feet, shin splints, or any condition that does not allow you to run or dance, then you should consider swimming. Karate, tennis, and golf are other sports you might consider to stretch yourself physically.

Mental
Learn to play a musical instrument

My eighteen-year-old son, Rasheed, started playing drums at the age of three. He could hardly sit on the stool, but he beat on that first junior set until it was destroyed (within three months). He now plays for various musical groups here in New York and in Atlanta, where he attends college.

There are several senior citizen musical groups in my community comprising men and women who learned to play an instrument in their youth. Since they are now retired, they have plenty of time to play for luncheons and other affairs. Many of them did not have time to play during their working years, but now they find enjoyment in dusting off their old instruments and making music for the pleasure of others.

Learn a language

The world today has become more multilingual than ever before. People travel and migrate to other countries in record numbers. Learning a second language may be your connection to your neighbor in the future. With the globalization that is occurring so rapidly, there will be a time in the near future when our telecommunication discourse will require some knowledge of a foreign language.

At the Allen School, we introduce Spanish as a second language in the first grade. Most of our eighth-grade graduates are competent enough in both spoken and written Spanish to receive advance placements in their high school language classes.

Do an art project

It is a shame that in many educational settings art has been expunged from the curriculum. Painting, sculpture, ceramics, and drawing are good ways of expressing your creativity. The arts are often used therapeutically to help people recover from strokes or other debilitating conditions. You need not wait until you get sick to start an art project. Be a bootstrapper and start today.

Read a good book

The market is full of very good fiction and nonfiction books. Reading is a great source of knowledge. Try reading one book each month. Start by taking a book with you on your next trip, whether it's to the bathroom or on a long flight. You will be surprised at how much you can learn in a very short time.

Spiritual
Attend regular worship services

Values for our life, families, and communities are generally taught through the medium of our religious worship experiences. Sermons, homilies, chants, inspirational songs, prayers, and meditation help us to take our focus off of the everyday issues of life. We are able to look within ourselves and find that special something that I call "the Spirit," which gives us courage to continue on in life's journey. We are also reminded of our own mortality and the special place that the Divine Creator occupies in our life.

Fast for one day each week

One day each week I abstain from food and sustain myself with liquids only. Fasting requires discipline; my experience has been that this period of abstinence from food allows me to be more focused on the things that are most important in my life.

Pray for one hour every day

Prayer should be an integral part of your daily activities from the moment you awake in the morning until you close your eyes at night. Do you remember that prayer your parents taught you as a child? It went like this: "Now I lay me down to sleep, I pray the Lord my soul to keep. If I should die before I wake, I pray the Lord my soul to take." Maybe you remember the grace that you were taught in kindergarten or first grade: "God is great, God is good, and I thank Him for my food. By His hands we all are fed, give us Lord our daily bread. Amen." It is interesting that no matter how old we get, we don't forget the prayers of our youth.

We should intermingle prayer with our daily activities—as we drive, ride, bathe, walk, run, deliberate, and so on. Our spiritual communion with God is a humbling experience that keeps us from going off the deep end and allows us to express gratitude and thanksgiving for the blessing of life.

ACTION STEP 9:
CREATE A LASTING LEGACY

Today's actions create tomorrow's legacy.

There was a time when history was not one of my favorite subjects in school. That was true until I met Mrs. Houston, who had a talent for making history come alive. In the past, we had the benefit of a rich oral tradition of family and community stories passed on by our parents and grandparents. They gave our history lessons context and relevance. Now I see, in retrospect, that it is many of those stories that have served to shape my perspective on life. My grandfather told me that his father was Negro and his mother was American Indian. They lived on a plantation during his youth. Later, my grandfather became a sharecropper and was able to purchase hundreds of acres in New Ulm, Texas, which is just outside of Bellville. He also managed to buy properties in Houston in the Third Ward area. As a matter of fact, the house in which I fell on the heater belonged to him. I was always fascinated that someone who had been born into slavery was able to amass so much property. Unfortunately, after the death of my grandfather, their land was lost in a prolonged legal battle among his sixteen children over how the land should be divided. The court ordered that the land be sold and the proceeds divided equally among the siblings or their descendants. After amassing huge legal bills over many years, each family received twenty-eight hundred dollars. The majority of the money from the sale went to the lawyers. The material portion of his legacy was lost because of greed.

I also remember the beautiful armoires, hutches, and other wood furnishings in the old farmhouse. It is too bad that we did not realize their value. Today, those types of furnishings garner thousands of dollars when sold as antiques. We must learn to claim our legacies; otherwise they will be lost.

Considering the advances that have been made by African Americans since the sixties in the social and political arenas, it is amazing how much we have regressed in land acquisition, retention, and ownership. Our foreparents left us a tremendous legacy of colleges that they built before the turn of the century, and communities that were developed by their labor. Yet those educational institutions are now struggling for survival, and homeownership among Black people is not growing in a significant way. FannieMae Foundation studies indicate that Black homeownership is at 43 percent compared to 72 percent for Whites. We must learn to claim and hold on to the legacies that we have received from those who made the sacrifice to build a foundation for future generations.

Fortunately, some of my grandfather's genetic legacy has been passed down to many of the members of my generation. Whenever the family got together while Grandpa was alive, we worshiped under the old oak tree. All of the kinfolk came around with their fiddles, harps, drums, guitars, and other musical instruments as we shared in family worship. In the year before I left for college, I preached for the family under that tree. In some families, money is the legacy that is passed down. Our foreparents bequeathed to us their property, values, work ethic, and faith.

People leave legacies in many ways. One example is Michael Jordan. Indisputably the greatest basketball player of all time, he recently retired from the National Basketball Association. The headline in *USA Today* read, "Alone at the Top Michael Bows Out." His retirement announcement was not a verbal statement of his historic and monumental achievements. He had already made that statement through his unprecedented successes. He had retired once before to pursue his dream of becoming a professional baseball player. But, eighteen months later, he returned to basketball. The sabbatical seemed to have done him some good, as he came back more determined than ever and led his team, the Chicago Bulls, to three consecutive championships.

At thirty-five years of age, he has retired after capturing ten scoring titles; snaring MVP awards; winning six NBA titles; and earning six

NBA finals awards, eleven all-NBA selections, and ten all-defensive team selections. His legacy had started to build even before his retirement as other professional, college, high school, and schoolyard players wanted to "be like Mike."

Michael Jordan moves to the top of the class of individuals in the sports world who were legends in their own time. The list includes but is not limited to Babe Ruth, Muhammad Ali, Joe DiMaggio, Billie Jean King, Jessie Owens, Wilma Rudolph, Willie Mays, Larry Bird, and Magic Johnson. What is Michael's legacy?

He was a quintessential professional. He was always physically, mentally, and emotionally prepared to give his best.

He was a great role model. He was articulate, sportsmanlike, well groomed, and likable. He did not have to brag because his game did the talking for him.

He set new standards. Michael was not content to rest on his laurels but worked diligently to raise every facet of his game from one year to the next. With all of his God-given talent, he still worked to improve in whatever area of his trade he considered himself to be weak in.

He appealed to all groups. He was comfortable with any group, whether young or old, rich or poor, Black or White, women or men. Michael made it hard not to love him, with that big happy smile and that impish look he had when he got into his game.

He had a strong work ethic. He kept his body in shape and his mind focused on his goals. Although his profession—basketball—is classified as a game, for Michael it was also his job and he treated it as such.

He understood family values. Michael learned his values from his late father, James, and his mother, Deloris. He earned millions of dollars as a player and through his many product endorsements. For many years, he felt that he was underpaid by the Bulls, but he said that he refused to renegotiate his contract so that he could teach his children a lesson. He stated in an interview with David Dupree of *USA Today*, "I've always taught my kids to be honest and keep their word. What kind of example would I be if I went back on mine?" His children are materially blessed for the rest of their lives, but more important, this man—their father—has given them a lasting legacy of values.

History is also an important part of a legacy. Today's children lack an inclusive context for their history. Thus, they do not feel a personal link to their studies. This is dangerous. When history becomes irrelevant, people become disconnected from the foundations on which they build. Benjamin Franklin was correct in stating, "When we do not learn from the lessons of the past, we are doomed to repeat them."

You can leave your children all the money in the world, but if they don't have the family and community stories and traditions that substantiate their inheritance, they'll be in danger of squandering all that you worked so long and so hard to achieve. They'll attach no value to the inheritance, except for what the money can buy them. And that is an empty promise. There is no energy in that.

Your legacy to your children and future generations is your personal story. Teach them the old stories, because without them, they'll end up repeating past mistakes and there will be no individual or collective progress.

If a culture stagnates, if there is no progress, it is because there is no direction. We get our direction from the past. We should not live in the past, but we must learn from it.

Why discuss history in a section about lasting legacies? Consider the laws of cause and effect. The decisions our parents made and the actions they took created our present day. Past, present, and future are not stand-alone segments of time but interconnected, interdependent, and overlapping. We change the future by the actions we take today. We atone for past mistakes by the actions we take today. Clearly, the present stands in the gap of past and future. We live our lives in the present; thus, it is our responsibility to be focused on the quality and integrity of our pursuit of success. In doing so, we honor our forebears and build for our children.

In 1961, Charles Gill decided to leave his job as an electronics specialist with the Lockheed Corporation to pursue his dream of owning a professional photography studio. He had worked for twelve years at Lockheed but decided that with the support of his wife, Carmen, they could make a good living and raise a family through the business.

Up to this time, Gill had done photography work part-time from his studio in the basement of their home. They borrowed money, using the home as collateral, and purchased a storefront on a busy street in St. Albans, Queens. They were successful in securing the loan only after being turned down by a number of banks. Their perseverance was rewarded when Charlie Sherwood of the Equitable Savings Bank chose to respond to their financial statement and character rather than their color.

The business grew, with Carmen working along with Charles for eighteen years while they raised a family of three sons. Over the years, the sons worked with Charles, but eventually the older two chose other fields. The Rev. Charles Gill, Jr., is a clergyman, and Carlton is a pharmacist. Now that he is 68, Charles Sr. has decided to go into semi-retirement. Fortunately, his youngest son, Christopher, and his wife, Sandra, have received the family legacy. Gill Photographers continues to prosper. The sacrifices that Charles and Carmen made in 1961 created a legacy that could live on far into the future. Christopher and Sandra have three children who will be introduced to the business as they grow up. I am proud that Gill Photographers is responsible for the picture that is on the cover of this book.

Bootstrappers, more than anyone else, should be concerned with legacy leaving—and not just for their own children but for all of our children! Bootstrappers are the movers and shakers of society. We build the institutions and corporations. We make the policies that govern human interactions. We're the ones with a strong sense of duty and national loyalty. We have a vested interest in ensuring that social norms and values continue into the future, because they will ensure the longevity of our creations.

Leaving a legacy is the cornerstone of a life filled with meaningful work, service, and joy. I cannot think of a better way to leave this life than to hear the words of scripture, "Well done, my good and faithful servant." The innovative architect Frank Lloyd Wright once said, "My building will last at least three hundred years." I'd like to know that what I put in place will endure. I was charged with the responsibility of building and serving within my realm of influence, and to the best of my ability, that is what I try to do. That's all any of us can do. That's a legacy that will live long after I am gone, and I find comfort in that.

Pull Yourself Up by Your Bootstraps

My four children have been able to live in a home where there was peace by virtue of the love that they have seen Elaine and me share. As we periodically look at the photographs of the children as they have grown, we realize that the role we have played in their lives has been a nurturing one. They need not look beyond us to know how family members ought to interact with one another. We hope that our legacy of love, care, discipline, and guidance will bring truth to the scriptural saying "Train up a child in the way that you would have them go and they will not depart from it."

We do not know whether any of our children will follow us into the ministry. They have not been pressured to do so. What we do know is that they have grown up in a home with parents who have demonstrated excellence in every endeavor that they have pursued. They receive a legacy of hard work, committed and focused energy in pursuit of goals, determination and desire to succeed, and a positive spirit. They have been taught that love is the only antidote for hate and that real power comes through performances that do not require bragging but stand on their own merit. Although they will receive a legacy of some material goods, their greatest legacy will be the religious foundation on which my faithwalk has been taken. They will know the way even if they choose not to follow it.

The final legacy that I leave to both my children and future bootstrappers is the inspiration that I have received through teachers, mentors, and others who have touched my life in very meaningful ways. I hope that this book has inspired you to pull yourself up by your bootstraps, knowing that you can be anything you want to be in life if you are willing to make sacrifices.

Leaving a positive, lasting legacy is more than just having your good name carried on into the next generations. What will you build, what will you grow for your children and your children's children? If you have not consciously considered your legacy, it's time to start. Get out your journal and respond honestly to the following questions:

1. What does legacy mean to you? How do you want to be remembered? What do you want to be remembered for?

2. What positive and negative legacies—emotional, spiritual, financial, and so on—were handed down to you from your parents and grandparents? How have they affected your life? How will you build upon or change those legacies?

3. Do you tell your children teaching stories about your childhood? Can you remember stories your parents and grandparents told you? Write them down or record them into a tape recorder. Begin today to tell your stories.

4. Do you have a legally binding will? If so, is it up to date? If not, when are you going to get yours done? Tomorrow is not promised to you. Get it done today.

5. Are you consciously building to last for future generations? If so, how are you going about doing this? If not, what are some of the ways that you will leave your legacy? Write them down, and get to work.

We are already in the birth pangs of the new era. The season of change is upon us. How will you respond? Will you be a voice of complaint or of opportunity? Will you get serious about helping to heal and uplift humanity? The world needs more bootstrappers, people who are willing to initiate and implement plans and programs that help people lead better lives. The way of the bootstrapper may sometimes be circuitous, but if the destination is known, you will arrive after a while. Bootstrapping can be used by everybody who wishes to bring their dreams to reality. If you are not a bootstrapper yet, now is the time to become one. The time for talk has passed. The time for action is *right now.*

May God richly bless your high aspirations and your actions. May your relationships be fruitful and your collaborations holy in God's sight. May your legacy be lasting and positive, and may it serve to elevate the quality of life for future generations. Amen!